Coalition Britain

MANCHESTER
1824

Manchester University Press

Coalition Britain

The UK election of 2010

Edited by

Gianfranco Baldini and Jonathan Hopkin

Manchester University Press
Manchester and New York

distributed exclusively in the USA by Palgrave Macmillan

Copyright © Manchester University Press 2012

While copyright in the volume as a whole is vested in Manchester University Press, copyright in individual chapters belongs to their respective authors, and no chapter may be reproduced wholly or in part without the express permission in writing of both author and publisher.

Published by Manchester University Press
Oxford Road, Manchester M13 9NR, UK
and Room 400, 175 Fifth Avenue, New York, NY 10010, USA
www.manchesteruniversitypress.co.uk

Distributed in the United States exclusively by
Palgrave Macmillan, 175 Fifth Avenue, New York,
NY 10010, USA

Distributed in Canada exclusively by
UBC Press, University of British Columbia, 2029 West Mall,
Vancouver, BC, Canada V6T 1Z2

British Library Cataloguing-in-Publication Data
A catalogue record for this book is available from the British Library

Library of Congress Cataloging-in-Publication Data applied for

ISBN   978 07190 83693 hardback
ISBN   978 07190 83709 paperback

First published 2012

The publisher has no responsibility for the persistence or accuracy of URLs for any external or third-party internet websites referred to in this book, and does not guarantee that any content on such websites is, or will remain, accurate or appropriate.

Typeset
by Action Publishing Technology Ltd
Printed in Great Britain
by Bell & Bain Ltd, Glasgow

Contents

List of figures

List of tables

List of contributors

Gianfranco Baldini is Associate Professor of Political Science at the University of Bologna and Deputy Director of the Istituto Carlo Cattaneo.

Roberto Bertinetti is Researcher in English Literature at the University of Trieste.

Patrick Dunleavy is Professor of Political Science at the London School of Economics and Political Science.

Elizabeth Evans is Lecturer in Politics and International Relations at Kingston University.

Richard Hayton is Senior Lecturer in Politics at the University of Huddersfield.

Jonathan Hopkin is Reader in British and Comparative Politics at the London School of Economics and Political Science.

Lucia Quaglia is Senior Lecturer in Contemporary European Studies at the University of Sussex.

Eric Shaw is Senior Lecturer in Politics at the University of Stirling.

Alan Trench is Honorary Senior Research Fellow at the Constitution Unit, University College London.

Martina Viarengo is a Post-doctoral Fellow at the John F. Kennedy School of Government at Harvard and Research Officer at the Centre for Economic Performance of the London School of Economics and Political Science.

Acknowledgements

This volume forms part of a series of studies of the major western democracies under the aegis of the Carlo Cattaneo Institute in Bologna, published in Italian by Il Mulino press of Bologna and translated into a number of other languages. The editors would like to thank the Cattaneo Institute and the Johns Hopkins Bologna Center and London School of Economics for their support in completing the project. Sonia Bussu did an excellent job translating three chapters from Italian to English. Tony Mason and Sarah Hunt of Manchester University Press were helpful and efficient in bringing this volume to press. Gianfranco Baldini would like to thank his family for support, and dedicates his contribution to the book to Daniela, Tommaso and Jacopo. Jonathan Hopkin would like to thank Silvia Evangelisti for her support and feedback, and dedicates his contribution to the book to Giulia Hopkin, for providing so many reasons for delaying its completion.

1

Introduction: an anomalous election, a surprising coalition

Gianfranco Baldini

Introduction

The 2010 elections will surely be remembered as a major event in recent British history. For the first time since the war, after the polls failed to give a majority of seats to any party, a coalition government emerged, with an agreement between the Conservatives and the Liberal Democrats. This marked a departure from the traditional dynamics of the Westminster model. The incumbent government, in defeat, found itself almost alone in opposition, alongside the small number of MPs representing non-statewide parties and the first ever Green MP elected to the House of Commons. The Tories and Lib Dems, who had often fiercely contested elections, formed an unprecedented alliance pushed through by their respective leaders, after days of negotiations. David Cameron and Nick Clegg both dragged their respective parties closer together than in the recent past (let's not forget that in 2001 the Lib Dems were perceived as being to the left of Labour – Heath *et al.* 2001) and tied their fates to a new 'liberal-conservative' coalition, as Cameron described it in the joint press conference on 12 May 2010. Less than a week after the elections, that conference put an end to speculation about the revival of the Lib-Lab formula or a new election.

This book analyses the 2010 elections and their implications for the British political system. Already this election is in the running to join the list of 'critical' elections over the past century: the Liberals' landslide victory 1906, the surprising victory of Clement Attlee's Labour in 1945, Margaret Thatcher's rise to power in 1979, the victory of Tony Blair's New Labour in 1997. The formation of a coalition government is a major development for the British party system and for British democracy more generally. It may mark the end of a phase of British politics – the half-century or so following the Second World War – when the Westminster model became consolidated after the upheavals of the 1920s and 1930s. Despite the failure of the promised referendum on the 'first past the post' (single-member plurality) electoral system, the birth of a coalition government has the potential to alter profoundly the workings of British government.

The changes that have unfolded can only in part be ascribed directly to the 2010 elections, and this book analyses the state of the political system from a long-term perspective. This introductory chapter, as well as outlining the structure of the book, describes the most important political shifts taking place under Cameron's administration in 2010 and evaluates the events that preceded the elections. Its aim, and that of the book as a whole, is to assess the British political context in 2010 and provide insights into the nature of the transformations of the British political system that are taking place.

A three-horse race?

When Gordon Brown visited Buckingham Palace on 6 April 2010 to request the dissolution of parliament, as protocol requires, opinion polls were already indicating a hung parliament. However, it would be misleading to conclude that the election campaign made little difference, because if nothing else it made Liberal Democrat leader Nick Clegg a household name. If at the beginning of the campaign he was barely known to the general public,[1] the first of three televised debates (broadcast on 15, 22 and 29 April) brought him huge – if short-lived – popularity. His party naturally benefited and for several days it rated above the fateful 30 per cent threshold, leaving Labour in third place and challenging the Conservatives for the lead. At least for a week or two of the election campaign the usual two-horse race between Labour and the Conservatives was subverted, and although an outright Lib Dem victory was never seriously contemplated (the electoral system historically penalises the Lib Dems),[2] the party's emergence to prominence disrupted the traditional two-party dynamic and familiarised many British voters with the third party.

The televised debates represented the main novelty of the 2010 electoral campaign and they appear to have had some effect in reviving citizen interest in politics, in decline over the recent years (Hay 2007; Stoker 2006). The degree of innovation entailed by these debates has been much discussed even during the campaign (Jones 2010), but there are doubts about their real impact on electoral behaviour, since the Lib Dems brought home a much more modest result than anticipated by opinion polls following the first debate. However, it appears likely that debates will also be held in future election campaigns.[3]

The televised debates briefly challenged the cycle of public cynicism, citizen disaffection and political disengagement, which has affected Britain, like many other advanced democracies, over the past two decades.

In the weeks preceding the debates, a survey by the Hansard Society seemed to confirm growing citizen mistrust towards politics, although, as it often happens, the press fuelled these feelings, through headlines that proclaimed the emergence of a new type of citizen: the 'bored and discouraged' voter (Curtis 2010). However, on careful examination, the study did not present particularly surprising findings on the trend of general mistrust towards politics, a trend observed across Europe. On the contrary, if one considers the impact that the parliamentary expenses scandal had on the press in May 2009, most voters seem to have viewed their representatives' behaviour more as celebrity gossip than of any real relevance for their attitude towards the political class (Flinders 2010a). The fact that disaffection and boredom with politics were more widespread among Labour rather than Conservative voters should be understood as part of the normal democratic dialectic of government and opposition, since New Labour was coming to the end of a long period in power.

The three parties faced the election in very different shape. Without going into the details of what emerged from Peter Mandelson's popular book of memoirs (2010), newspaper reports offered the image of a divided and worn out Labour Party (see Eric Shaw's chapter in this volume). In his three years of government, following his difficult succession to Blair, Brown showed the limits of his leadership, starting with the episode of the election planned for autumn 2007, but then abandoned after the plan had become effectively public knowledge. At that point, the party was flatly ahead of the Conservatives in the polls (see Figure 1.1). New elections would most likely have given Brown a fresh electoral mandate, which may have led to a more successful period in Number 10. However, in the following months unmistakable signs of deep internal divisions became visible. Faced with allegations of bullying, frequent (and clumsy) attempts to depose him and a gaffe-ridden electoral campaign, the incumbent PM was unable to capitalise on the international prestige he won through his skilful management of the economic crisis (see Lucia Quaglia's chapter in this volume) towards the end of 2009. Nor did Mandelson's return from Brussels revive a weak and exhausted government, which mirrored a party worn out by thirteen years in power, with a number of successes to its credit, but discredited by the Iraq war and the egocentric behaviour of some of its leading figures.

New Labour appeared unable to claim credit for its achievements (such as halting the widening of inequalities and preserving the welfare system; see Jonathan Hopkin and Martina Viarengo's chapter in this volume). The Conservative Party, in contrast, had freed itself from the ghosts of the failed leadership of the past decade, as Richard Hayton explains in chapter 4 of this book. The Tories were finally a modern party with a young and skilled leader. Elected as party leader at the end of 2005, Cameron had over four

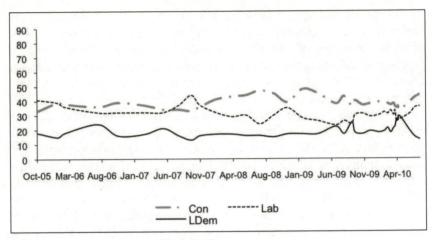

Figure 1.1 Voting intentions 2005–2010

years to build his own alternative to Labour and he was able to outline innovative policies in many sectors and to erase the party's negative image in key sections of the electorate. As stated by Theresa May, the new Home Secretary and one of the few women holding an important position in the current government, at the beginning of the new millennium the Tories were the 'nasty party', a hostile party, defined mainly by its being against Europe, immigrants or homosexual rights. However, the party that fought the 2010 elections was in many ways a reformed political force, with a new and captivating image, different from the previous two elections, which it had lost heavily under first William Hague and then Michael Howard (not to mention the two years of drift under Iain Duncan Smith, named Work and Pensions Secretary in the coalition government's first cabinet). One of the themes where the party remained consistent was Europe: with an increasingly Eurosceptic electorate, Cameron, at least before the elections, did not need to renounce his traditional Eurosceptic rhetoric (see Gianfranco Baldini's chapter in this volume).

Finally, the Lib Dems, often neglected and ignored, also presented a new image. For this party the role of their leader was also important (see Elizabeth Evans' chapter in this book; also Crabtree 2010). The party was courted by Labour,[4] which, before the vote, remained the closest political force to the majority of Lib Dem voters. However, Clegg believed he was evenly matched against the other two parties and gained the support of the progressive press (see Table 1.1). In a climate dominated by the expectation of a hung parliament, but with the Conservatives in the lead, some of the main UK newspapers endorsed different political parties than in previous elections, as Table 1.1 reveals.

In 2005 nearly 60 per cent of regular newspaper readers chose newspapers that supported Labour, against just above one third choosing newspapers supporting the Conservatives (the exact figures are 58.6 per cent and 34.4 per cent, see Bartle 2006). The situation in 2010 had changed radically in favour of the Tories, with the biggest selling paper, the tabloid *The Sun*, switching allegiance. The position of the two major centre-left newspapers, *The Guardian* and *The Independent*, expressed hostility towards any Conservative comeback, but failed to back Labour. Even *The Guardian*, staple of the educated left voter, advocated a vote for the Liberal Democrats, though after the elections, in the course of the coalition negotiations, *Guardian* columnists Polly Toynbee and David Marquand called for a Lab-Lib coalition.

Coalition of parties or leaders?

'A week is a long time in politics', was a phrase made famous by Harold Wilson, the last party leader to find himself winning a plurality, but not a majority of seats, in the February 1974 election. In May 2010, it took less than a week for David Cameron and Nick Clegg – the 'odd couple', as some in the British media described them – to appear at a joint press conference in Downing Street to announce the formation of a coalition government. There were a number of difficulties involved in reaching such an agreement: the ideological distance between some of the components of the two parties, the 'over-sized' nature of the coalition and the temptation to form a minority government, the presence of Gordon Brown in Number 10. Yet even critics of the Westminster model would have to concede that the party leaders were able to resolve the electoral deadlock in a rapid and effective manner, and the British institutions withstood the uncertainties of the week following the 6 May elections. The attitude of the two leaders made a difference, although the parliamentary arithmetic left them few alternatives, as a Lib-Lab coalition would have fallen short of the requisite 326 votes in the House of Commons. Cameron could have opted for a minority government, a rare scenario in Britain, yet workable, as the Scandinavian example demonstrates. However, the climate of the previous few months and the Lib Dem surge helped create momentum for a coalition, and the alliance had strategic value for Cameron, faced with an acute economic crisis.

For Nick Clegg, the press conference on 12 May was the culmination of an extraordinary few weeks. Less than a month earlier, after the first televised election debate, he was the new star, compared by some enthusiasts even with Churchill. Once the polls had delivered a hung parliament he became the king-maker, despite having gained only 23 per cent of votes

Table 1.1 Changes in party endorsement from British newspapers over the past five elections

Newspapers	Readers*	1992	1997	2001	2005	2010
The Sun	7751	Cons	Lab	Lab	Lab	Cons
Daily Mirror	3381	Lab	Lab	Lab	Lab	Lab
Daily Star	1617	Cons	Lab	Lab	–	Cons
Daily Mail	4881	Cons	Cons	Cons	Anti-Lab	Cons
Daily Express	1529	Cons	Cons	Lab	Cons	Cons
Daily Telegraph	1840	Cons	Cons	Cons	Cons	Cons
The Guardian	1124	Lab	Lab	Lab	Lab (with reservations)	Lib Dem**
The Times	1768	Cons	Eurosceptic	Lab	Cons	Cons
The Independent	635	Neutral	Lab	Anti-Cons	Lib Dem	Lib Dem**
Financial Times	418	Neutral	Lab	Lab	Lab	Cons

Sunday papers

News of the World	7642	Cons	Lab	Lab	Lab	Cons
Sunday Mirror	3826	Lab	Lab	Lab	Lab	Lab
The People	1331	Lab	Lab	Lab	Lab	Coalition
Mail on Sunday	5213	Cons	Cons	Cons	Anti-Lab	Cons
Sunday Express	1622	Cons	Cons	Lab	Cons	Cons
Sunday Times	3219	Cons	Cons	Lab	Cons	Cons
Sunday Telegraph	1677	Cons	Cons	Cons	Cons	Cons
The Observer	1212	Lab	Lab	Lab (with reservations)	Lab	Lib Dem
Independent on Sunday		Non conservative	Lab	Lab (with reservations)	Lib Dem	–

* (in thousands), **(tactical Lib-Lab voting), whereby Lib Dem voters were told to cast their vote for the candidate (either Labour or Lib Dem) that would stand the best chance against the Conservatives in a given constituency.

Sources: Kuhn 2007, author's updates from the National Readership Survey (www.nrs.co.uk/);

BBC (http://news.bbc.co.uk/2/hi/uk_news/politics/election_2010/8656552.stm), data refer to the period December 2009–March 2010, retrieved August 2010.

cast (1 per cent more than in 2005) and seeing his own parliamentary delegation shrink by six MPs. Notwithstanding speculation in the immediate aftermath, a progressive Lib-Lab coalition seemed a remote possibility and a risky one for all involved. The New Labour project seemed exhausted and Gordon Brown's reluctance to resign immediately as party leader gave Clegg the pretext for pursuing negotiations with the Conservatives. If an alternative leader had emerged to pursue a Labour-led coalition, they would have risked alienating public opinion and damaging their own prospects, especially since the parliamentary numbers would have required horse-trading with the Scottish, Welsh and maybe even Northern Irish parties. Although surveys show that the Lib Dem electorate is closer to Labour than the Conservatives (as confirmed by the British Election Study on post electoral data), Cameron and Clegg's cooperation was aided by the growing political convergence between the elites of their two parties over the period since 2005 (see the chapters by Elizabeth Evans and Richard Hayton in this book).

Cameron, for his part, skilfully seized the opportunity offered by the agreement with Clegg. Notwithstanding the personal attacks they launched at each other during the electoral campaign, the two leaders appeared to respect each other and quickly developed an ostensibly warm personal relationship. Although there is no doubt that the personal side played a pivotal role in the birth of the new government, the PM and his deputy both have to respond to their respective parties. For Cameron, after a liberal turn on many social policies, the alliance with the Lib Dems would provide him with valuable cover to resist pressures from the reactionary right of his own party. In this light, it is fascinating to observe how Cameron acted within the first week of the coalition government's existence to protect his leadership from his own MPs, by forcing a rule change allowing ministers to sit in the 1922 Committee of Conservative backbenchers. A coalition government restricts room for manoeuvre in some respects, but in others it also enhances the leadership's freedom to act.

The coalition relationship is even more complex for Clegg. At the head of his party only since 2007 (after a fiercely contested election) he leads a political organisation with a federal structure whose distinctive feature compared to most European parties is the full involvement of members (see Elizabeth Evans' chapter in this volume). Clegg was able to convince his party activists of the unique opportunity of an alliance with Cameron, which would allow the Lib Dems finally to enter in government. However, the costs of this decision became immediately apparent, with the party suffering a dramatic drop in its popularity, which saw its support in opinion polls collapse by more than half by the end of 2010 (see Figure 1.1). The smaller party in the coalition clearly faces the biggest risks, particularly in the context of economic austerity, characterised by deep public spending cuts and other unpopular decisions. The suggestion that the Lib Dems were being exploited by the Conservatives as cover for hardline policies was brutally expressed by Labour's Ed Balls, who described them a 'human shields' (BBC 2010a). The Lib Dems therefore have had to work hard to convince their voters that they are indeed exercising some influence in government, and a key plank in this strategy was the call of a referendum on the electoral system within the first year of government.

The political litmus test: the 2011 referendum

New Labour came to power in 1997 with a commitment to constitutional reform and quickly introduced significant changes, bringing devolution to Scotland, Wales and Northern Ireland (as examined by Alan Trench in chapter 9), introducing some more limited reforms of local and central government, and of the Westminster parliament. However, its reforming impetus faded after its first term of office. The Conservatives, for their part, have remained opposed to major constitutional change and have been trying to shake off their reputation as centralisers, built during the Thatcher years, when the Conservative government abolished the Greater London Council in 1986, curtailed the powers of local councils and staunchly opposed Scotland's increasing demands for devolution. The Lib Dems, in line with their federal structure and with their strategic interests, have been the most consistent supporters of institutional reforms at Westminster (Flinders 2010b), and one of their key demands in the coalition negotiations was for a referendum on changes to the voting system.

The single-member plurality system had traditionally guaranteed one-party majorities since 1945, with only one exception, in 1974. Governments were formed a few hours after the elections, and Conservatives and Labour alternated in power in a stable two-party system. However, the two main parties' vote share has progressively dropped from an average of above 90 per cent in the 1950s to 70 per cent in the past two decades (see Patrick Dunleavy in chapter 2). For this reason, one the promises of the 1997 Labour manifesto was the establishment of a commission to assess the possibility of reforming the electoral system. The Jenkins Commission completed its work in 1998 and suggested the adoption of a mixed system (the alternative vote (AV) – used in Australia – integrated with the proportional system to assign 15–20 per cent of seats from regional lists). Enjoying its 179 seat majority, Labour reneged on its commitment to hold a referendum on electoral reform, and rejected the findings of its own Commission. The issue was not raised again until 2009, when Gordon Brown committed the party to a referendum on the alternative vote. The Conservatives have maintained a firm opposition to electoral reform throughout this time, although its 2010 manifesto did contain a commitment to redraw the current electoral districts, which are skewed in Labour's favour.

The Lib Dems and their predecessor parties (the Liberal Party and the Social Democratic Party) enjoy an unenviable record as the party most heavily penalised by the electoral system. In all elections including those in 2010, the Lib Dems have been under-represented, with a difference of between 10–20 per cent between their vote share and their share of seats in the House of Commons (Baldini and Pappalardo 2009). As a result, the negotiations with the Conservatives, firm defenders of the status quo, touched a nerve and Clegg had to deal with a protest in Westminster by over a thousand Liberal Democrat activists demanding full electoral reform as a price for any coalition deal (BBC 2010b). For party activists electoral reform is a key political issue and, added to divisions over economic policy, could threaten the party's internal stability.

What Clegg obtained on institutional issues was a bland compromise which led to a major political failure for his party. In May 2011 a referendum was held on the alternative vote, with full proportional representation (PR) off the table. AV – a system in which voters would still elect one MP in each constituency, but by ranking the candidates in order of preference rather than through 'first past the post' – is very different from the single transferable vote (STV) used in Ireland, whose proportional system is favoured by the Lib Dems.[5] AV could have helped cement the Lib Dems' role as a pivot party, with the opportunity of allying itself with the most voted party, a bit like the German Liberals of the past, but there is no doubt that it was a far from ideal outcome for a party that has advocated full proportional representation. Another problem was that the Conservatives, who through junior minister Mark Harper helped draft the referendum proposal on AV, advocated a 'no' vote in the referendum. This scenario could have threatened the stability of the coalition, of Clegg's party and of the entire political system (Bogdanor 2010): British history of the past century reminds us that the Liberals already split on two occasions, in 1919 and in 1931. However, in the event the resounding victory of the 'no' camp simply confirmed the weakness of the Liberal Democrats within the coalition, removing electoral reform from the table for the foreseeable future.

Policy challenges: the Big Society and beyond

The formation of a centre-right coalition government marks a likely turning point in the public policy trajectory in the UK. For all the criticisms levelled at New Labour from the left, Blair and Brown's governments adopted distinctive policies that the new Conservative-Lib Dem government is unlikely to follow. The Labour period in office saw a major expansion in public spending with the aim of improving services such as education and health, which had been underfinanced and overburdened, and reducing poverty and inequality. The government target of eliminating child poverty within twenty years was a hugely ambitious Labour programme, given that levels of child poverty in the UK in 1997 were the highest in Europe. Some progress was made in achieving these aims: in the first few years after 1997, 1 million children were lifted out of poverty, and although the goal of halving child poverty by 2010 was not reached, between the mid-1990s and 2005 the numbers were reduced from 14 to 10 per cent, the biggest reduction of any OECD country (see Jonathan Hopkin and Martina Viarengo's chapter in this volume). There were also general improvements in the NHS (reduced waiting lists, better paid staff, more adequate structures) and in education, although in the latter case the emphasis on school drop-out rates, on tests results and increasing parents' choice proved controversial.

These policies are unlikely to be continued in any recognisable form, for two reasons. First, the economic crisis of 2008 on has left Britain with one of the highest deficits of any of the advanced democracies, leaving the coalition with the priority of reducing, rather than expanding, public spending. Second, even in more favourable economic conditions, the coalition would be unlikely to subscribe to Labour's spending priorities: although the coalition has promised to ring-fence health spending and protect current spending on schools, the Conservatives, and to an increasing extent also the Liberal Democrats, are hostile to high levels of public spending as a matter of political principle. The Conservatives, of course, have argued for a smaller state ever since the 1970s, and despite Cameron's initially compromising approach advocating 'sharing the proceeds of growth' between private and public spending, the period since the financial crisis has seen the party move back to a more traditional view of limited state spending, favouring instead the 'Big Society' – the idea of reducing the power of the central state in favour of local, preferably voluntary, initiatives.

The Liberal Democrats have also moved ground under their new leader, quickly abandoning the centre-left, pro-spending orientation of Clegg's predecessors. The new generation of Lib Dem leaders, such as Clegg and David Laws, sought to shift the party towards a more economically liberal stance, to move beyond, at least partly, its image in the past decade of the neutral party in defence of civil and environmental rights. This strategy, outlined in the 'Orange book' (Marshall and Laws 2004), made the party's collaboration with the Conservatives much easier than it would have been under leaders such as Charles Kennedy or Menzies Campbell, and suggests that the coalition may have a more coherent economic strategy than appeared at first glance. The loss of David Laws from the government in May 2010, forced to resign a few short weeks after being appointed Chief Secretary to the Treasury following an expenses scandal, weakened this strategy but Lib Dem support for the coalition's tough deficit-reduction policy proved strong, at least through 2010.

There are also a number of areas where agreement may prove more difficult to reach. For example, the debate on immigration and integration, heightened by the international tensions after 9/11, has the potential to divide the two parties, with the Conservatives committed to reducing net migration to the UK, a policy opposed by the Liberal Democrats in the election campaign (Roberto Bertinetti's chapter in this book analyses this very complex theme). In the past two years, particularly following the explosion of the economic crisis, the integration of foreign nationals clashed with growing unemployment. The controversy on 'British jobs for British workers' strongly influenced the European elections campaign in 2009, which gave the xenophobes of the BNP two seats in Strasbourg. The fact that Nick Griffin's party pocketed a result well below expectations did not quell controversies. In the coalition agreement, Cameron was able to keep his proposal for an immigration cap and ditch the Lib Dems' idea of an amnesty for illegal immigrants. The citizenship test introduced by Labour in 2005 will also remain in force.[6]

Another area of tension between the two governing parties is Europe and foreign affairs. In the first case (see Gianfranco Baldini in chapter 10), Cameron has so far displayed a pragmatic approach that has eased fears of a Eurosceptic stance, fears initially fuelled by the Tories' exit from the mainstream European Popular Party group in the European Parliament following the 2009 elections. As Prime Minister, Cameron moved to overcome the bad impression this made showing the polite and conciliatory face of diplomacy. Thanks to a climate of institutional paralysis where the most delicate issues, such as budget reform, remain unaddressed, Cameron has had the opportunity to avert the UK's marginalisation from European decision-making. In foreign affairs, the situation is less simple, as Cameron will have discovered during his long trip from Washington to Beijing at the end of July 2010. Gianfranco Baldini's chapter argues that Cameron has inherited a foreign and defence policy that still struggles to accept the new repositioning of the country in the international scene as a middle power.

Within this context, Cameron has attracted much criticism, particularly for his speeches in Turkey and India, when he showed he had not properly understood the fine art of diplomacy, as he waded into minefields without the necessary precautions. However, the costs for the government have been minimal, with most attention focused on domestic policy and particularly the economy.

The following chapters will discuss these issues in much greater detail, looking at the election results themselves, the state of the major parties, the major policy dilemmas facing the UK in 2010 and the changing dynamics of the British political system. In the conclusion we will go back to some of the most salient political and economic constraints and social aspects of the first months of a government that promised to change the country, starting with the economy and the first steps towards welfare reform. Some of our analysis will remain necessarily tentative, and we hope to resist the temptation to speculate on future events. What one can conclude, at least, is that the 2010 election will certainly be remembered as a key moment in British political history, and a valuable opportunity to assess the nature of British politics and society in the new century.

Notes

1 At the beginning of April 2010, a survey showed that Nick Clegg was known to only 36 per cent of the electorate. Furthermore, 19 per cent thought he was the other Nick, Griffin, the leader of the British National Party (BNP) (Meltzer 2010).
2 See chapter 2 by Patrick Dunleavy; also Curtis (2010).
3 In 2011 some of the smaller parties – and in particular the Scottish National Party – protested about their exclusion from the televised debates. There could be further problems if the next elections take place in May 2015, as set out in the coalition agreement. In fact in this case the national vote would coincide with elections in Wales and Scotland and the exclusion from the debates of nationalist political leaders who may hold governing responsibilities in Edinburgh and Cardiff would be even more controversial.
4 At the end of February 2010, former Labour minister Peter Hain wrote a letter published in *The Guardian* to advocate a new coalition between his party and the Lib Dems after the 2010 elections (Hain 2010).
5 The Electoral Reform Society (also in favour of STV) found that by applying the two electoral systems to the 2010 elections, AV would have given 281 seats to the Tories, 262 to Labour and 79 to the Lib Dems, while with STV the three parties would have gained 245, 207 and 162 respectively (as it stands the Tories have 306 seats, Labour 258 and the Lib Dems 57).
6 According to data published after the elections, in 2009 a third of immigrants failed this test. The failure rate was particularly high among Iraqi, Bangladeshi and Turkish nationals (BBC 2010b).

References

Baldini, G. and A. Pappalardo (2009). *Elections, Electoral Systems and Volatile Voters*. Basingstoke: Palgrave Macmillan.

Bartle, J. (2006). 'The Labour Government and the Media', in J. Bartle and A. King (eds), *Britain at the Polls 2005*. Washington DC: CQ Press, pp. 124–150.

BBC (2010a). 'Lib Dems United After Fees Rebellion – Clegg and Cable', *BBC News*, 10 December. www.bbc.co.uk/news/uk-politics-11967644 (last accessed 1 October 2011).

BBC (2010b). 'Demo Outside Lib Dem Meeting Demands Electoral Reform', *BBC News*, 8 May. http://news.bbc.co.uk/1/hi/uk_politics /election_2010/8670060.stm (last accessed 1 October 2011).

Bogdanor, V. (2010). 'Change the Voting System, Change the UK', *Financial Times*, 10 August.

Crabtree, J. (2010). 'Who Are the Liberal Democrats?', *Prospect*, 172: 31–35.

Curtis, P. (2010). 'Move Over Mondeo Man – Mr Bored and Ms Mistrustful Rule Road in 2010', *The Guardian*, 27 February. www.guardian .co.uk/politics/2010/feb/27/mr-bored-mondeo-man (last accessed 1 October 2011).

Flinders, M. (2010a). 'Happy Together for Now But Will it Turn Out to Be a Shotgun Wedding?', *Yorkshire Post*, 14 May.

Flinders, M. (2010b). *Democratic Drift. Majoritarian Modification and Democratic Anomie in the United Kingdom*. Oxford: Oxford University Press.

Hain, P. (2010). 'Think Lib Dem, Vote Labour – To Beat the Tories', *The Guardian*, 25 February. www.guardian.co.uk/commentisfree/2010 /feb/25/be-lib-dem-vote-labour (last accessed 1 October 2011).

Hay, C. (2007). *Why We Hate Politics*. Cambridge: Polity.

Heath, A., R. Jowell and J. Curtice (2001). *The Rise of New Labour*. Oxford: Oxford University Press.

Jones, N. (2010). *Campaign 2010. The Making of the Prime Minister*. London: Biteback.

Kuhn, R. (2007). *Politics and the Media in Britain*. Basingstoke: Palgrave Macmillan.

Mandelson, P. (2010). *The Third Man. Life at the Heart of New Labour*. London: HarperCollins.

Marshall, P. and D. Laws (eds) (2004). *The Orange Book. Reclaiming Liberalism*. London: Profile Books.

Meltzer, T. (2010). 'Cheer Up, Only 29 Days to Go. Tom Meltzer's Election Diary', *The Guardian*, 7 April. www.guardian.co.uk/politics/2010 /apr/07/tom-meltzer-election-diary (last accessed 1 October 2011).

Stoker, G. (2006). *Why Politics Matters*. Basingstoke: Palgrave.

2

The British general election of 2010 and the advent of coalition government

Patrick Dunleavy

Introduction

In many respects the May 2010 general election in Britain seems to be one of those cases where an election is lost, yet without any clear winner emerging. It was also a contest that led to a historic outcome, a further decline in support for the top two parties and the advent of the first peacetime coalition government in the UK since the 1920s. I begin below by considering the shape of the basic results and then look at how voting behaviour changed in response to changing party strategies. The third section looks at the operation of the electoral system and the longer term significance of the 2010 election for long-run trends towards multi-partism in British politics. The fourth section examines the transition to a coalition government between the Conservatives and Liberal Democrats, led by David Cameron and Nick Clegg, and the basic parliamentary arithmetic and electoral situation that it confronts. The final section considers the longer term potential for change in British politics that has opened up from the election and its aftermath, especially for another wave of constitutional reform.

The essential election outcomes

The governing Labour Party under Prime Minister Gordon Brown ended thirteen years in power on a low note, losing one in six of the votes they had gathered in the previous 2005 general election. Yet in the last two days of the campaign, the party rallied votes against the prospects of Conservative cuts in public expenditure and succeeded in coming in a clear second. The party outperformed the final opinion polls by 2 per cent, suggesting a hardening of the Labour vote in the last hours of the campaign. In the last two days of the campaign a drama over public spending cuts and violent street protests in Greece played out on TV screens helped to dramatise and underline Labour's argument that a Conservative government in charge of austerity measures would hurt many different groups. Or perhaps the push by some Labour ministers for progressive voters to vote tactically for them worked a little. In any case Labour lost but remained well ahead of the Liberal Democrats, limiting their vote loss to 6 per cent compared with 2005 and holding many seats against the odds in their surrounding regions. Overall, the party did enough to live to fight another day. By late autumn 2010, now in opposition, Labour was back at level-pegging with the Conservatives in terms of opinion poll support and actually ahead in a number of polls.

The Conservatives became clearly the largest party in the 2010 election, thanks to the operations of Britain's famously unproportional voting system. Called plurality rule, this historic system features local competitions in 650 small districts, in each of which the winning party is whichever one gathers the most votes (that is, a plurality of votes, but not necessarily or even usually a majority). In the UK's modern multi-party conditions this system is highly erratic, but it normally ends up awarding the largest party a strong 'leader's bonus' of seats, as it did in 2010. Thus the Tories gained 48 per cent of seats in the Commons on the basis of winning just over 36 per cent of votes. Yet David Cameron's party actually increased their vote share by only 4 per cent compared with the Tories losing performance in 2005 (see Table 2.1). And despite their 'unearned' seats bonus, the Conservatives failed to win an overall majority in the House of Commons and had to negotiate a coalition deal to gain power. One of the party's right-wing grandees (Lord Tebbit) noted acidly about David Cameron's leadership that given the recession and Gordon Brown's unpopularity as Prime Minister, the Tories should have been 15 per cent ahead of Labour: in fact they were 7 per cent ahead. This was not an impressive performance, despite the party's advances made in terms of winning seats. But the always centrist-sounding Cameron was insulated from criticisms from his right wing because of the haul of new MPs achieved and the coalition government's strong public spending cuts.

Many overseas observers follow the bulk of the UK media in picturing British politics as some form of 'two and a half' party system. This at least half-heartedly acknowledges the presence of the UK's longest-running third party, the Liberal Democrats, and of strong, nationalist fourth parties in Scotland and Wales. The chief justification for this characterisation has been that throughout the post-1945 period the Conservatives and Labour have monopolised governing power between them, despite some periods

Table 2.1 The vote share results for the 2010 general election in Great Britain

Great Britain share of the votes	% votes	Change in support (% points) since 2005	Compare 2005 % vote share	MPs in 2010	Other party representation
Conservative	36.9	+ 4	33	306	All forums
Labour	29.6	− 6	36	258	All forums
Liberal Democrats	23.5	+ 0.4	23	57	All forums
UK Independence Party (UKIP)	3.2	+ 0.9	2.3	0	EP, GLA, LG
British National Party (BNP)	1.9	+ 1.2	0.7	0	EP, GLA, LG
Scottish National Party (SNP)	1.7	+ 0.1	1.6	6	EP, SP, LG
Greens	1.0	− 0.1	1.0	1	EP, GLA, LG
Plaid Cymru (Wales only)	0.6	− 0.1	0.7	3	EP, WNA, LG
Other parties/candidates	1.6	− 0.1	1.7	0	–
Total	100%				

Notes: EP – European Parliament; GLA – Greater London Assembly; LG – local government councillors; SP – Scottish Parliament; WNA – Welsh National Assembly.

This table excludes 17 MPs elected in Northern Ireland for a completely different set of parties, specific to that province. The parties winning seats there were the Democratic Unionists (8 MPs), Sinn Fein (5 MPs, who never take their seats), the Social Democratic and Labour Party (3 MPs), Alliance (1) and an independent MP.

of minority or near-minority (tiny Commons majority) government in the mid-1960s and later from 1974–1979. Yet the 2010 election is chiefly significant as the point where this deceptive pattern finally broke apart and the Liberal Democrats became a formal partner in a peacetime coalition government for the first time since the 1920s. The party can trace its heritage back to the heyday of a previous Tory-Liberal two-party system, which dominated UK politics from the mid-nineteenth century until 1922, and began to break up in acrimonious Liberal splits during the First World War. Fuelled by a merger during the 1980s with the Social Democratic Party (SDP), a Labour splinter party, the Liberal Democrats' return to power was quite some comeback, and I discuss the coalition-forming process and its reverberations for future politics below.

Yet in specific electoral terms, measured by their vote shares won or their ability to elect MPs, 2010 was also something verging near to a disaster for the Liberal Democrats, made all the worse by the illusory signs of success that the party racked up during the campaign. Under their young and more right-wing leader, Nick Clegg, the Liberal Democrats at times achieved apparent parity in opinion polls with the other two major parties. Yet in the final vote counts they fell back to a clear third place, lost seats to the resurgent Tories and gained only a compensating few MPs from Labour. They also completely failed in their hopes of 'breaking through' to second party status, practically standing still in terms of vote share. Clegg probably reaped a whirlwind that he himself sowed in some unguarded and hubristic moments during the campaign, when he declared that he could not work with Gordon Brown; insulted the PM as being 'desperate'; proclaimed a 'two-horse race' between the Liberal Democrats and Tories, with Labour 'out of it'; and so on. Rejecting Labour calls for tactical voting in the last two days before polling also now looks unwise in electoral terms (although it may have reflected Clegg's already-settled determination to work with the Tories in a hung parliament). Tactical voting is a quid pro quo deal – with no quid, the Liberal Democrats lost out to a Tory-Labour squeeze in many seats that they might otherwise have won or kept.

Denying that the UK is a multi-party system, as the press, media and many political scientists still do, also ignores the existence of several other smaller parties in Table 2.1, with significant and growing vote shares in some forms of election. It is true that Westminster's highly unproportional voting system means that most of the smaller parties have never won Commons seats, although in 2010 the Greens broke through this barrier for the first time. Yet the smaller parties all have substantial representation elsewhere, especially in the UK's many proportional elections (for the European Parliament, Scottish Parliament, Welsh National Assembly and Greater London Assembly) and in local councils.

In 2010 the top-performing smaller party was the UK Independence Party (UKIP), which contested nearly 90 per cent of seats in Great Britain. Table 2.1 shows that it achieved the highest fourth party score ever in post-war British politics, but its average vote share fell slightly in its contested seats compared with 2005. UKIP's campaign was hampered by its members having elected as their party leader Lord Pearson of Rannoch, a highly obscure peer, who secured little publicity for the party and resigned a couple of months after the election. His chief claims to fame were admitting to a TV interviewer that he had not read his party's whole manifesto and was unfamiliar with its details, rather airily proposing draconian public spending cuts of 50 per cent, and launching his party's campaign by advising people to vote for other parties if they felt that they could better secure the UK's withdrawal from the European Union or limit immigration (UKIP's two central campaign issues). The anti-immigrant, anti-foreigner and generally far right British National Party (BNP) fielded candidates in more than half of the seats (338) in Great Britain, covering nearly three times as many seats as it did in 2005. Its national vote share increased to 2 per cent, but its vote share per candidate fell back in the seats that it contested. Finally, the Greens contested a similar number of seats as the BNP and showed a similar increase in candidacies. But their national vote share fell back compared with 2005, to just over 1 per cent, and their average vote per contested seat almost halved. However, the Greens concentrated their campaigning resources in just two seats, and their party leader, Caroline Lucas, succeeded in winning one of them in Brighton, to give the party its first ever MP at Westminster. In Wales the nationalist Plaid Cymru saw its vote fall back, perhaps reflecting its being in coalition in the Welsh Assembly government with Labour. In Scotland the Scottish National Party (SNP), running a minority government in the Scottish Parliament, increased its vote share by 2 per cent but won no more seats against Labour in Scotland, who staged a specific resurgence there under the Scottish Gordon Brown.

How voting behaviour responded to party strategies

The analysis of mass political behaviour in the UK has not changed markedly in recent decades. Most analysts have recognised a long-run 'dealignment' process in which there is a weakening of the traditional (two-party heyday) links between the non-manual people owning their own homes voting Conservative and manual workers and social renters voting Labour. A rearguard group of analysts argue that occupational class is still the most important sociological influence on how British voters are aligned (Evans 2000), but realignment denial has suffered from increasing strain as the voting patterns across different occupational classes have clearly become more similar. Table 2.2 (a) shows that this trend acquired particular force in 2010. The 'top' three occupational classes had near identical patterns of support for the Conservatives and Labour, with the proportion of voters in skilled manual worker (C2) households voting Labour falling from 40 to 29 per cent between 2005 and 2010. Splitting by class and gender suggests that this decline was in fact concentrated among C2 women and that unskilled men also abandoned Labour somewhat more – but otherwise the changes across occupational classes were surprisingly uniform. Table 2.2 (b) shows how the odds ratios for voting Conservative rather than Labour changed from 2005 to 2010, comparing the top three occupational classes with the DE group. The numbers for the two non-manual classes fell markedly, meaning that the difference between middle-class and working-class groups clearly reduced in 2010. Checking other potential bases for alignment in individual voting data from surveys

Table 2.2 Occupational class and voting behaviour in the 2010 general election

(a) Per cent of each occupational class voting for main parties

	Conservative	Labour	Liberal Democrat	Other parties	Total
Occupational class					
Upper non-manual (AB)	39	26	29	7	100%
Routine non-manual (C1)	39	28	24	9	100%
Skilled manual (C2)	37	29	22	12	100%
Unskilled manual/ not working (DE)	31	40	17	12	100%

Source: Ipsos MORI (2010).

(b) Odds ratios for voting Conservative rather than Labour, compared with the unskilled (DE) group

	2010	2005
Upper non-manual (AB)	1.94	2.54
Routine non-manual (C1)	1.80	2.22
Skilled manual (C2)	1.65	1.58

shows no other marked changes in the sociological or demographic influences on voting.

However, looking at voting patterns across constituencies (called 'aggregate data analysis') offers additional insights, with the recession clearly having most impact on the government's defeat: 'Labour particularly lost ground in seats where there were both many working class voters and there had been a large increase in unemployment; in these circumstances the drop in Labour's vote was as much as 9.4 [percentage] points' (Fisher *et al.* 2010: 6). These authors also show that Labour's support stood up far better in seats with large proportions of public sector workers, but was 4 per cent lower in constituencies with little public employment. This is a big difference from 2005 when no such effect was visible, and Fisher *et al.* conclude that 'a new political gap seems to have opened up in Britain's electoral geography' (2010: 7). Voters' fears about the more vigorous public spending cuts promised by the Conservatives largely explain both this effect and the hardening of Labour support in the last few days of the campaign.

Turning to the political issues dividing the parties, the British Election Study (BES 2010) undertook extensive polling during the campaign period and found that economic issues completely predominated with voters in the aftermath of the 2008 financial crisis and recession. Three-fifths of BES respondents rated an economic issue most important, with 41 per cent citing the economy as the key issue plus a further 11 per cent citing government debt (a strong Conservative theme in the campaign) and 7 per cent unemployment. The second ranked issue was immigration (chosen as most important by one in six voters). Clearly the primacy of economic issues created difficulties for Labour as the incumbent government, because voters especially blamed Gordon Brown for the economic crisis – he had been at the helm economically at the Treasury for ten years until 2007, and as Prime Minister since then. Yet the premier was also seen by many voters as competent economically and the Conservative rival team as flawed, so this was less damaging than might have been expected.

Immigration was a much more toxic issue for the government, with many working-class people resentful of the influxes of immigrants into housing stress areas of major cities and some smaller towns (such as Slough, for example), and of increased competition for low-paid jobs. Ministers were seen as unresponsive to these concerns, although the government had tightened immigration rules somewhat and could not restrict EU workers' inward migration. The issues flared into huge prominence when a Labour-supporting voter taxed Gordon Brown with it and the PM was heard calling her a 'bigoted woman' as he drove away in his car with a broadcaster's radio microphone still switched on and transmitting. This gaffe late in the campaign put the right-wing press into a frenzy of denunciation, demoralised the Labour campaign, put Brown on the defensive (he had to apologise in a humiliating way) and seemed to crystallise ministers' indifference to what their working-class voters were saying. But the affair seemed to change relatively few voters' minds about how they eventually voted.

Labour's biggest issue, the National Health Service, on which the party had lavished billions of pounds of extra public spending, was rated top by only one voter in twelve, partly because David Cameron succeeded in making credible the Tories' pledge to exempt NHS spending from looming public expenditure cutbacks. Other issues, such as the war in Afghanistan, terrorism and environmental concerns were rated unimportant by many voters and played little role in the campaign. Having withdrawn British troops from Iraq, the Brown government did successfully attract back some of the support among Muslim voters in major cities, support which the party lost under Tony Blair in 2005.

Many British political scientists traditionally invoked the controversial concept of 'party identification' (constructed from survey responses about 'feeling closer' to one party or another) in order to explain voters' alignments. Yet the BES study in 2010 found absolutely no change at all in the distribution of these responses compared with 2005, so presumably this mysterious construct played no part in the big electoral changes between the two contests. More recently this line of analysis has been changed into an emphasis upon 'valence issues', including voters' perceptions of efficacy and ratings of leadership or 'performance politics' (Clarke *et al.* 2009). The 2010 general election provides a perfect setting for evaluating the significance of such factors, since for the first time in the UK it was marked by three televised leadership debates between the top three party leaders, Gordon Brown, David Cameron and Nick Clegg.

These debates attracted saturation media attention before, during and after each occasion and they were seen by large proportions of voters (three fifths for the first, half for the last and two fifths for the middle one, which covered foreign policy and defence issues of less interest to most voters). Seven out of ten voters thought that Nick Clegg won the first debate, sparking a huge increase in Liberal Democrat support, with many polls putting them at around 30 per cent support for the next two weeks. However, the party's support fell back a little after that, as the right-wing press conducted their own highly biased version of 'due diligence' on its liberal policies on immigration. David Cameron was seen as winning the last leader's debate by around half of voters. Gordon Brown was seen as coming last in all three debates, but did not do disastrously in any of them, contrary to his general media persona.

In the end, the debates' influence on actual votes proved to be highly ephemeral. The Clegg/Liberal Democrat campaign bubble burst with no visible trace of any impact on the party's pre-campaign levels of support, although it may have helped them survive even more of a Conservative-Labour squeeze effect (evidenced under previous unpopular Labour administrations). Cameron did not seem able to win over more voters than he had before, nor to convince those doubting the Tories' competence to give him the benefit of the doubt. So the evidence seems to be that 'valence' issues made apparent differences at the campaign level, but not enough to influence how voters cast their ballots against their evaluations of what the parties' programmes (especially on the economy) meant for their interests.

The electoral system and the UK's transition to multi-party politics

As late as 1970, nine out of ten voters across the whole of the UK supported one of the main two parties (the Conservatives or Labour) and the salience of voting for any other party was low. As early as the February 1974 election this situation changed rapidly, with two-party support falling to three quarters of voters, as Figure 2.1 demonstrates. Since 1992 a slower but steady further decline of the top two parties' combined support has brought it in 2010 to less than two thirds of all voters (65 per cent). As early as the two 1974 elections, the Liberals alone gained almost a fifth of votes, and in 1983 in alliance with the Social Democrats nearly a quarter, a high water mark which they have sometimes come close to again, but have yet to improve upon. Meanwhile the total support for smaller fourth, fifth and subsequent parties started off at less than 2 per cent of the UK totals in 1970 (some of it in Northern Ireland), but ended the sequence in 2010 at 12 per cent. It is worth emphasising how much of a transition in voting behaviour this was by calculating the two-party lead over all other parties, which the numbers in Figure 2.1 show started off at 80 per cent but have now fallen to 30 per cent, especially steeply and consistently in the period since 1992.

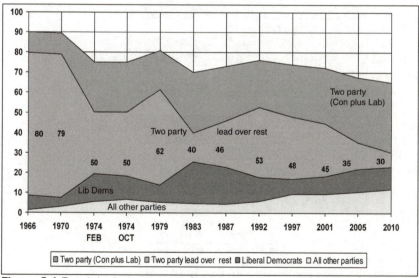

Figure 2.1 Trends in the vote shares for the top two parties and for smaller parties, 1970–2010

Note: The numbers in the grey area show the combined Conservative and Labour per cent support, minus the combined support for the Liberal Democrats and all other parties, that is the 'two party lead over the Rest'.

Another way of capturing this transition is to compute the 'effective number of parties' (ENP) score. This measure has some considerable problems of interpretation (Dunleavy and Boucek 2003), but it is simple to calculate and widely known. Figure 2.2 shows the ENP scores for all major elections in Great Britain since 1992, with the dark grey bars being plurality rule general elections for the House of Commons. The light grey bars are various forms of PR used in the UK for several other kinds of elections, including voting for MEPs to sit in the European Parliament (using a list PR system since 1999) and for the Scottish Parliament, the Welsh National Assembly and the Greater London Assembly (all using British variants of the 'additional member system' (AMS)) (Dunleavy and Margetts, 2001). It can be seen that all the general election ENP scores are always much smaller than those for PR elections. This is chiefly because voters know that in general elections the scales are stacked towards the bigger parties winning seats and the smaller parties being ineffective. This

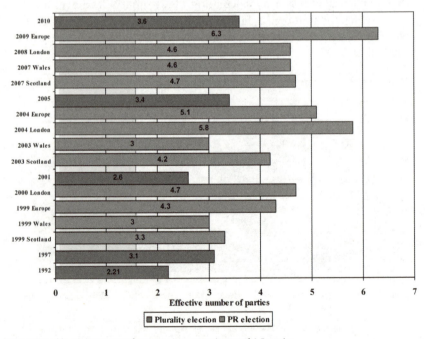

Note: Practicable minimum score for any voting system is around 1.5 parties.

Figure 2.2 The effective number of parties in terms of votes at major elections in Great Britain, 1992–2010

bias is still there in Britain's PR electoral system, but it is much less obvious and severe, so encouraging voters to support a wider range of parties more in line with their views.

The differences between PR and plurality rule elections can be seen vividly in the year 2009–2010. In the June 2009 European Parliament elections the PR system plus a surge of support for UKIP and the BNP (repeating almost exactly a 2004 surge) pushed the ENP score for Great Britain as a whole to 6.3 parties, while only eleven months later at the general election the number of parties fell to only 3.6. Yet the May 2010 result is a long way from the plurality rule starting position in Figure 2.2, with the Westminster ENP scores going from 2.2 in 1992, to 3.1 and 2.6 in 1997 and 2001, and then to 3.4 in 2005. Some political scientists dismiss the light grey bars in Figure 2.2 as data only from lower turnout, 'second order elections' of lesser importance. But there is no substantive basis for such a value-laden attitude and the light grey-bar elections have key implications for party performance in general elections, as 2005 rather strongly demonstrates. Another way of looking at this is that the electoral system 'reduced' the number of parties by 31 per cent when moving from the electorate's vote shares to the parties' seats shares in the Commons.

In addition to suppressing voting for smaller parties that are highly unlikely to win seats, the plurality rule electoral system of course takes the excluded parties' seat share nationally and awards it to others, normally to either the Conservatives or Labour. Whichever of the two is ahead characteristically gets a large 'leaders' bonus' in terms of winning seats that they are not entitled to in terms of their national vote shares. Figure 2.3 shows the combined effect of these processes in distorting the House of Commons from the breakdown of voters' preferences countrywide. I show here the 'deviation from proportionality' (DV) score, which can be construed as the proportion of all MPs whose party is not justified in holding these seats in terms of the party's national vote share. Figure 2.3 shows that in 2010 the DV score reached 23 per cent. This is a very high number indeed, for example, it is more than three times greater than the DV score for plurality rule in the USA, which is typically only around 7 per cent. Figure 2.3 also shows that all DV scores are much greater in general elections than in the UK's PR elections – where in the latest round of elections in Scotland, Europe and London DV scores were half or less than those in general elections. (This is not true of Wales, where there are too few 'top up' members to make the additional members system for the Welsh Assembly elections work proportionately. This feature was designed by the Labour government in the devolution settlement, in a bid to artificially maintain its historic party hegemony there.)

Advocates of electoral reform (and that included all parties at the 2010

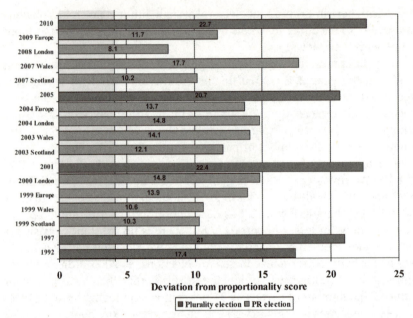

Note: Practicable minimum score for any voting system is around 4%.

Figure 2.3 Deviation from proportionality scores at major elections in Great Britain, 1992–2010

general election, except the Conservatives) generally argue that having a high deviation from proportionality is bad for electoral legitimacy, because voters know that their preferences are chewed up and served back to them only in a distorted fashion by the plurality rule voting system. Defenders of the status quo argue that plurality rule has two key virtues: it forms a strong link between a majority of local opinion and their MP; and nationally it produces 'clear' electoral outcomes where a 'swing of the pendulum' allows voters to choose between two credible single-party governments that give clear and unambiguous lines of electoral accountability. I look at the 2010 outcome of a hung parliament and a coalition government in the next section, but turn here to the arguments about strong links between MPs and their constituencies.

Figure 2.4 shows all the constituency outcomes in the 2010 general election, with each black square representing a single constituency outcome. The bottom axis shows the Conservative vote share minus the Labour vote share in each local area. So the further from the centre a constituency is to the right, the greater the Tory lead. And the more a constituency is on the left

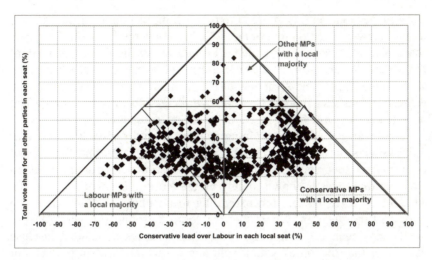

Figure 2.4 *The constituency outcomes in the 2010 general election, in Great Britain*

of the centre line, the more solidly Labour it is. The vertical axis here shows the combined share of votes going to all other parties, which we have seen in 2010 included the Liberal Democrats, UKIP, the BNP, the Greens, the nationalist parties in Scotland and Wales and all other candidates. All feasible outcomes must lie inside the overall double-triangle shape outlined here. There cannot be any outcomes outside this overall area.

The triangles inside and at the bottom of the overall feasible space in Figure 2.4 allow us to see immediately what proportion of MPs are from the top two parties and draw on local majority support in their constituencies. Every black square in the bottom right area is a Tory MP with local majority backing, and similarly Labour MPs with local majority support fall inside the bottom left triangle. (The top of the pyramid indicates the zone where Liberal Democrats, or the nationalists in Scotland and Wales, have some chance of enjoying majority support. It is set higher at a 60 per cent 'other' vote to allow for the fact that the 'other' vote splits across several parties.) The constituencies where MPs lacked majority support are those in the central inverted triangle – there are only a few tens of constituencies out of 650 seats in all.

Two-party contests completely disappeared in Britain in the 2005 general election and in 2010 there were also very few constituencies with only three parties contesting the seat. Figure 2.4 shows that right across the country support for parties other than the Conservatives and Labour is rarely less than a fifth of total votes, with exceptions occurring in only a few handfuls of seats. As a result the whole set of black squares showing constituency outcomes is located pretty much in the middle of the triangle, and a long way from the bottom axis – where Duverger's famous 'law' says that a plurality rule system should be. Instead, across the whole bottom third of the feasible area there are only a scattering of seats with total 'other party' votes below 20 per cent. Although the core band of seats is a long way up the chart, it still shows a marked Conservative versus Labour patterning – albeit at quite high levels of voting for third, fourth and subsequent parties.

Above all the advent of a hung parliament and the coalition government reflects the fact that the Liberal Democrats, SNP, Plaid Cymru and other parties now regularly win around 90 constituencies out of the 628 in Great Britain. This is shown mainly by the 'curling over' of seats on the sides of the distribution and extending in an upper swathe across the middle of the diagram. Where the total 'other party' vote is above 33 per cent, many seats are still won by the Conservatives or Labour, because remember that the 'other' vote is split across several different parties. But the higher up the squares occur on the chart, generally the less likely they are to be held by one of the top two parties.

To get an idea of how much change the 2010 results represent, suppose we flip back to the 1955 general election, a low point for Liberal party support and the heyday of the two-party Conservative-Labour system, shown in Figure 2.5. It is immediately apparent that it looks nothing like the 2010 results. In the vast majority of the 1955 constituencies there were no other candidates except the Conservatives and Labour. Hence in all those hundreds and hundreds of seats the outcome lies on the bottom axis itself – where seat after seat lies piled on top of each other, so many that the chart cannot possibly show them all. There were just 110 seats where the demoralised Liberals, and a few others, still put up candidates in 1955. Here the votes for 'other parties' still held up; these are the scatter of squares above the bottom axis, mostly concentrated in Conservative areas. However, even in these cases almost all the Conservative and Labour MPs were elected in local areas where they enjoyed local majority support, so that even these seats mostly fell inside the bottom left or bottom right triangles in Figure 2.5. Only around 40 seats are located in the central inverted triangle signifying that the MP elected there did not have local majority support. The contrast between Figures 2.4 and 2.5 shows how far the argument that the British voting system secures local accountability has degenerated, chiefly under the contemporary pressures of rising multi-partism among voters.

A final aspect of how the modern British system works in practice is the creation of what the 1999 Jenkins Commission on voting reform called 'electoral deserts' for the top two parties at the regional level, an effect shown in Figure 2.6. The same diagram discussed above is used to show

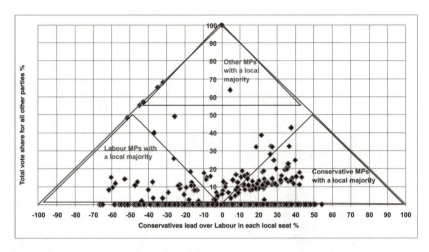

Figure 2.5 *The constituency outcomes in the 1955 general election, in Great Britain*

four contrasting regional political systems. In the top row, the south-east region reverted sharply to the Conservatives in 2010, so that Labour lost all but a handful of the seats that it had held there since 1997 (Diamond and Radice 2010). In the north-west, however, Labour MPs fought tenaciously and the party hung on to the bulk of its seats. In the bottom row of Figure 2.6, the Scottish system was orientated as a battle between Labour and the SNP (or Liberal Democrats in some specific areas), while the Conservative Party had little impact still. In Wales, however, Plaid Cymru, the Liberal Democrats and the Conservatives were all contenders in the middle, north and southern suburban areas with Labour holding its south Wales valley and industrial bastions.

After the election, the advent of coalition government

The last solid argument of plurality rule defenders has generally been that the system produces clear outcomes, so that the alleged 'complexities', 'delays', 'deals' and 'bargaining in smoke-filled rooms' associated with European-style coalition government formation can be avoided. Yet in 2010 with 645 MPs (excluding the five Sinn Fein MPs who never take their seats and so do not vote), the election result was a hung parliament. Table 2.3 shows that there were only six possible results in terms of forming a government (which would need at least 323 votes).

The only possible governments that were actually subject to serious negotiation were the top three, because they all involved only one or two

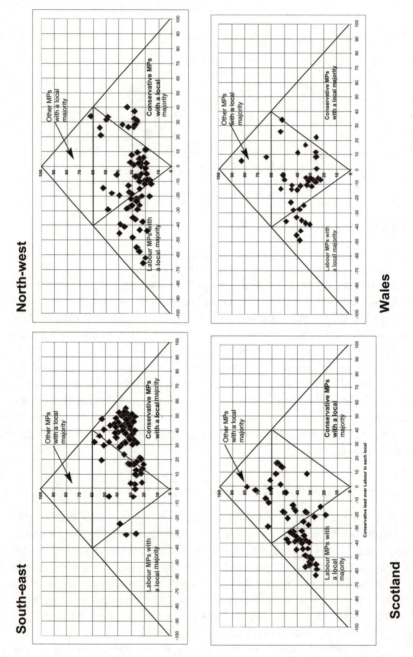

Figure 2.6 The patterns of constituency outcomes across four different regions in 2010

Table 2.3 Feasible governments that could have formed in May 2010

Possible government	Parties involved (number of MPs)	Overall seats (majority)
1. Two-way coalition government with a majority	Conservatives (306) + Liberal Democrats (57)	363 majority: 85
2. Two-way coalition government with no majority	Labour (258) + Liberal Democrats (57)	315 short by 8 seats
3. Single-party minority government	Conservatives only (306)	306 short by 17 seats
4. Multi-way coalition government with bare majority	Labour (258) + Liberal Democrats (57) + SNP (6) + Plaid Cymru (3) + SDLP (3)	327 majority: 13
5. Two-way minority government	Conservatives + Democratic Unionists (8)	314 short by 9 seats

parties being in government, with minority government (option 3) being what might happen if negotiations failed (the 'reversionary' position). The possibility of larger, multi-way coalitions was generally discounted by the leaders of all the three major parties, because a complex government relying on multiple parties for support could quickly collapse. In addition, the parties from Great Britain were very wary of becoming dependent upon any of the Northern Ireland parties for support – given the history of sectarian-influenced politics in that province. Beside options 1, 2 and 3, a Tory minority government was possible (this is what happened in February 1974 and again in 1977–1979). But it would almost certainly have meant another general election within a year or at most two, a timing that the PM would not necessarily be able to control. It was also an unattractive basis for dealing with the public spending cutbacks made necessary by the UK's ballooning budget deficit and huge borrowing to counteract the financial crisis and subsequent recession.

For David Cameron's Conservatives, a coalition deal with the Liberal Democrats seemed to offer the prospect of a five-year government with a secure majority. Meanwhile the Liberal Democrats had effectively only a choice of joining the same majority coalition or of forming a minority government with Labour, requiring that Gordon Brown resign and a new Labour leader be elected. Even then a Lab-Lib government would have had no majority and would have had to negotiate every piece of legislation with nationalist MPs and some Northern Ireland MPs to secure its passage. Since Nick Clegg was himself temperamentally on the right wing of the Liberal Democrats (with many free market as well as social liberal values) and since he had openly disparaged a failing Gordon Brown in the election campaign, it was predictable from early on in the negotiations that he would accept David Cameron's offer and reject Labour's.

Political scientists have also developed a way of estimating what share of power each party has in this situation in terms of its coalitional potential or C-score. (If you're already an expert, I am using here the 'normalised Banzahf score', see Taylor 1995: chapter 4.) Essentially this approach looks at every conceivable way in which a majority coalition could come about and then works out how many times each party's joining or leaving is critical for retaining a majority. For each party their C-score is given by the number of times they are vital to winning, divided by the total number of possible coalitions. Thus we get a share of all 'power as coalitional potential' that goes to each party.

We can use this approach to analyse the distribution of power in the House of Commons before and after the formation of the coalition government. The 'before' situation is shown in Table 2.4. The fourth column shows that although the Tories had over 47 per cent of MPs, they actually had only 37 per cent of the overall coalitional potential. It also shows that although Labour had five times as many MPs as the Liberal Democrats, on this basis the two parties' coalitional power was exactly the same, at just under a quarter each. The smaller parties all had smaller C-scores, but these were in each case several times bigger than their shares of MPs. The fifth column in Table 2.4 shows each party's total coalitional potential share divided by the number of its MPs, to give the average 'power' weight of each MP. It can be seen that this is lower for Labour. (In fact the second largest bloc almost invariably comes off worst on C-scores.) This measure also suggests that before the coalitional deal was done the Liberal Democrat MPs were individually each three times more influential over the coalitional outcome than were the Tory MPs.

Of course, a great many critics in political science argue that comprehensive coalitional potential scores are not good indicators of a broader concept of political power. C-scores are completely situational and locked into the present – they do not take any account of the past or future of the parties making deals. And small changes in the numbers of blocs (e.g. some backbench dissenters from any of the main parties) can make exaggerated differences to C-scores. Above all coalitional potential scores do not work very well in predicting what will happen empirically. In Table 2.4, Labour and the Liberal Democrats are assigned the same C-score – so if a Lab-Lib cabinet were to form this seems to predict that it would include equal

Table 2.4 Before the coalition – the coalitional potential and power scores for all parties in the House of Commons

Party	MPs	Resource weight: % of all (voting) MPs	C-score: % share of coalitional potential score (normalised Banzahf index)	C-score: per MP ratio	P-score: % share of power	P-score per MP ratio
Conservative	307	47.6	36.7	0.77	42.1	0.89
Labour	258	40.0	22.0	0.55	31.0	0.78
Liberal Democrat	57	8.8	22.0	2.49	15.4	1.75
Democratic Unionist Party (NI)	8	1.2	7.3	5.92	4.3	3.46
Scottish National Party	6	0.9	5.5	5.92	3.2	3.46
Plaid Cymru	3	0.5	1.8	3.95	1.2	2.47
Social Democratic & Labour Party (NI)	3	0.5	1.8	3.95	1.2	2.47
Green	1	0.2	0.9	5.92	0.5	3.46
Alliance Party (NI)	1	0.2	0.9	5.92	0.5	3.46
Others	1	0.2	0.9	5.92	0.5	3.46
Total	645	100 %	100 %		100 %	

Note: With separate Conservative and Liberal Democrat parties, there are a total of ten blocs in this situation.

numbers of ministers for both parties, which of course would greatly overstate Liberal Democrat influence. Empirically we might have expected that in a minority government coalition between the two parties Labour would get the large majority of cabinet seats and the Liberal Democrats a minority (perhaps five or six posts out of a cabinet of twenty-three).

To cope with such problems the last two columns in Table 2.4 show an extended conception of parties' power scores (the P-score), introduced here for the first time. This is essentially an average of each party's C-score plus their resource weight (in this case their percentage share of all MPs). The logic of this measure is twofold. First, resources are built up over time. A party's representation in parliament, for instance, is normally added to or lost only partly at any given general election. And the party's influence with the media, public opinion, the government apparatus and interest groups reflects how many seats it holds now (which bears on how much it can influence legislation) – but also how much the party might hold in the future, given its historical record and the prospects at the next general election. So averaging coalitional potential in the present with parties' resources in parliament (i.e. their percentage shares of all MPs) gives a much better guide to real, empirical power.

A second reason to prefer P-scores is that the C-scores assign all power to a majority government as soon as it has 51 per cent of MPs, and zero power to the opposition, which is clearly completely unrealistic. By contrast, the reformulated power score in the last two columns of Table 2.4 only gives a 'total power to the government' reading if the top party controls all seats in the Commons. So long as the opposition parties have MPs, in the P-score they also have a share of power – and this share is greater the closer the opposition is to matching the government lobbies. Again the P-score is far better than just looking at comprehensive coalitional potential, because parties' resource weights reflect their longer-term power, while the coalitional potential index taken on its own is very immediate and short term.

Looking at the 'before' coalition situation in Table 2.4, the P-score (real power) shows that again the Tories fell short of a winning position, but it places the Labour Party as having twice as much power in the hung parliament as the Liberal Democrats. It also marks down the influence of the smaller parties compared to the C-score. However, in terms of P-score per MP they still do well, as do the Liberal Democrats at the expense of the two largest parties' MPs. These power readings are also still the ones that will apply on issues that are handled via free votes during the 2010–2015 parliament, especially on certain issues that were exempted from the coalition agreement between the Conservatives and Liberal Democrats.

To see what changes occur after the Conservative-Liberal Democrat coalition is formed, Table 2.5 recalculates the C-scores and P-scores on the basis that these two parties now operate as a single bloc in the House of Commons. Power and influence scores are highly sensitive to blocs coalescing with each other and hence to reductions in the total number of blocs that are competing with each other. So when the largest and the third-largest blocs (i.e. the Conservatives and the Liberal Democrats) coalesce into one bloc for most voting purposes, thus reducing the total number of blocs to nine, we can expect to see big changes. And in this 'after coalition' picture, everything has indeed changed in a dramatic way.

The comprehensive coalition potential score now assigns all power to the coalition government with a score of 100 per cent and gives zero per cent to all the opposition parties, making not the slightest differentiation

Table 2.5 After the coalition – the coalitional potential and power scores for all parties in the House of Commons with the Conservative and Liberal Democrats treated as a single bloc

Party	MPs	Resource weight: % of all (voting) MPs	C-score: % share of coalitional potential score (normalised Banzahf index)	C-score per MP ratio	P-score: % share of power	P-score per MP ratio
Conservative-Liberal Democrat government	364	56.4	100	1.77	78.2	1.39
Labour	258	40.0	0	0	20.0	0.50
Democratic Unionist Party (NI)	8	1.2	0	0	0.6	0.50
Scottish National Party	6	0.9	0	0	0.5	0.50
Plaid Cymru	3	0.5	0	0	0.2	0.50
Social Democratic & Labour Party (NI)	3	0.5	0	0	0.2	0.50
Green	1	0.2	0	0	0.1	0.50
Alliance Party (NI)	1	0.2	0	0	0.1	0.50
Others	1	0.2	0	0	0.1	0.50
Total	645	100%	100%		100%	

between them. Essentially, the score is just saying 'I give up' at this point, because the combined Conservative and Liberal Democrat MPs do not need to coalesce with anyone else in order to win. But my revised power score keeps on working fine here, because we can still average the coalitional potential of a winning bloc and its resource weight. (We can in principle average it in many different, weighted ways: but for simplicity here I assume that we just take the mean of the two scores.) On this basis, the Cameron-Clegg government has more than three quarters of the total power in parliament, with Labour a long way behind on a fifth and the small parties sharing less than 2 per cent of power between them.

When the coalition first formed, many media commentators waxed lyrical about the disruptive potential of an 'awkward squad' of MPs on the Conservative right. But in ideological terms the Tory right are highly unlikely to vote with the opposition Labour Party on many issues, so that the most Tory dissidents can do is abstain. The maths of the situation show that a massive 84 out of the 307 Tory MPs will need to abstain before the government could lose a single Commons vote – which seems highly unlikely to happen. And even at this stage, the government would be the largest actor and its power score would not be dented greatly. Not until the government faced 100 abstainers would its power score fall below half.

We can use the same approach to assess the possibilities of rebellion from MPs on the left of the Liberal Democrats, who may feel pressured by party members anguished by the loss of the party's centre-left credentials and be unconvinced of the need for the massive public spending cuts that quickly became coalition policy. These dissenters could easily vote with Labour in ideological terms, thereby swelling the opposition ranks as well as depleting government support. But it would require forty-two of them before the government would be at all imperilled – that is, nearly three quarters of the Liberal Democrats MPs before losing any vote. Finally the government can probably rely on the eight votes of the Democratic Unionist Party from Northern Ireland most of the time, so that its insulation from defeat is even greater than I have allowed.

In other words, the Cameron-Clegg coalition looks remarkably strong in parliamentary power terms. And in the period since its formation to the time of writing it has proved remarkably cohesive and coherent in its various stances, with Conservative and Liberal Democrat ministers working well together. At this point, it seems certain to go whatever distance the two leaders and two sets of cabinet ministers want it to go, busting many paradigms in our thinking about British politics. Indeed it seems that single-party government is not at all needed for cohesive government, but that it is rather the product of a particular elite political culture, one that the Liberal Democrats' MPs share as much as the elites running the Conservative and Labour parties. The formal agreement between the Conservatives and Liberal Democrats says that the government will last a full parliamentary term of five years – and ministers will probably need that long to make the austerity cuts, weather unpopular times and come out on the other side. This suggests that the next UK general election will be held between May 2014 and May 2015, unless the coalition unravels in some spectacular fashion through internal splits before then.

The Labour Party tried hard to form coalition number 2 in Table 2.3 with the Liberal Democrats. But having been rejected, Labour moved swiftly to reconstruct its leadership. Gordon Brown announced his retirement as party leader almost as soon as the election results were clear, triggering a leadership election, which Ed Miliband narrowly won over his older and more experienced brother, David Miliband. Under its new leader, Labour may have to prepare for a long and frustrating opposition. If the coalition is still in being, a 2014 or 2015 election could easily spell a new electoral disaster for Labour, suggesting that the party needs to adjust its mindset to begin to compete effectively.

Longer term changes and voting reform

Three central elements of the coalition agreement between the Liberal Democrats and the Conservatives concerned constitutional reform. The parties first agreed to hold a referendum in May 2011 on changing the voting system at Westminster to the alternative vote system as used in Australia. This compromise proposal (also proposed by Labour in its 2010 manifesto) would keep the UK's local constituencies but allow voters in each area to number their preferences across parties in order (1, 2, 3 etc.), instead of just marking an X for their top preference (Travers *et al.* 2010). All the first (top) preferences that voters have given are counted, as now. If any candidate gets majority support (i.e. 50 per cent + 1), they immediately win the seat. If not, the candidate who has the fewest first preference votes is knocked out of the contest and we look at the second preferences of this party's voters, redistributing these votes to the remaining candidates in the race. This process of knocking out the least popular candidate and redistributing their voters' choices as voters intended continues until one candidate gets 50 per cent. In the USA this system is called 'instant run-off' and this is a good summary of what AV does – it delivers a run-off election when no one gets an outright majority on first preference votes.

Looking back to Figure 2.4, it should be clear that AV will make a clear difference in the more than two thirds of constituencies shown against a white background, where in 2010 the winning MP lacked local majority support. Figure 2.7 shows how the BES study team project that voting outcomes would have changed, based on their large survey. The AV system would have given the Liberal Democrats thirty-two more seats, two thirds coming from the Tories and one third from Labour, creating a considerably more proportional distribution of seats in parliament. However, this effect would not necessarily apply in other circumstances. Equally detailed studies of AV's impact on the 1992 and 1997 general election results show that at that time the Liberal Democrats would have gained 15 to 20 more seats. But in 1997, when Labour was in the ascendant, Blair's party would also have benefited, creating an even greater under-representation of Tory MPs than in fact occurred in that year. In other words, the impact of AV is rather volatile, depending on the fine distribution of opinion. For example, in a 2014 or 2015 election if the Conservatives and Liberal Democrats are still in coalition or have any kind of electoral pact, then AV could be very damaging for Labour.

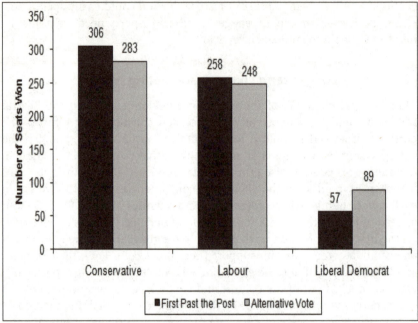

Source: BES (2010).

Figure 2.7 How the alternative vote would have worked at the 2010 general election

In the event, the alternative vote was decisively rejected by voters in the 2011 referendum. The Conservatives agreed to holding the referendum, but were free to campaign against any change and many prominent Tories did so. Some 'old style' Labour MPs joined the Tories in opposing any changes in Westminster voting. The official Labour position was in favour of the 'yes' vote, but the party did not campaign too strongly for any change, partly in the hope that the referendum defeat could increase the strain between the two coalition parties. And for the Liberal Democrat activists, AV was anyway only a pale shadow of the PR system that they have long campaigned for, which is the single transferable vote system already used in Northern Ireland and in Scottish local government.

The second key constitutional reform element of the coalition agreement concerned changing how Westminster seats are allocated across the country. The Conservatives wrote into the coalition agreement that the House of Commons must be reduced in size to 600 MPs and that these seats must be rigorously designed so as to have the same average size, plus or minus 5 per cent. Constituency redrawing must occur every five years in response to population changes and the previous long-winded boundary review inquiries are to be abolished. These changes will not be easily implemented (Baston 2010; Johnston 2011). They will clearly tend to reduce Labour's advantage in recent elections and the party accordingly bitterly opposed the changes, especially in the House of Lords where a filibuster almost prevented the law passing in time for a referendum to take place in May 2011. However, some analyses suggest that it is in fact the Liberal Democrats who may lose most seats from the changes, because reducing the number of seats is disruptive for their MPs holding 'isolated' seats (Baston 2011).

The third key constitutional reform element of the coalition agreement was reform of the House of Lords to make it a wholly or mainly elected chamber, the Conservatives favouring only 80 per cent elected members and Liberal Democrats tending towards universal election. The government will outline proposals for changes in early 2011 and they are likely to include using a proportional representation voting system of some kind, opening up new opportunities for the Liberal Democrats and smaller parties to perhaps win enhanced representation at Westminster. What yet remains uncertain is whether there is any realistic prospect of the government giving sufficient priority to Lords reform to enact these changes before the end of its term in office. Before the general election David Cameron described Lords reform as a 'third term priority', i.e. a long way down his list of priorities.

Conclusion

Despite the outcome of the AV referendum and Lords reform, it seems likely that Britain will continue to develop electorally towards essentially a European-style multi-party system. The Tories and Liberal Democrats hope to weather the political storm anticipated around public spending reductions and emerge in 2014 with a renascent economy and a case for re-election. By autumn 2010 the Liberal Democrats were already suffering a crisis of support, with only around half their general election support in some opinion polls, locking them ever more tightly into depending upon the coalition, while the Conservatives were so far little affected. In midterm elections at least, it is likely that momentum will swing towards Labour for a time as the spending cuts bite. But other smaller parties are also likely to revive if economic conditions worsen, especially the far-right UKIP and BNP, while the Greens' political presence might also grow. The lasting impact of the 2010 election is likely to be that it made explicit in governmental terms a series of trends towards greater political diversity, which I hope to have shown are deep-rooted in the British society and polity. A great deal now depends on whether the coalition's hopes for extended cooperation in government can be sustained and on whether this cooperation lasts up to and into the next general election.

References

Baston, L. (2010). 'Do Turkeys Vote for Christmas? Yes, When it Comes to Liberal Democrat MPs and the Boundary Review for Westminster Constituencies. Nick Clegg's Party Will Lose a Fifth of All its MPs', British Politics and Policy blog, 9 December. http://blogs.lse.ac.uk /politicsandpolicy/2010/12/09/do-turkeys-vote-for-christmas-yes-when-it-comes-to-liberal-democrat-mps-and-the-boundary-review-for-westminster-constituencies-nick-clegg%E2%80%99s-party-will-lose-a-fifth-of-all-its-mps/ (last accessed 1 October 2011).

Baston, L. (2011). 'Britain's Unequally Sized Constituencies Are a Non-existent Problem, to Which the Coalition Government Has Adopted an Extreme and Perhaps Unworkable Solution', British Politics and Policy blog, 7 January. http://blogs.lse.ac.uk/politicsandpolicy /2011/01/07/britain%E2%80%99s-unequally-sized-constituencies-no -problem/ (last accessed 1 October 2011).

BES (2010). 'British Election Study 2009–10'. http://bes.utdallas .edu/2009/ (last accessed 1 October 2011).

Clarke, H., D. Sanders, M. Stewart and P. Whiteley (2009). *Performance Politics and the British Voter*. Cambridge: Cambridge University Press.

Clarke, H., D. Sanders, M. Stewart and P. Whiteley (2010). 'Electoral Choice in Britain, 2010: Emerging Evidence from the BES', 25 June. http://bes.utdallas.edu/2009/report/elecchoicever7june25.ppt (last accessed 1 October 2011).

Diamond, P. and G. Radice (2010). *Southern Discomfort Again*. London: Policy Network. http://pn.winonaesolutions.net/uploads/media/154 /7134.pdf (last accessed 1 October 2011).

Dunleavy, P. and F. Boucek (2003). 'Constructing the Number of Parties', *Party Politics*, 9 (3): 291–315.

Dunleavy, P. and H. Margetts (2001). 'From Majoritarian to Pluralist Democracy: Electoral Reform in Britain since 1997', Journal of Theoretical Politics, 13 (3): 295–319.

Evans, G. (ed.) (2000).'The Continued Significance of Class Voting', *Annual Review of Political Science*, 3: 401–417.

Fisher, S., J. Curtice and R. Ford (2010). 'The British General Election of 2010: The Results Analysed', paper to the American Political Science Association Conference, Washington DC, 3 September. http://papers.ssrn.com/sol3/papers.cfm?abstract_id=1643443 (last accessed 1 October 2011).

Ipsos MORI (2010). 'How Britain Voted 2010'. Data slides at www.ipsos-mori.com/researchpublications/researcharchive/poll.aspx?oItemId=26 13 (last accessed 1 October 2011).

Johnston, Ron (2011). 'Why Are Labour Lords Keeping Their Peers Up Late? Opposition to the Coalition's Plans for Fewer MPs and More Equal Constituencies', British Politics and Policy blog, 18 January. http://blogs.lse.ac.uk/politicsandpolicy/2011/01/18/labour-house-of -lords-and-the-reform-bill/ (last accessed 1 October 2011).

Taylor, A. D. (1995). *Mathematics and Politics: Strategy, Voting, Power and Proof*. Berlin: Springer-Verlag.

Travers, T., P. Dunleavy and C. Gilson (2010). 'The LSE's Simple Guide to Voting Systems', British Politics and Policy blog, 12 May. sshttp://blogs.lse.ac.uk/politicsandpolicy/?p=2356 (last accessed 1 October 2011).

3

The Labour Party

Eric Shaw

Introduction

The general election of 6 May 2010 brought to an end the longest ever period of Labour government. To have secured a third substantial majority in 2005 was a remarkable achievement and most in the party were aware that to notch up a fourth victory would not be easy. But five years later Labour's score had sunk to 29 per cent, its second worst in ninety years and only marginally better than the disastrous result of 1983. What had gone wrong?

In fact, it had won the 2005 election with only 35.2 per cent of the vote, compared to 43.2 per cent in 1997 and 40.7 per cent in 2001, netting a loss of millions of voters. It garnered less support in England than the Conservatives and benefited heavily from an electoral system skewed in its favour. The dominance the party had enjoyed under Tony Blair's leadership was coming to an end, Blair was dogged by the backwash of his highly unpopular war in Iraq and faced unrelenting pressure from his Labour rival Gordon Brown to resign (Rawnsley 2010: 361–362). But Brown, once he had taken over as Prime Minister, failed to reverse Labour's electoral decline. He enjoyed a short honeymoon of popularity in the summer of 2007, but after planning and then pulling out of a snap autumn election Brown's premiership, and indeed the whole of Labour's third term, were overshadowed by two events – a hugely embarrassing political expenses scandal and, even more serious, the most severe economic crisis since the Great Depression. These two events effectively sealed Brown's, and the Labour government's, fate.

New Labour, Giddens declared shortly after the election, was 'dead' (Giddens 2010). It is too early for a full autopsy but a preliminary coroner's hearing focusing in particular on its final years may be useful. What did New Labour stand for? What were its ambitions for British society? What were its guiding principles? How far did it succeed in achieving its political objectives? And what is the party's political future? This chapter seeks to answer these questions by looking at Labour's attempts to manage the economy and reconcile the sometimes conflicting goals of economic growth and social justice. Until 2007, competent management of the economy was regarded as one of New Labour's major strengths and Gordon Brown, as Chancellor of the Exchequer for the first decade of Labour's period of office, took particular personal credit for the apparent success of Labour policies. But the onset of the credit crunch blew these claims apart and Labour was forced to grapple with the worst economic crisis since the 1930s. The next section of this chapter examines the main components of Labour's political economy.

New Labour and social justice

During the Blair years it became commonplace in the media to dismiss New Labour as all soundbites and focus groups, image and tinsel. New Labour did indeed exhibit an acute sensitivity to the shifting currents of public opinion and rarely was an initiative unveiled without thought about how it would play with the media. But, equally, it was a government that 'built its policies on the basis of careful and complex analyses of the origins and character of the problems that those policies [were] designed to redress' (Coates 2005: 185). All politicians, Jack Straw averred, need a 'framework of belief ... so that there is some template for the scores of individual decisions which they have to make every day' (Straw 1998). There has been much debate about the nature of New Labour's 'framework of belief'. Few could doubt the far-reaching alterations in the party's ideological physiognomy over the years but opinions differed about whether this entailed the shedding of the party's core values. For some commentators, the metamorphosis was so drastic that, in effect, a new political organism emerged, one that could more accurately be characterised as 'centre-right' (Levitas 2005: ii). Acting 'massively in favour of capital to promote growth' by disciplining the labour force and 'little concerned with inequalities' it was 'certainly not a classical social-democratic government' (Faucher-King and Le Gales 2010: 41). Other commentators disagreed. For Giddens, the Labour government stood firmly by the values of 'solidarity, a commitment to reducing inequality and protecting the vulnerable, and a belief in the role of active government' while understanding that 'the policies designed to pursue these ends had to shift radically because of profound changes going on in the wider world' (Giddens 2010). By the close of its second term it had 'become a recognisably social democratic government' though one 'that only half-heartedly admits to beings so' (Riddell 2005: 67. For other views see, for example, Bevir 2005; Coates 2005; Driver and Martel 2006; Shaw 2007).

There is, as we shall see, truth in both these views. The key theme of this chapter is that the New Labour programme can best be understood as a sustained and comprehensive effort to marry together social justice with neo-liberal economics – to advance what might be called 'marketised social democracy'. It remained strongly committed to the pursuit of social justice, though with the accent on 'fairness' rather than equality. By fairness it meant the adoption of policies that would enable all people, whatever their background disadvantages, to realise their potential. This would entail a sustained expansion in public expenditure, which could only be financed by economic growth. The 'Old Labour' preference for regulation and intervention had to be scrapped and replaced by a hard-headed acknowledgment of 'the wealth-creating potential of markets' (Buckler and Dolowitz 2000: 310). It followed that Labour's object should not be to curtail or restrain the operations of the market but to utilise the power of the state to create the conditions in which a market economy could flourish.

What New Labour stood for above all was the socially inclusive meritocratic society where all, irrespective of background, would have the opportunity to advance themselves and fulfil their goals. The principal institutional means for securing this goal was the creation of an 'enabling state'. As two senior New Labour advisors put it, the role of the state as enabler was that of 'ensuring people are able to develop their capabilities, increasing social mobility by breaking the insidious link between parental origins and destinations, and giving people new opportunities throughout their lives' (Diamond and Liddle 2009: 235).

A whole battery of policies was put in place to realise this vision. Here we can only briefly review some of them. The various New Deals (e.g. for the long-term unemployed, for the young, for single mothers) helped to ease transition to the labour market – a vital part of New Labour's strategy, which saw paid work as the best way to build a socially inclusive society. For the government the main cause of joblessness was not (as Keynesians tended to argue) deficiency in demand for labour but supply-side factors such as lack of skills or appropriate qualifications, inadequate information and advice, poverty traps and the absence of child-care facilities. Its response was twofold: enhancing 'employability', that is equipping people with relevant skills which facilitated their integration into paid employment; and 'welfare to work', that is gearing the organisation of the welfare system more tightly to the needs of the labour market.

Vital to employability and the amassing of 'human capital' was access to good quality education. A huge amount of funding was committed to this end. A major building programme renovated schools, the numbers of teaching staff grew, pay was raised and facilities greatly improved. A myriad of initiatives was devised to raise the standards of primary and secondary education, including reductions in class sizes, and the introduction of numeracy, literacy and science hours and Education Action Zones. A pivotal role was assigned to the Sure Start programme whose aim was 'to improve the nurture and parenting of disadvantaged children through the provision of advice, support and nursery places' (Levitas 2005: 52).

The government was upbraided by some critics for failing to do more to help the disadvantaged. But it did confront a tricky political problem since the evidence suggested that the amount of public support for redistribution fell during the years of the Labour government (Horton and Gregory 2009: 99).[1] For this reason benefits were targeted at the politically most appealing groups, the young and the elderly (Diamond and Liddle 2009: 229). The minimum wage played a major role in raising the income levels of the poorly paid by providing a wage threshold. Millions benefited. Further the government enacted legislation that procured significant improvements in the working conditions and entitlements of many employees (mainly by enacting EU directives into British law), and took steps to protect the rights of workers transferred from the public to the private sector. However, low rates of pay and insecure employment remained major problems, which, if anything, the government's policy of encouraging migration flows from new EU members – as a device to dampen inflationary pressures – tended to exacerbate. Trade union ability to push wages up was, in addition, restrained by the government's resolve to maintain intact much of the employment law framework it inherited from the Tories.

Reforming the public sector

The Labour government's strong commitment to much heavier investment in public services was coupled with an insistence on the need for reform. A central tenet of New Labour thinking was that public services did *not* have to be delivered by public organisations. What mattered was that key services (such as schooling and healthcare) should be provided according to need and free at the point of consumption. Rather than insisting on its right to provide all services directly, 'the enabling state' should, the Prime Minister's Strategy Unit maintained, 'help to empower citizens by introducing much greater diversity of service provision – extending the choices available to users and ensuring that the best providers (whether from the public, private or voluntary sector) are used' (PMSU 2007:14). Choice became the mantra of New Labour. Choice within a competitive system – the so-called internal or quasi-market – would empower the service-user (or consumer) and ensure that service improvement would be self-sustaining. Services delivered by public sector monopolies, it was felt, tended to be wasteful and inefficient, resistant to innovation and prone to 'producer capture'. Choice and competitive pressures – including from private providers – would have a galvanising effect on public services, enhancing the quality of services and ensuring more efficient use of resources (see Shaw 2009b). The government drew upon many other techniques and practices associated with so-called 'new public management', such as targets, performance indicators, audits, appraisal mechanisms and performance-related pay, which were intended to both simulate or mimic market pressures and impose sanctions upon laggardly service providers.

The evidence that such market-oriented policies would achieve their objectives was not at all conclusive and there were many within the public sector who felt that scarce resources were being squandered by both the pace and the direction of the changes (see Shaw 2009a). These doubts appeared to be shared at the highest levels within the government. Blair encountered persistent obstruction from his Chancellor and many within his entourage were convinced that Number 11 had helped foment massive rebellion against such market-oriented initiatives as 'foundation' hospital trusts and (after 2005) the expansion of (partly independently run) 'City Academies'. But it soon became evident that Brown was no less enthusiastic a proponent of 'modernisation' than his predecessor. In a heavily trawled and widely publicised article in the *Financial Times* he promised 'a greater diversity of providers, more choice and in many areas more competition'. He made his position on public service reform unequivocally clear: 'there can be no backtracking on reform, no go-slow, no reversals and no easy compromises'. He promised a faster expansion of the contentious City Academies programme, more personal budgets and more participation by the private sector in the delivery of NHS care (Brown 2008).

Notwithstanding the controversies over public service reform, the overall thrust of New Labour's policies on tax, benefits and public services was decidedly redistributive. Coates concluded that 'it is difficult to think of a single area of government intervention since 1997 which has not been related to questions of poverty and inequality' (Coates 2005: 187). Although open redistribution was rarely celebrated by the government, the effect of increases in investment in public services clearly benefited those poorer citizens which tended to be the heaviest users of them.

New Labour and business

While New Labour strove to raise the living standards of the poor, the narrowing of inequality *per se* was not an important policy objective. Its vision was that of 'an aspirational Britain' in which 'the talents and potential of all the British people [are] fulfilled: social mobility for the majority' (Brown 2010) – not an egalitarian society. What was important was not *how* resources were distributed but providing all people, irrespective of social background, with the ability to rise in the world. Inequality was indeed seen as a functional requisite in complex market economies operating in a highly competitive globalised world economy. New Labour's 'key philosophical principle' was thus not equality as an end in itself but to ensure that the less well off should have the resources to compete for success.

Equality of outcome was discarded because it was seen as neither practicable nor particularly desirable. It was not practicable because steeper tax rates on business and the wealthy were seen as self-defeating. The view was taken that if Britain's entrepreneurs and bankers were faced with higher tax bills they would simply relocate to countries with more lenient tax regimes. Business, investment and valuable talent would all be lost and the net effect would be an actual fall in tax revenues. Equally, greater equality of outcome was not really desirable since high rates of corporate and individual tax were economically damaging. As Blair and Schroeder explained, tax cuts for business and the wealthy raised profitability and strengthened the incentives to invest: 'higher investment expands economic activity and increases productive potential. It helps create a virtuous circle of growth' (Blair and Schroeder 1999). Enterprise, profit-seeking and the willingness to take risks, upon which the future of the economy depended, required the spur of substantial personal incentives. The government largely accepted 'trickle-down theory', which held that society as a whole ultimately benefited from the dynamism imparted to the economy by fostering the entrepreneurialism of the wealthy (Lansley 2008: 33).

Brown was the principal architect of New Labour's business-friendly tax regime. 'Rewarding risk takers, valuing entrepreneurial talent and celebrating successful wealth creators as role models' were, he declared, central to New Labour economic policy (Brown 2005). He noted with some satisfaction in 2004 that his government, 'unique in terms of Labour's history', had cut capital gains tax from 40 per cent down to 10 per cent, corporation tax from 33 to 30 per cent and small business tax from 23 to 19 per cent (Brown 2004). Generous pay, bonuses, fees and capital gains poured into the coffers of bankers, hedge-fund founders and private-equity partners, all of which were lightly taxed. 'Non-doms' (residents non-domiciled for tax purposes) were also generously treated. Under New Labour the UK had 'one of the most generous tax regimes for creators of businesses, for entrepreneurs, of any developed economy' (Peston 2008: 59). Tax avoidance – upon which a younger Brown had threaten to crack down – burgeoned and the UK evolved into a 'gigantic tax haven for the internationally mobile business elite' (Peston 2008: 339). According to an estimate by HMRC officials tax evasion and tax avoidance were diverting a massive £40bn each year from public revenues (Inman 2010). The net result was under New Labour the riches of the wealthiest 1 per cent soared into the stratosphere, while incomes at the lowest levels did little more than stagnate. 'The really striking phenomenon under New Labour', the BBC's business editor commented, 'has been the triumph of the super-rich' (Peston 2008: 7). For Brown none of this mattered as long as the economy grew and the Treasury's coffers bulged with rising tax receipts from the City.

In fact, the evidence that high pay and bonuses and lenient tax regimes for the rich had actually benefited the economy, in terms of output growth and productivity, was always scanty (Lansley 2008: 24; Peston 2008: 343–344, 346; Toynbee and Walker 2008: 46). Indeed the opposite may well have been the case. Adair Turner, chair of the Financial Services Authority (FSA), argued that vast rewards available in the City had actually damaged the economy by sucking talent from its more productive sectors (Treanor 2009).[2] A high reward system had indeed, as intended, encouraged risk taking and 'financial innovation' – but this had disastrous consequences. In February 2008, a report from the Financial Stability Forum (composed of central bankers and regulators) concluded that among the causes of the financial crisis was 'the lavish performance-pay regimes on Wall Street and the City which encouraged disproportionate risk taking with insufficient regard to longer term risks' (quoted in Lansley 2008: 22). None of this had been remotely anticipated by New Labour. To understand why we need to explore its political economy.

The political economy of New Labour

In no area did New Labour depart more sharply from the traditional party thinking than in economic strategy. Its reasoning ran as follows: the interventionist approach favoured by the party in the past, with its commitment to a regulated market economy, high public spending financed by a steeply progressive tax regime and close collaboration with trade unions within a corporatist framework had reached a total impasse by the end of the 1970s. 'Those on the right', Blair told bankers at Goldman Sachs, had 'correctly identified the obstacle of Big Government as holding people back: too much bureaucracy, too high taxes, too much trade union power, insufficient room for individual initiative and enterprise' (Blair 2004). In key areas of political economy – deregulation of the economy, privatisation, the importance of monetary and fiscal discipline and the new industrial

relations legal framework – New Labour accepted the Thatcherite settlement (Riddell 2005: 201). This was not a tactical shift. 'The decision to
accept the broad outlines of what Thatcher had wrought', Cronin has
pointed out, was 'not just a reluctant concession to what was politically
feasible but a recognition that much of what the Conservatives had said
and done in the 1980s was effective and in some sense appropriate'
(Cronin 2004: 394).

The cornerstone of New Labour policy was stability in macroeconomic
management – particularly price stability. This was seen as vital to secure
the confidence of the financial markets – without which, Brown endlessly
reiterated, no government could survive – and hence the essential foundation for sustainable long-term growth. The problem, as key New Labour
policy-makers saw it in 1997, was how to convince the markets that a
Labour government could be trusted to act 'prudently'. The answer was for
it to constrain its own behaviour – to limit its capacity to act in ways that
the financial markets would deem as ill-judged. Self-restraint was to be
achieved in two ways: monetary policy run independently of government
and a rules-based fiscal policy. The first was achieved by transferring
control over interest rate policy to the Monetary Policy Committee of the
Bank of England which, in turn, was charged with meeting an inflation
target of 2.5 per cent. The second took the form of constraining the government's fiscal discretion by setting firm rules. These were: (1) the so-called
'golden rule', which stipulated that 'over the economic cycle the government will borrow only to invest and that current spending will be met from
taxation'; and (2) the 'sustainable investment rule', which held that public
debt as a proportion of national income would be held at a prudent and
stable level (at about 40 per cent) over the economic cycle (Brown 1997).

For some commentators, all this demonstrated that New Labour now
subscribed, in its essentials, to new right political economy. According to
Cerny and Evans it had embraced the notion of the 'competition state' with
its focus on maximising economic competitiveness by freeing-up markets,
supply-side policies, strict control of public expenditure and tough anti-
inflationary policies (Cerny and Evans 2004: 55). Similarly Jessop
contended that New Labour 'has largely followed in the tracks of the neo-
liberal regime shift it inherited ... It has maintained the broad strategic line
embodied in ... neoliberal economic strategy' (Jessop 2003). Having
accepted 'fiscal discipline as an unavoidable constraint over policy making'
it had left itself with 'no option but to adopt public expenditure cuts in the
core areas of the welfare state, like pensions, unemployment or disability
insurance' (Bonoli 2004: 205).

This is a one-sided rendering of New Labour strategy. For the government it was precisely its success in securing credibility in the eyes of the

financial markets that would allow it to achieve its social goals – to make substantial inroads into poverty and educational disadvantage, improve the range and quality of healthcare and embark on a comprehensive assault on squalor and deprivation (Balls 1997; Peston 2005: 172, 190–191). Once the confidence of global and domestic investors had been won, and the government had gained a reputation for sound economic management, it would have more leeway – not least to relax fiscal policy by creatively interpreting its own rules. As Watson comments, 'the game-keeper, in effect, had turned poacher' (Watson 2008: 585).

The problem, for New Labour, was this. It wanted (and it believe the public wanted it) to establish high quality public services. This required a steady increase in public spending. Equally, it felt (perhaps wrongly) that raising taxes to meet the bill would be politically dangerous. So, after 2003–2004, it allowed the public finances to take the strain through increased public borrowing. The bond markets, now willing to repose confidence (for the first time) in a Labour government, saw nothing amiss. Ironically, the Keynesian economics that New Labour so disparaged would have advised, in a period of sustained economic growth, counter-cyclical policy, that is building up surpluses or at the very least reducing the deficits. Instead, Brown allowed the budget deficit to grow and in his final budget, in preparation for his imminent arrival in Number 10, Brown not only kept the spending taps running but chose, in an extraordinarily short-sighted if politically popular move, to cut income tax by 2 per cent. And, crucially, there was hardly a murmur in the financial markets (Rawnsley 2010: 439).

Public spending could grow because an expanding economy generated the tax revenues while the bond markets were happy to make up the shortfall. Nominally, New Labour's strategy for growth was the 'social investment state' (Giddens 2000: 52). This concept was grounded in so-called new growth or (somewhat misleadingly) 'New Keynesian' theory. The UK (along with other developed economies) could only compete with third world low-cost producers by specialising in high value-added, infor-mation-rich goods and services. In this new information economy human capital – the skills, expertise and adaptability of the workforce – was the vital factor of production (Giddens 2000: 52). The state would retreat from its role as owner, controller and regulator of economic processes, but expand its role in the provision of social and public infrastructure, and strategic investment in education, training and research. The idea of the knowledge economy, within New Labour discourse, in effect operated 'as the corner stone of a modernisation narrative around information technol-ogy, education and lifelong learning, innovation and entrepreneurship' (Andersson 2007: 2).

Such, at least, was the theory – actual performance fell short. Compared to countries such as Germany and France a much higher proportion of the UK workforce (about a third it was estimated in 2006) lacked any recognised skills at all (Taylor 2007: 234). A 2004 Office of National Statistics study noted that 'in recent years the aggregate amount of spending on research and development in the UK has lagged behind that of our international competitors'. The eminent economist and senior government advisor Lord Layard felt that policy on skills and training had been 'a major failure' (both quoted in Taylor 2007: 235). 'After 12 years of progressive competitiveness', David Coates concluded, the UK economy remained 'one which – in comparative terms – is scarred by low productivity, long hours of work, low wages and skill levels' (Coates 2009: 428).

But there *was* an underlying rationale to Labour policy – a coherent, well thought-out strategy for steady economic expansion. There was one area where the UK had a definite competitive edge – the financial services sector. The City, Brown proudly boasted, is 'a great example of a highly skilled, high value added, talent driven industry that shows how we can excel in a world of global competition' (Brown 2007). The centrepiece of New Labour economic policy was to enhance London's standing as a major hub of global financial activity. A rapidly swelling financial sector would attract inward flows of capital, boost growth, create jobs and, above all, supply the tax revenues that would enable the government to finance its ambitious schemes for renovating the country's run-down public services and curtailing poverty and social deprivation. 'Wary of the power of global capital', *The Guardian* economics editor Larry Elliott wrote, 'Brown decided the only thing to do was to allow the City to make a mint, cream off the tax revenues and use them for socially useful purposes such as higher public spending and tax credits' (Elliott 2010).

As a result the Labour government pledged itself to reducing the fiscal and regulatory burdens on financial bodies. The key to City growth was unleashing its spirit of enterprise, its creativity and its appeal to foreign investors through 'light-touch regulation'. Economic Secretary to the Treasury Ed Balls stated flatly that the government would do its utmost 'to safeguard the light touch and proportionate regulatory regime that has made London a magnet for international business' (Balls 2006). All this reflected a profound change in Labour's economic philosophy. New Labour eagerly endorsed the view that 'markets were always rational and self-equilibrating, that market completion by itself could ensure economic efficiency and stability, and that financial innovation and increased trading activity were therefore axiomatically beneficial' (Turner 2010).

Until 2007 all went well. The share of a thriving financial services sector in national economic activity grew rapidly from 6.6 per cent in 1996 to 9.4 per cent in 2006 and an estimated 10.1 per cent in 2007 (Lansley 2008: 14). Over 40 per cent of the world's foreign equities and over 30 per cent of the world's currencies exchanges were traded in London (Brown 2007). Tax levied on ballooning City profits flooded into the Exchequer's coffers to fund expanding public programmes. Compared with other major countries in the European Union, New Labour's economic record seemed impressive. Unemployment was consistently less than in Germany and France, the growth rate higher, interest rates were low and inflation was well under control. Not least, the UK was a favoured destination overseas for business investment and a honey-pot for global capital flows. And the money was domestically recycled – though at a cost. 'Given their head by the government, banks and building societies doled out unlimited quantities of cheap credit, artificially pumping up the housing market and consumer spending' (Elliott 2008). By 2008 Brown could proudly claim that as both Chancellor and Prime Minister he had presided over the longest period of uninterrupted economic growth that the UK had ever experienced.

The financial hurricane that struck the world in 2007 and 2008 caught the Labour government (like most others) totally unprepared. Initially, the government was loath to accept the severity of the crisis. When Northern Rock failed – the first failure of a British bank since the nineteenth century – in September 2007, its main concern seemed to be to avoid the obvious solution, of immediate nationalisation: this would be so 'Old Labour'. The Bank of England was equally slow to respond. But then with the collapse of Lehman Brothers in 2008 the financial tornado struck. The money markets froze as banks refused to lend to each other and stock markets plunged. The City minister, Lord Myners, feared 'a systemic collapse of the banking system' (Rawnsley 2010: 591). The entire global financial system seemed to be on the verge of disintegration and another Great Depression beckoned.

Yet, ironically, this was to be Brown's finest hour. Flinging aside his customary prevarication and timidity and abandoning the gods of economic orthodoxy that he had so venerated, he unveiled a bold and imaginative package. Noble prize-winning economist Paul Krugman lauded him as displaying a 'combination of clarity and decisiveness' unmatched by other western governments (Krugman 2008). Banking nationalisation, Keynesian-style reflation, cuts in interest rates and quantitative easing all represented a dramatic repudiation of the neo-liberal script to which Brown had previously so scrupulously adhered. Eventually the Royal Bank of Scotland was over 80 per cent publicly owned, the Lloyds Group over 40 per cent and some smaller banks were nationalised outright. The government's ability in the short term to head off a total financial meltdown brought a brief boost in Gordon Brown's popularity.

But the price tag for all this was disturbingly large. The level of public debt rose dramatically, partly because the government had run a structural deficit in the good times, partly because of the massive cost of the bank bailouts and partly because (as a result of the financial crisis) the economy went into headlong decline, squeezing tax receipts and pushing up welfare costs. Unemployment in the UK rose rapidly (though not as steeply as some had feared, in part because of government action). By the time Labour left office it was at its highest level since 1994 – all the progress in the years of the Labour government apparently wiped out. With tax revenues plummeting and spending commitments rising the government felt it had no option but to announce major cuts in public spending (and some hikes in the taxes) though for the main part these cuts would only bite in 2011.

Brown had responded pragmatically, but intellectually and politically he found it difficult to free himself from the old verities. In particular, he was loath to subject the City to a much tougher regulatory framework. The Treasury's proposals for reforming the institutional architecture of financial regulation in the White Paper of July 2009 were 'limited and cautious' (Froud *et al.* 2010: 31). Nor, as part of the bank bailouts, had firm conditions – about pay or lending – been attached. Towards the end of 2009 and in 2010 a spate of announcements about bank bonuses and remuneration levels indicated that the appetite among the ultra-wealthy for richly rewarding themselves had hardly been slaked. The government's response was lame and ineffectual. With the financial crash the chickens came home to roost.

From the onset of its third term, the New Labour government struggled. This was partly because the distorting effects of the electoral system created a totally exaggerated picture of its real support in the country. At first there were hopes that a Brown premiership would inject new purpose and a more radical spirit into the government. This was always unlikely. 'New Labour's main domestic policies during the ten years of Blair's premiership were in large measure policies designed or agreed to by Gordon Brown himself' (Coates 2009: 423). The New Labour regime had always been a dual monarchy. For Brown as for Blair, social mobility, not material equality, was 'the defining mission of New Labour' (Brown 2008).

Whether the mission could ever succeed was another matter. New Labour's presumption was that opportunities could be equalised while the structure of income and wealth remained, in its essentials, very uneven. The problem was that, as one of the country's leading experts commented, equality of opportunity was very hard to achieve when the gap in the resources individuals commanded was so wide (Hills *et al.* 2010: 386). New Labour was always reluctant to acknowledge this, not only for electoral reasons but because it was convinced that an efficiently functioning and competitive economy required an incentive system that inevitably generated large disparities in rewards. New Labour's political economy was grounded in a faith in neo-liberal precepts and an unremitting confidence in the virtues of a liberalised, financially driven world economy. For a decade it seemed that what two former senior New Labour aides labelled a new 'Anglo-social model' was working (Diamond and Liddle 2009: 216). The fabric of once-fading public services had been restored, the quality of healthcare and education was significantly higher and the tax and benefit regime had redistributed income to the more disadvantaged sections of the community. But all this turned sour after the financial crisis as the virtues of unfettered markets no longer seemed so self-evident. Animating the New Labour project was a wager – that neo-liberal economics and social demo-cratic social policy could be yoked together. The wager failed. The punishment was meted out on 6 May 2010.

The party after defeat: the election of Ed Miliband

Almost immediately after Labour's eviction from office it was plunged into another electoral contest – this time an internal election for the party leader. Five candidates garnered sufficient nominations to compete for the leadership: Diane Abbott, Ed Balls, Andy Burnham and the Miliband brothers, David and Ed. It soon became clear that the race was between the latter two. Initially it was expected that David, the elder and more experi-enced brother, would cruise to victory and David was backed by virtually the whole of the press and what might be called the New Labour establish-ment (though this may have been a double-edged sword). Ed, for his part, was backed by the major trade unions – Unite, Unison and the GMB – and more left-leaning groups in the party.

The electoral college that elected the leader was divided into three sections, party members, parliamentarians (MPs and MEPs) and members of affiliated organisations, mainly trade unions. The younger Miliband only carried the third of these sections but by a sufficient margin to render him, very narrowly, the overall winner. Much was made of this. Many in the media and some disenchanted Blairites claimed that Ed Miliband lacked a democratic mandate since he had effectively been 'imposed' on the party by the union 'barons'. The argument was misleading, for a number of reasons. First, the union vote was not cast in blocks by trade union leaders but by individuals. Second, on the first ballot the majority of affiliated members had *not* in fact voted for the candidate the union leaders had endorsed – he only secured a majority after first and second preferences had been redistributed. Equally it took no note of the fact that the younger Miliband had attracted more individual voters by a significant margin (over

30,000) than his brother. And finally the claim chose not to take into account the fact that the elder Miliband had not only benefited from the support of the press but also that his campaign had been the most generously funded – including by some wealthy donors.

What might the election of Ed Miliband as Labour's new man at the helm signify? What clues does it offer for the party's future sense of direction? The contest between the two brothers was framed by some media commentators as between 'Continuity New Labour' and 'Red Ed'. In reality, no evidence exists that major differences in outlook separated the two brothers. David was never a died-in-the-wool Blairite while his brother had spent well over a decade toiling within the New Labour inner circles. If David had won he too would have sought to disengage himself from 'New Labour' though probably more circumspectly than Ed. Furthermore both brothers would have had to accommodate the preferences of the others' supporters. This was precisely what the new leader did in his shadow cabinet appointments, selecting for the key posts those who had voted for David or who had otherwise played prominent roles in the Blair and Brown administrations. Very few were associated with more left-oriented currents in the party.

Claims that 'Red Ed' would provoke a 'lurch to the left' (whatever that meant) were clearly specious. But it does not follow that the election of Ed rather than David had no significance. It plainly did. It marked a definite shifting away from the Blairite strand of New Labour. For this strand (eagerly espoused by such Blairite true believers as Peter Mandelson, Alan Milburn, Patricia Hewitt, John Reid as well as the former Prime Minister himself) what was most valuable about New Labour was what most sharply distinguished it from traditional Labour thinking, notably the introduction of choice, competition and profit-seeking corporations in the public services; a tax regime that looked benignly upon the accumulation of large fortunes; light regulation of financial and labour markets; lack of interest in promoting greater equality; a more restrictive approach to social welfare and a tough line on law and order issues.

In his first leader's speech to conference, Ed Miliband made clear that he found many (if not most) of these policy stances unpalatable. In a long catalogue of New Labour faults he almost certainly went further than his brother would have done in disowning key aspects of the Blair/Brown governmental legacy: its naivety about the beneficence of the market, its timidity over City regulation, its creation of an economy too dependent on financial services and its promotion of flexible labour markets that facilitated employer exploitation of migrant labour in order to undercut wages. New Labour, he continued, had failed to grasp that alleviating the plight of the poor was not enough – its failure to reduce the very wide gap between the rich and the poor which it had inherited from the Conservatives and its apparent ease with the massive piling-up of wealth at the top harmed not only the disadvantaged but society as whole. 'What does it say about the values of our society', he declared, 'that a banker can earn in a day what the care worker earns in a year? It's wrong, conference' (Miliband 2010).

Not all within the party accepted it was so wrong. For one former Blair advisor, Tim Allan, this was the 'most damaging line' in the speech. It appeared to signal that Miliband was 'against success, against wealth creation, and wants to dictate economic outcomes for the wealthiest rather than provide economic opportunities for all' (Allan 2010). Stripped of its exaggeration, there was an element of truth in this comment. Miliband was indicating that he (unlike his two predecessors as leader) was *not* – in Mandelson's oft-quoted remark – 'intensely relaxed about people getting filthy rich'. New Labour had seemed too often to be in thrall to wealth, giving the impression 'that we know the price of everything and the value of nothing'. It was time to resurrect the values of 'community, belonging and solidarity' as guiding principles of Labour's mission (Miliband 2010).

Advocates of the old regime countered that Labour had lost not because it had stuck too rigidly to New Labour prescriptions but because, under Gordon Brown's leadership, it had begun to dilute them. As Brown's chief pollster Deborah Mattinson argued, it had stopped listening to voter concerns in particular, over immigration and social security fraud (Mattinson 2010). The answer to regaining the public's confidence was not a move to the left but a sharper articulation of voter anxieties over these issues – and, by implication, the adoption of tougher policies. To abandon the party's pro-business and pro-market stance would, they claimed, be dangerous. To the contrary it must – the New Labour magazine *Progress* averred – reaffirm that it stood for aspiration, wealth creation and economic efficiency as well as equality, redistribution and social justice: all code words for continuing to tack to the right.

Labour (the 'New' has effectively been dropped) has yet to engage in a systematic analysis of why it lost and it is far too early to predict the direction that the inevitable review of policy will take. Doubtless Ed Miliband will strive to balance and reconcile rival trends of thought within the party. But his election did represent both a psychological blow and a symbolic repudiation of the New Labour 'project' and, for the first time in almost two decades, the hold of the ascendant right of the party has been shaken. Beyond that, one can only speculate. The battle, in the foreseeable future, will in any case be dominated by the struggles over the coalition's plans for an unprecedented wave of cuts in public spending. Never has a new Labour leader confronted a more uncertain and unpredictable future.

Notes

1 The Institute for Fiscal Studies reported 'widespread public ignorance of the scale of inequality … Most people are unaware … of the true scale of differences between the high paid and the low paid' (Hills *et al.* 2010: 398).

2 'In the years running up to 2007, too much of the developed world's intellectual talent was devoted to ever more complex financial innovations, whose maximum possible benefit was at best marginal, and which in their complexity and opacity created large financial stability risks' (Adair Turner, in Treanor 2009).

References

Allan, T. (2010). 'An Open Letter to Ed Miliband: If You Bury the Lessons of New Labour You Will Bury the Party', *The Observer*, 3 October.

Andersson J. (2007). 'Socializing Capital, Capitalizing the Social: Contemporary Social Democracy and the Knowledge Economy', *Centre for European Studies Working Paper Series*, 145.

Balls, E. (1997). 'Open Macroeconomics in an Open Economy', *Centre for Economic Performance Occasional Papers*, No.13.

Balls, E. (2006). 'Speech by the Economic Secretary to the Treasury to the British Bankers Association', 11 October.

Bevir, M. (2005). *New Labour: A Critique*. London: Routledge

Blair, T. (2004). 'Speech on the Economy to Goldman Sachs', 24 March.

Blair, T. and G. Schroeder (1999). 'The Third Way/Die Neue Mitte'. http://adampost.home.xs4all.nl/Archive/arc000006.html (last accessed 1 October 2011).

Bonoli, G. (2004). 'Social Democratic Party Policies in Europe: Towards a Third Way?', in G. Bonoli and M. Powell (eds), *Social Democratic Party Policies in Contemporary Europe*. London: Routledge.

Brown, G. (1997). 'Budget Speech by the Chancellor', July.

Brown, G. (2004). 'Speech by the Chancellor of the Exchequer', Mansion House, London, 16 June. http://webarchive.nationalarchives .gov.uk/+/http://www.hmtreasury.gov.uk/press_56_04.htm (last accessed 1 October 2011).

Brown, G. (2005). 'Speech by the Chancellor of the Exchequer at the CBI', 18 May.

Brown, G. (2007). 'Speech by the Chancellor of the Exchequer', Mansion House, London, 20 June.

Brown, G. (2008). 'Time for the Third Act in Public Sector Reform', *Financial Times*, 9 March.

Brown, G. (2010). 'Speech by the Prime Minister', Fabian New Year Conference, 16 January.

Buckler, S. and D. Dolowitz (2000). 'Theorizing the Third Way: New Labour and Social Justice', *Journal of Political Ideologies*, 5 (3): 301–320.

Cerny, P. G. and M. Evans (2004). 'Globalisation and Public Policy under New Labour' *Policy Studies*, 25 (1): 51–65.

Coates, D. (2005). *Prolonged Labour*. Basingstoke: Palgrave.

Coates, D. (2009). 'Chickens Coming Home to Roost? New Labour at the Eleventh Hour' *British Politics*, 4: 421–433.

Cronin, J. (2004). *New Labour's Pasts: The Labour Party and its Discontents*. London: Longman.

Diamond, P. and J. Liddle (2009). 'Conclusion: The Challenge of Renewal', in P. Diamond and J. Liddle (eds), *Beyond New Labour*. London: Politico's.

Driver, S. and L. Martel (2006). *New Labour*. Cambridge: Polity, 2nd edn.

Elliott, L. (2008).'Brown Damned by His Faustian Pact', *The Guardian*, 12 May.

Elliott, L. (2010). 'Labour Needs to Admit What It Got Wrong', *The Guardian*, 3 May.

Elliott, L. and D. Atkinson (2007). *Fantasy Island*. London: Constable.

Faucher-King, F. and P. Le Gales (2010). *The New Labour Experiment*. Stanford: Stanford University Press.

Froud, J., M. Moran, A. Nilsson and K. Williams (2010). 'Wasting a Crisis? Democracy and Markets in Britain after 2007', *Political Quarterly*, 81 (1): 25–38.

Giddens, A. (2000). *The Third Way and Its Critics*. Cambridge: Polity.

Giddens, A. (2010). 'The Rise and Fall of New Labour', *New Statesman*, 17 May.

Hills, J. *et al.* (2010). *An Anatomy of Economic Inequality in the UK: Report of the National Equality Panel*. London: Government Equalities Office/Centre for Analysis of Social Exclusion (LSE). http://sticerd.lse.ac.uk/dps/case/cr/CASEreport60.pdf (last accessed 1 October 2011).

HM Treasury (2008). *Embracing Financial Globalisation*. London: HM Treasury, May.

Horton, T. and J. Gregory (2009). *The Solidarity Society*. London: Fabian Society.

Inman, P. (2010). 'Under Pressure: Tax Inspectors Turn Up the Heat on the Rich', *The Observer*, 21 February.

Jessop, B. (2003). 'From Thatcherism to New Labour: Neo-Liberalism, Workfarism, and Labour Market Regulation'. www.lancs.ac.uk /fass/sociology/papers/jessop-from-thatcherism-to-new-labour.pdf (last accessed 1 October 2011).

Krugman, P. (2008). 'Gordon Does Good', *New York Times*, 12 October.

Lansley, S. (2008) 'Do the Super-Rich Matter?', *Touchstone Pamphlets*, No. 4. London: TUC.

Levitas, R. (2005). *The Inclusive Society? Social Exclusion and New Labour*. Basingstoke: Palgrave.

Mattinson, D. (2010). *Talking to a Brick Wall*. London: Biteback.

Miliband, E. (2010). 'Speech to the Labour Party Conference'. www.bbc.co.uk/news/uk-politics-11426411 (last accessed 1 October 2011).

Peston, R. (2005). *Brown's Britain*. London: Short Books.

Peston, R. (2008). *Who Runs Britain?* London: Hodder and Stoughton.

PMSU (Prime Minister's Strategy Unit) (2007). *Building on Progress: Public Services Policy Review*. London: Cabinet Office.

Rawnsley, A. (2010). *The End of the Party*. Harmondsworth: Penguin Viking.

Riddell, P. (2005). *The Unfulfilled Prime Minister*. London: Politico's.

Seldon, A. (2007). *Blair Unbound*. London: Simon and Schuster.

Shaw, E. (2007). *Losing Labour's Soul? New Labour and the Blair Government*. London: Routledge.

Shaw, E. (2009a). 'The Consumer and New Labour: The Consumer as King?' in R. Simmons, M. Powell and I. Greener (eds), *The Consumer in Public Services*. London: Policy Press.

Shaw, E. (2009b). 'The Meaning of Modernisation: New Labour and Public Sector Reform' in J. Callaghan, N. Fishman, B. Jackson and M. McIvor (eds), *In Search of Social Democracy*. Manchester: Manchester University Press.

Straw, J. (1998). 'Speech to the Nexus Conference on Mapping Out the Third way', July.

Taylor, R. (2007). 'New Labour, New Capitalism', in A. Seldon (ed.). *Blair's Britain 1997–2007*. Cambridge: Cambridge University Press, pp. 214–240.

Toynbee, P. and D. Walker (2008). *Unjust Rewards*. London: Granta.

Treanor, J. (2009). 'Pay Packet Envy: The Greed That Drove the City's Bonus Culture', *The Guardian*, 28 January.

Turner, A. (2010). 'Speech by Chairman, Financial Services Authority', 14th Chintaman Deshmukh Memorial Lecture, Reserve Bank of India, Mumbai, 15 February.

Watson, M. (2008). 'The Split Personality of Prudence in the Unfolding Political Economy of New Labour', *Political Quarterly*, 79 (4): 578–589.

4

The path to (sharing) power: the Conservative Party

Richard Hayton

Introduction

It goes without saying that general elections are events of utmost importance to all major political parties. Nonetheless, some general elections matter more than others, and a few come to be seen as pivotal turning points in the economic, social and political trajectory of the nation. Britain witnessed arguably three such defining moments in the twentieth century: the Liberal landslide of 1906; the election of the first majority Labour government under Clement Attlee in 1945; and the installation in Number 10 Downing Street of Margaret Thatcher in 1979. For the Conservative Party, the first two of these represented calamitous defeats that initially appeared to threaten its future as a potent political force. The third ushered in eighteen years of Conservative government and marked not only the end of the post-war consensus but the beginning of the neo-liberal transformation of Britain.

The Thatcherite legacy shaped and constrained Conservative political thinking, communication, policy-making and statecraft. Thatcher brought her party electoral success and a sense of strategic direction, particularly in response to the perceived crisis of the 1970s. However, Thatcherism was the subject of fierce criticism both within and outside Conservative circles, and ultimately had the unintended effect of prompting a deep intellectual uncertainty in the party about its purpose and future direction. It was against this backdrop that a long period of Conservative electoral dominance was brought decisively to an end by the election of New Labour under Tony Blair. Debate continues as to whether 1997 can take its place as a fourth date of comparable magnitude to the three noted above (Griffiths and Hickson 2010: 3). Nevertheless, whatever its long-term significance for the country as a whole, for the Conservative Party the 1997 general election was a hugely traumatic defeat, which marked the onset of a period of abject electoral failure for the party. Having been reduced to just 165 MPs in 1997 (their worst performance since 1832) the Conservatives were able to add just one seat to this total after four years of opposition under the leadership of William Hague. Under Michael Howard in 2005 the Conservatives did better, adding thirty-two seats to win 198 in total, in an election that saw the government's majority more than halved. However, only in the context of abysmal expectations could this be presented as an electoral success: the 33.2 per cent of the vote received by the Conservatives represented an improvement of only 0.5 per cent on 2001, and after three different leaders and eight years in opposition the Conservatives still returned fewer MPs than Labour managed at their nadir in 1983.

The 2010 general election marked a highly significant moment for the Conservative Party if nothing else for bringing this long period of opposition to an end. By succeeding where William Hague, Iain Duncan Smith and Michael Howard failed, developing an effective opposition strategy and entering Number 10, David Cameron has secured his place in Conservative Party history. In an effort to contextualise this change in Conservative fortunes and to understand its implications this chapter provides an overview of the Conservatives' efforts to recover power since 1997, culminating with their return to office in May 2010. It then sketches out a number of possible scenarios for the 'new politics' of coalition that have emerged from the election and offers some thoughts on the trajectory of the Conservative Party in government.

The long road to renewal: the Conservatives in opposition, 1997–2010

Under the leadership of David Cameron, the Conservative Party sought to present itself to the electorate in May 2010 as a modernising, liberal, even progressive force for change. This was consistent with the strategy Cameron had outlined during his 2005 leadership election campaign, when he vowed that he would radically reshape the Conservative Party should he be elected. Yet in order to secure the leadership Cameron needed to win the support of two groups more renowned for their traditionalist, rather than modernising, instincts – the Parliamentary Conservative Party (PCP) and the wider party membership. As such his triumph was unexpected and given his youthful inexperience and lack of public profile (he only entered the Commons in 2001) was in many ways 'a remarkable achievement' (Heppell 2008: 193).

The election of Cameron did mark a significant shift in the direction of Conservative politics, but it would be wrong to view it as a decisive break with the party's past. As Denham and Dorey cautioned, while it might be tempting to interpret Cameron's victory as the 'final exorcism' of the ghost of Thatcherism, it can be more convincingly attributed to his exceptional communication skills and a belief among the PCP and party members that he was the candidate most likely to prove attractive to the electorate (Denham and Dorey 2006: 41). A willingness to vote according to such a conviction did nonetheless mark a step change from the leadership elections of 1997 and 2001, when the party eschewed the candidates with the greatest electoral appeal in favour of those it found the most ideologically palatable. For Heppell this contrast is clear – with the election of Cameron 'the era of ideology was ending and Conservatives were re-engaging with the merits of pragmatism in the pursuit of power' (Heppell 2008: 193). While it would be a mistake to view Cameron as somehow un-ideological or to see his election as marking the death of ideology in the Conservative Party, it is true to say that ideology played a less overt role in his election and has been further tempered by his leadership. As a thoughtful analysis by Matt Beech (2009) has demonstrated, in a number of areas Cameron has moved his party's ideas and policies towards the centre, to the extent that he cannot be accurately categorised as a Thatcherite.

To understand how this has been possible requires us to look back beyond 2005, situating Cameron and his modernising approach in relation to his three immediate predecessors: Michael Howard, Iain Duncan Smith and William Hague (Hayton, forthcoming). Although for the Conservatives the 1997–2005 period was characterised by strategic mistakes and electoral failure, it is vital to any understanding of the development of the party under Cameron. Most obviously, one effect of this lengthy period of opposition was to make Cameron's leadership pitch of 'change' more attractive in 2005. Following three heavy election defeats both the parliamentary party and the wider membership were more acquiescent to his determination to transform the party's image, messages and strategy. After all, as Michael Howard frankly admitted, under his leadership the Conservatives had 'tested the alternative theory to destruction in the 2005 election, and lost' (interviewed in Portillo 2008).

A key feature of Conservative Party politics between 1997 and 2005 was an intra-party debate over whether, how and to what extent the party should seek to modernise in an effort to rejuvenate its image and broaden its appeal. An embryonic modernisation agenda can be discerned in William Hague's early leadership strategy in 1997–1998. Hague was elected on the promise of a 'fresh start' (his campaign slogan) having effectively presented himself as a youthful unity candidate, generally perceived as a 'non-ideological figure' who had avoided the factional infighting of the 1990s (Taylor 2003: 230). Hague hoped that changes of tone and language would provide distance from the Thatcher–Major era and improve the party's image, and his early speeches demonstrated his desire to develop a more inclusive brand of conservatism, epitomised by his well-publicised but widely ridiculed visit to the Notting Hill Carnival. Internal strategy documents also reveal recognition at the time of the need for the Conservatives to make radical changes to both their image and policies. For example in 1998 Kitchen Table Conservatism (KTC) suggested a new Conservative narrative 'about much more than economics', addressing issues such as the future of the public services. Hague was enthusiastic about the KTC strategy and quickly adopted it at shadow cabinet level (Snowdon 2010: 54). In spite of this, it was soon abandoned and Hague reverted to a core vote strategy based on the unholy 'Tebbit trinity' of tough talk on Europe, immigration and tax.

Two key events prompted this move away from 'reaching out' to 'shoring up' the base Conservative vote. The first was the 1999 R. A. Butler Memorial lecture given by the then deputy leader Peter Lilley, in which he called for a rhetorical shift to a narrative that recognised the value of welfare as well as the value of free markets. The furious reaction to the speech suggested the Conservative Party was far from ready for such a change. At first Hague attempted to weather the storm, but the furore weakened his leadership and made him wary of further attempts to forge a more 'inclusive' narrative of conservatism. This was reinforced by the results of the 1999 elections to the European Parliament, which the Conservatives won on the back of a strongly Eurosceptic manifesto and campaign. The electoral success secured Hague's position as leader and he used the opportunity to reshuffle his shadow cabinet and evict his deputy. The Conservatives' language and campaigning grew gradually more hysterical as the parliament dragged on, culminating in Hague's warning in March 2001 that Britain risked becoming a 'foreign land' and that the forthcoming election was the 'last chance to vote for a Britain that still controls its own destiny' (Hague 2001). This reactionary scaremongering left the electorate unimpressed and Hague promptly resigned after the inevitable general election defeat in June 2001.

The debate over modernisation returned with renewed intensity in the leadership contest to succeed Hague, with the doyen of the cause, Michael Portillo, standing on an uncompromisingly reformist candidature. Portillo had come to believe that if the Conservatives were ever again to be seen as electable they needed to radically liberalise their stance on social issues (notably racial, sexual and cultural equality) to better reflect twenty-first century Britain. The first candidate to enter the race, he quickly secured the endorsement of most of the shadow cabinet and was the strong favourite with the bookmakers. However, Portillo's conversion to social liberalism caused unease and distrust among his former admirers on the right of the parliamentary party and he was beaten into third place by the traditionalist Iain Duncan Smith (Hayton and Heppell 2010: 428).

To the surprise of many both within and outside of the Conservative Party Duncan Smith showed an appreciation of the limitations of Hague's core vote strategy and attempted to re-orientate the party to broaden its appeal. Under his leadership the Conservatives finally began a more serious policy renewal process, and in spite of his initial move to harden European policy (to permanently rule out ever joining the single currency) he downplayed the core vote issues of Europe, immigration and taxation. Most strikingly he sought to establish social justice as the centrepiece of his party's narrative, declaring that combating poverty was its 'greatest mission'. Duncan Smith was, however, an abject failure as leader of the opposition, he lacked the requisite skills and was unable to persuade his party, or even many members of his shadow cabinet, of the merits of his approach (Hayton 2010a).

Duncan Smith's brief tenure as Conservative Party leader reached its ignominious conclusion when he was ejected in a vote of no-confidence from his parliamentary colleagues in October 2003. Keen to avoid another acrimonious contest, the PCP disregarded the new election procedures and installed his replacement, Michael Howard, unopposed without consulting the wider membership. Howard possessed key leadership attributes that Duncan Smith demonstrably lacked: heavyweight experience, effective debating skills and the force of character to impose discipline on the party. His arrival appeared to signal that the Conservatives were finally getting their act together – unity and morale were transformed and factionalism diminished (Heppell 2008: 173).

Howard was presented with the opportunity to push forward with Duncan Smith's efforts to broaden the party's policy framework and narrative. However, with an election looming he chose instead to revert to a core vote strategy, abandoning the project of renewal. As one comparison of Hague, Duncan Smith and Howard noted, the latter 'had the easiest task, and his failure was thus the greatest' (Seldon and Snowdon 2005: 143). The relatively fortuitous circumstances he enjoyed were not transformed into a coherent strategy and were ultimately reduced to a 'mean-spirited and reactionary' election campaign (Portillo 2005). It was therefore left to Cameron to pick up the themes of social justice, poverty and the public services first raised by Duncan Smith (Hayton and Heppell 2010: 436–441).

Howard's most lasting legacy resulted from the way he engineered the process leading to Cameron's election to the party leadership. The day after the 2005 defeat Howard announced his intention to step down as leader, but not until the party had had the chance to review its leadership selection procedures. This meant that the contest would effectively last for seven months, the longest ever held by a British political party (Denham and O'Hara 2008: 173). This delay allowed Howard to promote favoured members of the 'Notting Hill set' in a shadow cabinet reshuffle – most strikingly George Osborne to Shadow Chancellor and David Cameron (apparently at his own request) to Shadow Education Secretary (Denham and O'Hara 2008: 115).

In the event, the new rules Howard proposed for selecting the leader (which were essentially designed to give the final say back to MPs) failed to achieve sufficient support and did not come into force (Bale 2010: 272). The 2005 contest therefore took place under the framework utilised in 2001. It was widely assumed that the ideological leanings of the PCP meant that this system would favour the candidates from the right – David Davis and Liam Fox – and work against those from the centre, namely David Cameron and Kenneth Clarke. Davis was the initial favourite, garnering an early lead in terms of endorsements from fellow MPs. However, the race was transformed by the hustings, which took place at the October 2005 party conference. In what was soon labelled 'a tale of two speeches' Cameron wowed delegates with an accomplished performance, while Davis was generally perceived as having done poorly, outshone not only by Cameron but also by Fox and Clarke (Denham and Dorey 2006). On the back of the conference Cameron leapt ahead of his rivals in the opinion polls and his campaign continued to gather momentum, leading to victory in the second ballot of the PCP and his triumph over Davis by a margin of two to one in the vote by the party membership.

Cameron's Conservative Party: Thatcherism vanquished or varnished?

Since his election as leader much academic debate has focused on the question of whether Cameron's arrival marked the end of the ideological dominance of Thatcherism within the Conservative Party or merely the beginning of another neo-Thatcherite chapter. Analysis of the 2005 leadership election suggests that Cameron's appeal 'transcended ideological categorisation' as his backers came from all sections of the party (Heppell and Hill 2009: 398). For Heppell and Hill this marks a significant departure from previous Conservative leadership elections in which ideology was a key determinant of voting behaviour. But as Tim Bale has noted, one explanation of Cameron's victory – that 'he was the candidate who aroused least opposition and was thought most likely to be able to unite the Party' – also holds for all Conservative leadership contests since 1990 (Bale 2010: 280).

Cameron's modernisation rhetoric did not ease once he had secured the leadership; if anything, it intensified. This was central to his strategy of 'detoxifying the Tory brand' (Reeves 2008: 63). By emphasising policies and issues not traditionally associated with the Conservatives Cameron hoped to demonstrate that he was qualitatively different from his predecessors and that he was impressing change on his party. As Neil Carter has noted, he 'quickly made the environment his signature issue' (2009: 233), perhaps most memorably being photographed with a pack of huskies on a Norwegian glacier, ostensibly as part of his campaign to raise awareness of climate change. This project of brand decontamination was seemingly vindicated by research suggesting that the Conservatives' problem since 1997 had been one of image rather than policy or ideology. According to one analyst, popular perceptions of the party placed them further to the right than a dispassionate policy analysis, indeed since 1997 Conservative policy positions 'have often been only marginally different from New Labour's' (Quinn 2008: 195). Consequently, rather than undergo a radical policy repositioning, to compete effectively on the centre-ground the Conservative Party needed to follow Cameron's lead in combating the view that it was backward-looking, out of touch and illiberal. A further aspect of this strategy was 'to render the Conservative Party more socially representative (and inter alia more electorally attractive) by seeking the adoption of more women and ethnic minority candidates' (Dorey 2007: 153). Cameron enjoyed only partial success in this regard, but his chosen mechanism (a priority candidates list) did help ensure that the Conservatives returned by far their highest ever number of female MPs (forty-eight) to Westminster in 2010.

A change of image and new personnel does not, however, amount to an ideological about turn. Indeed, a plausible case can be assembled to suggest that like Hague, Duncan Smith and Howard before him, Cameron has steered the Conservative Party within, rather than against, Thatcherism's wake. For example, Stephen Evans (2010) suggests that the unmistakable imprint of Thatcher can be seen on Cameron's leadership – a consequence of both pressure from the right of his party and his own commitment to Thatcherite ideals. Perhaps more surprisingly, Evans (2010: 330) also suggests that Cameron has made repeated public statements of his admiration for Thatcher and his wish to follow in her footsteps, not least in an effort to strengthen his own credibility with the Conservative right wing. Such an approach would appear to run contrary to Cameron's modernisation rhetoric and his strategy of transforming the Conservative Party's image. However, Cameron has been careful to use references to Thatcher to try and reinforce rather than undermine his status as an advocate of change, for example by suggesting that he intends the

Conservatives under his leadership to be as radical in the field of social policy as they were under Thatcher in the field of economic policy. Rather than overtly reject Thatcherism, particularly in the early years of his tenure, Cameron tended to sidestep the issue, praising Thatcher's approach as appropriate for the problems of the 1980s, but arguing that times and the challenges facing the country have changed.

Following the financial crash in 2008 and during the subsequent recession this became a harder position for Cameron to maintain. In the early years of his leadership Conservative economic policy was driven by the need to neutralise Labour's strong lead on the issue – at the time of the 2005 general election, for example, 46 per cent of voters thought that the incumbent government was best able to manage the economy, compared to 21 per cent who favoured the Conservatives (Dorey 2009: 259). Recognising this weakness, Cameron pledged to match Labour's spending plans on key public services such as health and education, and offered no substantive critique of the government's economic policy. Six months after becoming leader Cameron famously went as far as suggesting that: 'It's time we admitted that there's more to life than money, and it's time we focused not just on GDP, but on GWB – General Well-Being' (Cameron 2006). This was both a tacit acknowledgement that the Conservatives broadly concurred with Labour's economic approach and part of Cameron's strategy of moving his party (and public debate) on to other policy issues. However, as Dorey notes, this left the Conservatives 'unable to offer a convincing response to the financial and economic crisis facing the country, beyond attacking the government for not having taken appropriate measures to prevent it in the first place' (Dorey 2009: 263). Bereft of any new thinking on the issue the Conservatives resorted to a purely Thatcherite excoriation of Labour's policy approach, particularly the fiscal stimulus and the deficit in the public finances. Cameron's language in 2009 and 2010 came to more closely echo that of Thatcher as the Conservatives settled on a policy of advocating much greater fiscal austerity to deal with the crisis. The 2010 Conservative election manifesto thus promised a strong dose of Thatcherite medicine – spending cuts, reduced welfare bills and tax incentives for businesses – purportedly the only way to 'get the economy moving' (Conservative Party 2010: 19).

Even before the credit crunch prompted a reassertion of neo-liberal economics over other aspects of Conservative Party policy there were clear indications in his party management strategy that Cameron was unable (or unwilling) to ignore the Thatcherite wing of his party. Indeed, during his leadership election campaign he pledged to withdraw Conservative MEPs from the main centre-right grouping in the European Parliament (the European People's Party) in order to secure the backing of Eurosceptic MPs

(Lynch and Whitaker 2008: 34). Cameron was also reminded of the latent power of the right of his party by the internal row over grammar schools policy in May 2007. Having initially pledged that a future Conservative government would not increase the number of selective state schools, under pressure from MPs and party members Cameron soon reversed his position, in what was widely perceived as a defeat for the modernisers (*The Independent*, 1 June 2007). Later he demoted the Shadow Education Secretary David Willetts, who was blamed for the blunder.

Writing in 2008, Tim Bale observed that as leader Cameron 'has not encountered much internal opposition' but concluded that this was because 'he has not really pushed things very far' (2008: 295). Cameron's idea of modernisation, in other words, had never meant that Thatcherism must be vanquished, but rather that it be reconstituted and repackaged in an electorally palatable manner. As Alan Finlayson has noted, Cameron represents an amalgam of twenty-first-century mores with clear links to the Thatcher years: 'he combines his acceptance of contemporary standards in personal morality, and his embrace of do-gooder liberalism, with familiar Conservative commitments: to the family, to social entrepreneurs rather than the state, to individual freedom, aspiration and national pride' (2007: 4). Under Cameron's stewardship as leader of the opposition the Conservatives moved on from Thatcherism in a number of important ways, notably in the way concerns such as poverty, social issues and the environment were discussed. However, core elements remained. An opinion poll conducted shortly after the general election suggested that Cameron had got this balancing act 'about right'. While 30 per cent of respondents believed that he 'did not do enough to modernise the Conservative Party' and 11 per cent thought that he had 'abandoned too many traditional Conservative policies', a greater proportion, 36 per cent, thought he had struck the right balance. It also appeared that his approach had won over Conservative supporters – just 12 per cent thought he had gone too far and 6 per cent not far enough, with 68 per cent backing his approach (YouGov 2010).

The election and its aftermath

The 2010 general election took place against the backdrop of the parliamentary expenses scandal and the deepest recession since the Second World War. Given that the Labour Party had been in office for thirteen years and was led by an unpopular Prime Minister who had struggled to connect effectively with the public, the Conservatives under Cameron might reasonably have expected to be quietly confident of victory. Under the leadership of Gordon Brown Labour had suffered its lowest ever approval ratings while in office: in mid-2008 things were even worse than during the 1976 IMF crisis and Brown's personal approval ratings hit a low of minus 58 per cent (Grice 2010). Yet as the election drew near it was widely anticipated it would be the closest for many years and there was much speculation about the possibility of a hung parliament. In part this reflected a modest recovery by Labour in the opinion polls since late 2009, but it also signalled that in spite of the widespread feeling that it might be time for a change of government, the Conservatives under Cameron had failed to 'seal the deal' with the electorate.

The most striking feature of the campaign itself was the extraordinary surge in support for the Liberal Democrats, triggered by the stellar performance of Nick Clegg in the first of the three televised debates between the party leaders. Opinion polls were unanimous in reporting that the public regarded Clegg as the clear winner of the debate by a considerable margin (Winnett and Porter 2010) and this was soon reflected in backing for his party. Before the first debate on 15 April, support for the Liberal Democrats had been hovering around 20 per cent. Afterwards it jumped to around 30 per cent, with several polls even giving the party a small lead over the Conservatives, with Labour in third place. This increase came at the expense of both the major parties, threatening Labour with the humiliation of finishing third on polling day (in terms of votes if not seats) and ominously for David Cameron suggesting that the Conservatives would fail to win an overall majority. Elements of the right-wing press seized the opportunity to criticise the Conservative leader, first, as he was regarded as having performed below expectations in the first debate, and second, as it had been persistent public pressure from Cameron that had been instrumental in forcing Gordon Brown to concede to the televised debates in the first place. Keen to exploit his telegenic advantage over the Prime Minister, Cameron had seemingly failed to anticipate the risk of providing an unprecedented platform for the leader of the third party.

Much of the praise heaped on Clegg's performance appeared to centre on the fact that (unlike Brown and Cameron) he spent much of the first debate looking straight at the camera, addressing the audience watching on television rather than the relatively small number of people in the studio itself. Cameron in particular took this lesson to heart, gazing intently into the nation's living rooms during the second and third debates. Both he and Brown raised their game, and the public verdict on the final two debates was much more divided and roughly reflected the strength of each party's support. The Conservatives and Labour also attempted to turn the tide on the Liberal Democrats by warning of the 'danger' of a hung parliament. The Conservatives even went as far as to issue a spoof manifesto and party election broadcast on behalf of 'the hung parliament party', which variously suggested that such an outcome would lead to 'behind closed door politics ... indecision, inaction and half measures', and would spook the markets and 'paralyse the economy' (conservatives.com 2010). In spite of these attacks most opinion polls continued to suggest that the Liberal Democrats were maintaining their increased support as the election approached. Nick Clegg appeared to have cornered a gap in the market, offering a 'vote for change' (the Conservatives' slogan) without the need to support Cameron's party. Beyond the televised debates the election struggled to capture the public imagination, despite the prospect of a close result. In part this reflected cynicism towards the pledges by all parties to 'clean up politics' in the light of the expenses scandal, but it also stemmed from a deeper malaise affecting British politics, namely the rise of disenchantment with the political system itself (see Stoker 2006).

Although Cameron proved unable to lead his party to an outright victory, the Conservatives were the clear winners on election night as both Labour and the Liberal Democrats lost seats. On a respectable swing from Labour of 5 per cent the Conservatives gained ninety-seven seats, their biggest advance since 1931 (see chapter 2). This still left the party nineteen short of the 326 required for an overall victory, and Cameron swiftly moved to open discussions with the Liberal Democrats about a possible coalition. This was a brazen move by the Conservative leader, who had to make significant concessions on electoral reform and taxation policy in order to secure the agreement of Clegg's party. The prospect of governing in coalition caused unease among backbenchers in both parties, although publicly at least things were more strained among the Liberal Democrats, most of whom regarded Labour as their more natural bedfellows. Dissent on the Conservative side was surprisingly limited, kept in check by the tantalising prospect of power. When the coalition was formed some right-wing commentators immediately condemned the 'betrayal' of the Conservative Party by its leadership (Heffer 2010) but those sharing such reservations in the parliamentary party largely kept them out of the newspapers. The next section explores how the coalition might impact on intra-party dynamics and what it might mean for Conservative politics more broadly.

New politics for old? What coalition means for the Conservatives

In one respect at least Cameron's modernisation of his party in opposition has been shown to have gone far enough: it enabled him to strike a deal for coalition government with the Liberal Democrats under Nick Clegg, who became his Deputy Prime Minister. Had the 2005 result made it a mathematical possibility, such a deal between the then party leaders Michael

Howard and Charles Kennedy would have been totally unthinkable. This serves as a reminder that Cameron has overseen significant change in his party and moved it towards the fabled centre-ground of British politics. Clegg and Cameron were brought together in part by their professed desire to forge a 'new politics' to reform the political system, economy and society, which they declared 'broken'. So what might the coalition mean for the future of Conservative politics? This section briefly sketches some possible scenarios, distinguishing between outcomes leading to a return to established patterns of Conservative politics ('old politics') and transformative change ('new politics').

Old politics: another Conservative century?

Such was the dominance of the Conservative Party in British politics that it became known (and regarded itself) as 'the natural party of government', and historians came to refer to the twentieth century as 'the Conservative Century' (Seldon and Ball, 1994). Analysts sought to explain its success and pointed to an apparent aptitude for modifying itself in pursuit of power. As Addison comments, the Conservatives 'have long been renowned for their ability to adapt to new conditions while retaining something of their old identity' (1999: 289). This idea is at the heart of the most influential explanation of Conservative electoral dominance, namely Bulpitt's statecraft thesis. Bulpitt highlighted the importance of leadership strategy for understanding Conservative Party politics, stressing 'the need to examine the activities of party leaders in terms of their statecraft – namely the art of winning elections and, above all, achieving a necessary degree of governing competence in office' (1986: 19). In other words, statecraft embodied the idea that the Conservative Party existed to govern and that its leaders enjoyed a high degree of flexibility to pursue the electoral success required to fulfil that role.

On such a reading Cameron could be comprehended as a return to this tradition of pragmatic statecraft, modernising his party sufficiently to return to office. The period 1997–2005 might come to be seen as something of a blip in the history of Conservative politics, perhaps best explained by the public desire for something different after eighteen years in office and the political skill and electoral appeal of Tony Blair. As Andrew Gamble noted back in 2007, it 'remains to be seen whether New Labour will eventually be recognised as a stepping stone to a renewed progressive politics in Britain, or merely an interruption before Britain's long Conservative political hegemony resumes again' (Gamble 2007: 35). The decline in Labour's vote share to just 29 per cent and the willingness of the Liberal Democrats to coalesce with the Conservatives might be taken to indicate the final collapse of the vision of a permanent realignment of British politics onto more progressive lines.

Understood in terms of statecraft, the coalition agreement may be regarded as an astute piece of 'high politics' by Cameron. While conceding some specific points to his junior partner (most notably a referendum on electoral reform) the Conservative leader secured for himself and his party all the key prizes: the major offices of state; control of the public finances and the direction of economic policy; and a large majority in the Commons to ensure the passage of the government's legislative programme. Statecraft would suggest a continued willingness on Cameron's part to compromise to hold the coalition together – at least until such a time as he adjudges it to be electorally rewarding to allow it to break down, prompting a general election. It also implies a governing approach driven by pragmatism rather than ideology, characterised, for example, by Cameron and Clegg's claims that they have no wish to slash public spending, but that cuts are simply 'unavoidable' because of the size of the government's deficit. If such an approach is successful, it could mark a return to the Conservative dominance of the last century.

Another possibility worth considering is Cameron's Conservative Party emerging as a direct descendent of the Thatcherite hegemonic project. In his early portrayal of Thatcherism as 'the great moving right show', Stuart Hall argued that it was a dangerous combination of 'the resonant themes of organic Toryism', such as the nation, authority and the family, with the 'aggressive themes of a revived neo-liberalism', primarily anti-statist competitive individualism (Hall 1983: 29). It is this latter element that Cameron made great efforts in opposition to dispel from the electorate's mind: his oft-repeated refrain that 'we are all in this together' is a direct appeal to a sense of collective belonging. Learning from Blair and New Labour, Cameron appreciated that the harsher side of Thatcherite individualism left the Conservatives appearing uncaring and 'only in it for themselves', so he consistently tempered this aspect of his party's language. Yet it is difficult to avoid the conclusion that the Conservatives under Cameron remain fundamentally neo-liberal in their economic viewpoint, as illustrated by their response to the financial crisis. Indeed, as one analyst recently argued:

> Conservative economic policy under David Cameron's leadership has remained wedded to Thatcherism's core assumptions about the respective roles of the state and market. In particular, both Cameron and Osborne have shown in their rhetoric and actions to be adherents to a political economy and economic policy agenda which continues to identify individual entrepreneurial initiative as the prime agency of economic and social change. (Lee 2009: 78)

Cameron's neo-liberal critique of the state is not merely confined to economic policy – indeed, it underlies his social policy agenda too. The nebulous concept of the 'Big Society' is much more clear about what it is not (the state) than what it would actually involve. As outlined in the Conservative general election manifesto, the concept flows from a belief that '[t]he size, scope and role of government in the UK has reached a point where it is now inhibiting, not advancing, the progressive aims of reducing poverty, fighting inequality, and increasing general well-being' (Conservative Party 2010: 37).

If one agrees with John Gray (2010) that 'an ideologically driven Conservatism is here to stay' then it is difficult to avoid the conclusion that it will be Thatcherite ideology at the steering wheel. On this reading, just as Thatcher seized the opportunity provided by the economic crisis of the late 1970s, the Conservatives under Cameron will exploit the current crisis to impose a new regime of austerity, perhaps rolling back the state much further than Thatcher managed. From this perspective, the coalition with the Liberal Democrats can be seen as little more than a convenient fig leaf to help mask the scale of the retrenchment. In his speech to the 2008 party conference, Cameron declared that: 'The central task I have set myself and this party is to be as radical in social reform as Margaret Thatcher was in economic reform' (*The Guardian*, 2 October 2008). If the great moving right show gets back on the road, he could indeed signal a return to the radicalism of old.

New politics: a new progressive politics?

From a rather different perspective, some analysts have heralded the Conservative-Liberal Democrat coalition as a new dawn for progressive politics. For Anthony Barnett, it finally 'brought the period associated with Margaret Thatcher after her election in 1979 to an end' (2010: 1). With one move, he suggests, Cameron has 'broken the spell' of Thatcherism that had captivated his party and returned it to 'its one-nation Whig tradition' (2010: 2). From this viewpoint, Cameron's audacious move into coalition confirms that he was always committed to modernisation and saw the opportunity to marginalise the right of his party and fully complete this project in a way he had been unable to do in opposition. Forming the coalition was a strategic choice by Cameron that entailed the rejection of other options such as a minority government, which was favoured by many in his party and the Conservative press. For the former Labour Minister David Lammy, this ranks alongside the transformation of the Labour Party under Tony Blair:

The coalition with the Liberal Democrats is therefore hugely significant. It has done more to rebrand and modernise the Conservative party than anything during my time in politics. The new Prime Minster not only has a working majority, he has the opportunity to govern free from his party's rightwing – Nick Clegg has handed Cameron his Clause 4 moment. (Lammy 2010)

But to suggest that the Conservative Party has been transformed overnight by the formation of the coalition is too hasty: it will very much depend on how the coalition government performs – indeed whether or not it can survive. For many Conservative backbenchers the coalition is on an extended period of probation. Only if it is able to govern effectively for a number of years will it bring about any significant shift in the culture of the party towards more liberal and cooperative lines. One way that Cameron could have demonstrated his commitment to a progressive politics to close the chapter on Thatcherism would have been to support electoral reform. Although a referendum on the alternative vote was part of the coalition agreement, Cameron campaigned in favour of the status quo 'first past the post' system. This allowed Nick Clegg to assume the mantle as the leading advocate of 'new politics', although the triumph of the 'no' vote suggested a waning appetite for change among British voters.

As a debate between two academics in one newspaper highlighted the day after the coalition was formed, its implications were immediately hotly disputed. For one, it marked 'a historic watershed as the embodiment of the emergence of a genuinely multi-party politics at Westminster' (Hayton 2010b). For another, 'Although both partners were keen to present this as a "historic and seismic shift in British politics", it is really little more than a grubby shotgun wedding' (Flinders 2010). Such disagreements are unlikely to dissipate for quite some time to come. But coalition politics has the potential to have a significant transformative effect on Conservative politics and British politics more generally.

Since becoming Conservative leader, Cameron has demonstrated a desire to be seen as a modern, compassionate and liberal Conservative. His enthusiasm for coalition reflects the fact that it offers him the opportunity to strengthen these aspects of his electoral appeal and to further the modernisation of his party with less hindrance from its right wing. Like Blair's 'big tent' before it, the coalition provides Cameron with the opportunity to present himself as a leader standing slightly apart from his party, seeking to govern in the national rather than party interest.

Coalition politics also has the potential to transform the dynamics of party competition, perhaps in ways that are difficult to predict. Cameron might hope, for example, that it will split Liberal Democrat support (and perhaps even the party itself), with a chunk of third party voters returning to the Conservative fold. If he can broaden the Conservative appeal to once again regularly command the support of over 40 per cent of the electorate, Cameron will have laid the ground for another lengthy period of Conservative electoral dominance. The referendum on electoral reform, had it prospered, might have signalled the normalisation of multi-party coalition politics in Britain. Such a change would have moved the UK decisively towards a more European political system, undermining the foundations of the Westminster model. The 'no' vote in the referendum means that it falls to other reforms promised by the coalition – notably more open government, greater devolution and decentralisation, an elected upper house and fixed term parliaments – to change the political settlement in Britain.

Conclusion

David Cameron's Conservatives face a raft of difficult challenges in office. The pain of public spending cuts might become too much for his new Liberal Democrat partners and break his government apart. Other issues such as European integration, an unforeseen foreign policy crisis, banking reform or university tuition fees all have the potential to irrevocably damage the coalition. Indeed, the age of austerity we are entering will put stress on the future integrity of the United Kingdom itself, not least because the Conservatives hold just one seat in Scotland and the Liberal Democrats only eleven. This will inevitably lead nationalists north of the border to question the legitimacy of cuts imposed from Westminster. Nonetheless, as Conservative leader Cameron has already enjoyed significant success. He has brought to a close one of the most prolonged and painful periods of opposition in the history of his party and changed its image, personnel and positioning in a number of significant ways. Perhaps under his leadership the Conservatives are finally starting to emerge from Thatcherism's long shadow.

References

Addison, P. (1999). 'The British Conservative Party from Churchill to Heath: Doctrine or Men?', *Contemporary European History*, 8 (2): 289–298.

Bale, T. (2008). '"A Bit Less Bunny-Hugging and a Bit More Bunny-Boiling"? Qualifying Conservative Party Change under David Cameron', *British Politics*, 3: 270–299.

Bale, T. (2010). *The Conservative Party: From Thatcher to Cameron*. Cambridge: Polity.

Barnett, A. (2010). 'The End of Thatcherism', www.opendemocracy .net/anthony-barnett/end-of-thatcherism (last accessed 1 October 2011).

Beech, M. (2009). 'Cameron and Conservative Ideology', in S. Lee and M. Beech (eds), *The Conservatives Under David Cameron: Built to Last?* Basingstoke: Palgrave Macmillan, pp. 18–30.

Bulpitt, J. (1986). 'The Discipline of the New Democracy: Mrs Thatcher's Domestic Statecraft', *Political Studies*, 34 (1): 19–39.

Cameron, D. (2006). 'Improving Society's Sense of Well Being Is Challenge of Our Times', speech, 26 May. www.conservatives.com/News /Speeches/2006/05/Cameron_Improving_societys_sense_of_well_ being_is_challenge_of_our_times.aspx (last accessed 1 October 2011).

Carter, N. (2009). 'Vote Blue, Go Green? Cameron's Conservatives and the Environment', *Political Quarterly*, 80 (2): 233–242.

Conservative Party (2010). *Invitation to Join the Government of Britain: The Conservative Manifesto 2010*. London: Conservative Party.

Conservatives.com (2010). 'An Election Broadcast from the Hung Parliament Party', 26 April. www.conservatives.com/Video /Conservatives_TV.aspx?id=5fab8efd-8b85–497b-8fc9–cbd168b2384a (last accessed 1 October 2011).

Denham, A. and P. Dorey (2006). 'A Tale of Two Speeches? The Conservative Leadership Election of 2005', *Political Quarterly*, 77 (1): 35–42.

Denham, A. and K. O'Hara (2008). *Democratising Conservative Leadership Selection*. Manchester: Manchester University Press.

Dorey, P. (2007). 'A New Direction or Another False Dawn? David Cameron and the Crisis of British Conservatism', *British Politics*, 2: 137–166.

Dorey, P. (2009). 'Sharing the Proceeds of Growth: Conservative Economic Policy under Cameron', *Political Quarterly*, 80 (2): 259–269.

Evans, S. (2010). 'Mother's Boy: David Cameron and Margaret Thatcher', *British Journal of Politics and International Relations*, 12 (3): 325–343.

Finlayson, A. (2007). 'Making Sense of David Cameron', *Public Policy Research*, May: 3–10.

Flinders, M. (2010). 'Happy Together for Now But Will it Turn Out to Be a Shotgun Wedding?', *Yorkshire Post*, 14 May.

Gamble, A. (2007). 'New Labour and Old Debates', in G. Hassan (ed.), *After Blair: Politics After the New Labour Decade*. London: Lawrence & Wishart, pp. 26–36.

Gray, J. (2010). 'Thatcher, Thatcher, Thatcher', *London Review of Books*, 32 (8): 19–21.

Grice, A. (2010). 'Poll: This Is the Least Popular Labour Government Ever', *The Independent*, 3 July.

Griffiths, S. and K. Hickson (eds) (2010). *British Party Politics and Ideology after New Labour*. Basingstoke: Palgrave Macmillan.

Hague, W. (2001). 'Speech to Conservative Spring Forum', 4 March.

Hall, S. (1983). 'The Great Moving Right Show', in S. Hall and M. Jacques (eds), *The Politics of Thatcherism*. London: Lawrence & Wishart, pp. 19–39.

Hayton, R. (2010a). 'Leadership Without Authority: Iain Duncan Smith as Leader of the Conservative Party', paper presented to the 'Leaders of the Opposition from Churchill to Cameron' conference, University of Leeds, 9 July.

Hayton, R. (2010b). 'Happy Together for Now But Will it Turn Out to Be a Shotgun Wedding?', *Yorkshire Post*, 14 May.

Hayton, R. (forthcoming). *Reconstructing Conservatism? The Conservative Party in Opposition, 1997–2010*. Manchester: Manchester University Press.

Hayton, R. and T. Heppell (2010). 'The Quiet Man of British Politics: The Rise, Fall and Significance of Iain Duncan Smith', *Parliamentary Affairs*, 63 (3): 425–445.

Heffer, S. (2010). 'David Cameron Will Rue the Day He Betrayed the Conservatives', *Daily Telegraph*, 21 May.

Heppell, T. (2008). *Choosing the Tory Leader: Conservative Party Leadership Elections from Heath to Cameron*. London: IB Tauris.

Heppell, T. and M. Hill (2009). 'Transcending Thatcherism? Ideology and the Conservative Party Leadership Mandate of David Cameron', Political Quarterly, 80 (3): 388–399.

Lammy, D. (2010). 'Clegg Has Given Cameron His Clause 4 Moment', *The Spectator*, 19 May.

Lee, S. (2009). 'Convergence, Critique and Divergence: The Development of Economic Policy Under David Cameron', in S. Lee and M. Beech (eds), *The Conservatives Under David Cameron: Built to Last?* Basingstoke: Palgrave, pp. 60–79.

Lynch, P. and R. Whitaker (2008). 'A Loveless Marriage: The Conservatives and the European People's Party', *Parliamentary Affairs*, 61 (1): 31–51.

Portillo, M. (2005). 'Cameron Mania Could Be an Election Too Soon', *Sunday Times*, 9 October.

Portillo, M. (2008). 'The Lady's Not for Spurning', documentary programme, first broadcast 25 February, 9pm, BBC4.

Quinn, T. (2008). 'The Conservative Party and the "Centre Ground" of British Politics', *Journal of Elections, Public Opinion and Parties*, 18 (2): 179–199.

Reeves, R. (2008). 'This Is David Cameron', *Public Policy Research*, June: 63–67.

Seldon, A. and S. Ball (eds) (1994). *Conservative Century: The Conservative Party Since 1900*. Oxford: Oxford University Press.

Seldon, A. and P. Snowdon (2005). 'The Barren Years: 1997–2005', in

S. Ball and A. Seldon (eds), *Recovering Power: The Conservatives in Opposition Since 1867*. Basingstoke: Palgrave Macmillan, pp. 243–275.

Snowdon, P. (2010). *Back from the Brink: The Inside Story of the Tory Resurrection*. London: Harper Press.

Stoker, G. (2006). *Why Politics Matters: Making Democracy Work*. Basingstoke: Palgrave Macmillan.

Taylor, I. (2003). 'The Conservatives, 1997–2001: A Party in Crisis?', in M. Garnett and P. Lynch (eds). *The Conservatives in Crisis*. Manchester: Manchester University Press, pp. 229–247.

Winnett, R. and A. Porter (2010). 'TV Election Debate: Nick Clegg's Star Rises in Great Showdown', *Daily Telegraph*, 16 April.

YouGov (2010). 'Cameron Balance Right', 1 June. http://today.yougov .co.uk/politics/Cameron-balance-right (last accessed 1 October 2011).

5

The Liberal Democrats

Elizabeth Evans

Introduction

The 2010 general election proved to be both a blessing and a curse for the UK's third party. While Liberal Democrat leader Nick Clegg described the election as a 'disappointing result', no party had a large enough majority to govern alone. A hung parliament meant that Nick Clegg was in the position of king-maker. Decades of opposition had led many within the party to place their hopes in a hung parliament, which would finally allow Liberal Democrats to wield influence. Following five days of negotiations a coalition with the Conservatives was announced. For the Liberal Democrats, this was their first ever taste of power, and their precursor party, the Liberals, had been out of government since the Second World War. While the Liberal Democrats seemingly did well out of the coalition negotiations, securing five cabinet posts and numerous junior ministerial positions, the principal tensions surrounding the coalition agreement related to policy, most notably the referendum on the electoral system.

Although many within the party were deeply uncomfortable at the 'unholy alliance' that had been formed between the two parties, there was no more than a small flurry of defections and resignations from the party (Grayson 2010). However, the long-term implications of the coalition agreement for the party's electoral fortunes and for internal party cohesion remain unclear. This uncertainty is compounded by changing dynamics within the party, which has become both increasingly professional and more leadership-oriented. More important, perhaps, is the continued frustration at the party's repeated failure to make the much anticipated 'electoral breakthrough', despite seemingly favourable political climates in both 2005 and 2010. This chapter explores the internal dynamics and electoral fortunes of the party in the run-up to, and the immediate aftermath of, the 2010 general election. Focusing on party organisation, electoral strategy and the coalition process, the chapter offers an assessment of the challenges facing the party, including the difficulties of maintaining a unique identity and appeasing grassroots activists.

Party organisation: from participation to professionalisation?

Since their formation in 1988, the Liberal Democrats have consolidated their third party status in the UK. Although frustrated by the majoritarian system used to elect the national parliament, recent years have seen them win control of key local authorities in some of the UK's largest cities, while also forming coalition governments with Labour at the devolved level in both Wales and Scotland. Moreover, being on the side of public opinion on two key issues – opposing both the war in Iraq and the introduction of tuition fees for university students – has ensured their continued relevance in UK politics (Russell 2005). The party has also attempted to demonstrate their credibility (where credibility is judged to be adherence to fiscal orthodoxy) to the electorate, by adopting less controversial policies, for instance by scrapping a commitment to introducing a 50 per cent income tax for those earning over £100,000. Cumulatively, these electoral achievements and strategic decisions highlight the evolution of the Liberal Democrats, from Westminster's largest pressure group to serious political players.

The Liberal Democrats cut a distinctive shape in UK politics. Organisationally, the party has a federal, bottom-up organisational structure that allows party activists and members the opportunity to participate in the policy-making process. While their commitment to community politics, best illustrated through their successful campaigning methods, would once have set them apart, their strategies and emphasis on localism have now largely been adopted by the other main parties (Russell and Fieldhouse 2005). However, the Liberal Democrats remain a clearly less hierarchical and centralised party than the Labour and Conservative parties.

Despite this distinctive organisational ethic, the Liberal Democrats have undergone a process of professionalisation, both in terms of their organisation and the image they present to the electorate (Evans and Sanderson-Nash 2011). This professionalisation can be illustrated by the increasing centralisation of decision-making processes within the party and the erosion of grassroots influence. It is therefore within the context of an increasingly compliant membership, dovetailed with an increasingly centralised party, that Nick Clegg was able to lead his party into a coalition government with the Conservatives. Following the 2005 general election there were two successive leadership elections, contributing to a sense that the party had somehow lost its direction. The rapid change of personnel at the top of the party, coupled with a raft of damaging headlines regarding the personal lives of its senior politicians, made 'selling' the party a much harder task (Hurst 2006).

The emphasis on credibility has been part of the professionalisation of the party in recent years (Russell and Fieldhouse 2005). The party has sought to present a more credible face to the public, which has led to greater direction from party headquarters in Cowley Street. The professionalisation of the party's central office, notably through investment in opinion research and the increasing influence of the party leadership, has been key to the party's development (Evans and Sanderson-Nash 2011; Russell and Fieldhouse 2005; Russell et al. 2007; Webb 2000; Whiteley et al. 2006). This professionalisation has, in part, exacerbated tensions between the federal party and the party's grassroots activists, with the latter keen to protect their autonomy (Evans 2007; Russell and Fieldhouse 2005).

Despite the efforts on the part of successive leaders to centralise decision-making processes the federal structure of the party ensures that the grassroots can still inflict humiliating defeats upon the party leadership (Russell and Fieldhouse 2005). The distinctive structure of the Liberal Democrats is a result of the party's commitment to community politics. Theoretically, the structure facilitates grassroots and democratic decision-making processes through the election of party activists to federal bodies. So, according to the party constitution, policy, elections and fundraising, as they apply specifically to England, Scotland and Wales, are the responsibility of the state parties. Federal structures deal with federal matters such as funding for party groups and overseeing internal party elections. Additionally, there are four directly elected UK wide federal committees: the Federal Executive (FE); the Federal Policy Committee (FPC); the Federal Conference Committee (FCC); and the Federal Finance and Administration Committee (FFAC).

The organisation of the Liberal Democrats ensures that party activists are able to help shape policy through two annual conferences, the sovereign decision-making body within the party. While the federal structure has at times enabled the membership to thwart the party leadership (Russell and Fieldhouse 2005) in particular through the removal of not one but two leaders, recent years have seen the party become increasingly loyal to the party leadership (Grayson 2010). This loyalty has inevitably changed the dynamics of the relationship between party activists and the leadership, with the latter now able to secure the support of members for policies previously rejected by conference. For instance in 2005, Liberal Democrat members rejected a policy calling for the part privatisation of Royal Mail; however, when it was reintroduced to conference in 2009 by Vince Cable, the popular Liberal Democrat Treasury spokesperson, the party gave its approval.

Following Nick Clegg's election as party leader in 2007 he commissioned a review of the party's internal organisation and established the Chief Officer's Group (COG).[1] Given that the function of this group is to manage, coordinate and direct the work of the party, much of the power that used to lie with the FE has now been ceded to this newly centralised group. The creation of the COG was part of a wider attempt on the part of Clegg to streamline the party's existing committee structure and to create one clear decision-making body. Despite Nick Clegg's claims that this new committee was in place to reduce inefficiency and bureaucracy, it led many to speculate that it was a deliberate attempt on the part of the leader to wrest power away from the then chief executive, Lord Chris Rennard (*The Times*, 16 July 2008). While this was denied by the party leadership, ongoing tensions between senior party officials based at the party's headquarters and senior parliamentarians have been observed (Evans and Sanderson-Nash 2011).

The conscious attempt by the leadership to professionalise the party was also underpinned by an internal party review, the Bones Commission. Its remit was to explore reform of the party's internal practices. The report identified a 'collective mission creep' for some of the bodies within the party's democratic process, something they believed had led to confusion and needless obfuscating of the party's strategic focus (Bones *et al.* 2008). Intra-party tensions between senior party activists, parliamentarians and professional staff regarding accountability are also compounded by the broader ongoing tensions between the party's elite and grassroots. Indeed, the Bones report highlights the resentment felt by activists as being regarded simply as part of a 'leaflet delivery cult' (Bones *et al.* 2008: 38). For the Liberal Democrats then, the need to professionalise conflicts with the need to placate the party's vocal grassroots, who currently enjoy more influence within their party than Conservative or Labour party activists. These tensions are likely to be exacerbated not only by the coalition agreement but also by the election results, which were disappointing for the wider party. Despite overall declining party membership, the Liberal Democrats with relatively fewer material resources rely heavily on their activists to help campaign, and keeping their support will be critical for the party (Whiteley *et al.* 2006).

Centre-left or centre-right? Party strategy and the 2010 election

In addition to tensions around the balance of influence between leaders and activists, broad policy disagreements also exist within the party. Although research has noted increased cohesion among the parliamentary party (Cole 2009), recent internal debates over the renewal of Trident and university tuition fees have highlighted splits within the wider party. Furthermore, ideological differences based upon a social-classical Liberal divide have led to the perception that the Liberal Democrats have not reconciled the two wings of their party that emerged from the Liberal Party and SDP. Illustrative of this is the recent publication of two very different ideologically motivated books by parliamentarians and senior party activists: the economically liberal *Orange Book* (Marshall and Laws 2004) and the socially liberal *Reinventing the State* (Brack *et al.* 2007).

The ideological divisions between the economic and social liberals have to a certain extent been exaggerated, and it is certainly true that both factions share much common ground (Grayson 2010). However, tensions within the party also emanate from broader disagreements concerning the overall direction of the party. Although many in the Liberal Democrats consider the party to be on the centre-left of British politics, research has shown that they benefit electorally when they have been able to brand themselves as a centrist party (Nagel and Wlezien 2010). As such, internal disputes regarding policy positions directly impact upon the electoral fortunes of the party. This is obviously difficult for a party whose leadership is generally seen to be to the right of the party membership (Grayson 2010). The difference in emphasis between leadership and grassroots attitudes has at times meant that totemic policy pledges, emblematic of the party's position on the left of British politics, have come under fire, for instance dropping the 50 pence income tax pledge. The implications of the 2010 election result for these internal tensions are potentially significant.

Just as in the aftermath of the 2005 election, there was a perception, both internally and externally, that in 2010 the party had missed an important opportunity to make a significant electoral breakthrough. Two years out from the election Nick Clegg signalled his intent to target the top fifty Labour marginal seats. In a pre-election pamphlet, *The Liberal Moment* (2009), Nick Clegg argued that the time had come for progressives to 'regroup under a new banner'. Despite his studious avoidance of the terms 'centre-left' or 'left-wing', the intention of the pamphlet was clear: to appeal to disaffected Labour voters. This was both in response to a resurgent Conservative Party under David Cameron and the declining popularity of Gordon Brown. This decision was reminiscent of the party's 2005 campaign where the Liberal Democrats had made much of their

'decapitation' strategy to target senior Conservative politicians, also ultimately unsuccessful (Curtice 2007; Russell 2005).

The election results were a particularly bitter pill for the Liberal
Democrats to swallow given their seemingly successful election campaign.
The 2010 campaign marked a departure from previous general elections
with the televised leaders' debates offering Clegg the opportunity to
compete on a level playing field. Nick Clegg's success during the debates,
which at its peak resulted in opinion polling of over 30 per cent for the
party, even giving it the lead in some opinion polls, was not however eventually translated into seats. Although the party managed to secure the
support of *The Observer* and *The Guardian*, the Conservative supporting
press, notably *The Sun*, launched a series of personal attacks on the party
leader. Despite a modest increase in their share of the vote, the number of
Liberal Democrat seats actually went down.

As Table 5.1 highlights the Liberal Democrats have not substantially
increased their number of seats outside of their heartlands, Scotland and
the south-west, and where their share of the vote did increase it was only
by a small amount. The geographical unevenness of the Liberal Democrats'
seats also makes it harder for the party to sell itself as a 'credible' option to
voters nationwide, which is critical to any future breakthrough (Russell and
Fieldhouse 2005). The party's capacity to appeal to all British regions is
hindered by the lasting purchase of the 'wasted vote syndrome', which kept
them out of second place electorally despite being the second choice for
many voters (Russell and Fieldhouse 2005).[2] While the party is disadvan-

Table 5.1 Lib Dem share of the vote and seats won by region, 1997–2005

Region	1997		2001		2005		2010	
	seats	vote (%)	seats	vote (%)	seats	vote (%)	seats	vote (%)
Eastern	1	17.1	2	17.5	3	21.8	3	23.5
E Mids	0	13.6	1	15.4	1	18.5	0	20.9
London	6	14.6	6	17.5	8	21.9	7	21.6
Nth East	1	12.6	1	16.7	1	23.3	2	24.6
Nth West	2	14.5	3	16.7	6	21.4	6	22.0
Scotland	10	13.0	10	16.3	11	22.6	11	19.0
Sth East	7	23.3	8	23.7	6	25.4	5	26.7
Sth West	14	31.3	15	31.2	16	32.5	15	33.2
Wales	2	12.3	2	13.8	4	18.4	3	20.0
W Mids	1	13.8	2	13.8	3	18.8	2	19.9
York/Hum	2	16.0	2	17.1	3	20.7	3	21.9
Total	46	16.8	52	18.3	62	22.1	57	23.0

Source: updated from Russell and Fieldhouse, 2005

taged by the UK's majoritarian electoral system (Curtice and Steed 1982; Denver 2007) and a relative lack of material resources, the party's problems have also been compounded by organisational upheaval and internal disputes over policy and the future direction of the party.

The pattern of the party's successes at the 2010 election was mixed. Going into the election the Liberal Democrats had a number of seats they were hoping to win, some of these included newly created seats, such as the City of Durham, while others were seats they had previously held, such as Guildford. In total the party had some thirty-one seats that required a swing to win of 5 per cent or less (excluding those held seats which under redrawn boundaries were notional Conservative or Labour seats), of those seats the party won just three. Moreover, the party lost thirteen held seats with even some high profile MPs losing out.[3]

The 2010 election campaign was conducted within the shadow of the expenses scandal, which had seriously damaged public confidence in Westminster. Although all three parties were hit by the scandal, the Liberal Democrats remained relatively unscathed with few high profile MPs seriously damaged, Accordingly, the election offered the party a unique opportunity to sell their vision of a 'new politics' to a largely alienated and distrustful electorate. Indeed, throughout the campaign Clegg repeatedly referred to the 'duopoly' of the 'two tired old parties'. Furthermore, the number of MPs standing down, rather than face re-election, was uncommonly high allowing the Liberal Democrats a rare opportunity to capitalise on the relatively high number of seats with no incumbent.[4]

The Liberal Democrat campaign was based upon two core strands: fairer taxes and cleaner politics. However, the spectre of a hung parliament overshadowed much of the detailed policy debates with repeated calls from senior Labour politicians for Liberal Democrats supporters to vote tactically in an anti-Conservative alliance (see for instance *The Scotsman* 10 April 2010). Nick Clegg appeared to encourage this narrative, when on 11 April he called the possibility of a hung parliament a 'good thing'. While opinion polling looked favourable for the party, particularly at the start of the campaign, by the last of the TV debates a sense of ennui surrounded reactions to the Liberal Democrat leader's performance. Within the context of an unpredictable election campaign, which undoubtedly appeared to benefit Nick Clegg and the Liberal Democrats, the party's performance at the ballot was disappointing. Given the hype of 'Cleggmania' that dominated much of the media coverage of the election, there is a suspicion among some party activists that the party got carried away and failed to follow the targeting strategy effectively. For instance, it has been suggested that Oxford West and Abingdon was lost partly because it was thought to be a relatively safe seat and so resources were directed to the neighbouring seat of Oxford East. Notwithstanding the inequities of the electoral system, the party's overall share of the vote increased by just under 1 per cent.

Forming a government: the Liberal Democrats and coalition politics

In the immediate aftermath of the 2010 general election Nick Clegg stuck to his pre-election pledge to allow the party with the biggest mandate to make the first attempt to form a government. Luckily for the Liberal Democrats, the Conservatives secured both the highest percentage share of the vote and number of seats, meaning that the party did not have to decide what actually constituted the 'biggest mandate'. Although a few meetings were held with Labour politicians, some senior Labour figures including David Blunkett and John Reid had warned against a coalition deal (BBC 2010). Consequently, negotiations with the Conservatives moved on apace with frequent discussions between David Cameron and Nick Clegg underpinning the formal negotiation process, which was led by teams of senior politicians from both parties.

The choice of politicians for the Liberal Democrat negotiation team was telling. David Laws, Danny Alexander, Chris Huhne and Andrew Stunnell between them represented key groups or sections within the party: David Laws, a key proponent of economic liberalism; Danny Alexander, Nick Clegg's chief of staff; Chris Huhne, the defeated leadership contender; and Andrew Stunnell, a former local councillor accustomed to negotiating coalitions. Between them Clegg and his negotiating team sought to reassure the rest of the parliamentary party and party activists that they had secured a workable deal from the Conservatives that would be in the best interests not only of the country but also of the Liberal Democrats. On 11 May 2010 the Liberal Democrats formerly entered into coalition government with the Conservatives, marking a historic moment not only for the party but also for the UK political system.

For many within a party traditionally viewed as being on the centre-left of British politics, a coalition with the Conservatives was a surprising and not wholly welcome development (Grayson 2010). Indeed, during the coalition negotiations many senior party activists sought to highlight the importance of securing a progressive alliance between the Liberal Democrats and Labour. Despite the open opposition of some within his party, Nick Clegg was able to secure the support of both his parliamentary party and the Federal Executive, the minimum necessary requirement for the party to enter into coalition government. The party does have a 'triple lock' mechanism in place to protect the party's grassroots against a change in strategy or direction. The triple lock, passed at the party's Federal

Conference in 1998, was introduced by the party to safeguard against the possibility that the then leader Paddy Ashdown would seek to form a formal alliance with Tony Blair. The mechanism requires 75 per cent of both the FE and parliamentary party to support key strategic decisions such as coalition agreements (Evans and Sanderson-Nash 2011).

Nick Clegg did secure 75 per cent of both bodies, but the leadership also sought to legitimise the agreement by organising a special conference of members. Despite the party's much vaunted federal structure and grass-roots oriented and democratic decision-making processes, party members were only consulted on the coalition agreement five days after it had been signed. The special conference called for party members on 16 May over-whelmingly approved the decision to enter into coalition with the Conservatives.[5] This support was secured in spite of the much publicised 'unease' about the coalition on the part of former leader Charles Kennedy, who himself was unable to vote in support of the agreement.

The coalition agreement itself contained a few concessions to the Liberal Democrats: restoring the earnings link for the basic state pension with a 'triple guarantee' that pensions are indexed to the higher of average earnings or prices; a 'Great Repeal Bill' to reverse many of the Labour government's policies surrounding security and civil liberties; and of course the much sought after referendum on electoral reform, albeit on the far from proportional AV system. However, it is clear that many within the party were far from satisfied with the coalition agreement's 'get out clause' for Liberal Democrats to simply abstain on any legislation introduced to increase tuition fees for higher education.

The first real test for the Liberal Democrats came with George Osborne's emergency budget. Contained within the budget was a commit-ment to increasing the rate of VAT from 17.5 per cent to 20 per cent. Despite the fact that during the election none of the parties explicitly ruled out a rise in VAT, the Liberal Democrats had made much of the likely VAT 'tax bomb' that would occur under a Conservative government. This proved to be embarrassing for the Liberal Democrats, with the Business Secretary Vince Cable forced to concede that the party had used the issue to 'score points' during the election (Walker 2010). Despite the reservations of many within the party, in the end only two Liberal Democrat MPs (Mike Hancock and Bob Russell) voted against the government, although four MPs also abstained from the vote.

A striking aspect of the budget debate was the inclusion of the Liberal Democrat response, a speech delivered by senior MP Sir Alan Beith. That the party felt it important to deliver a response on behalf of the Liberal Democrats to the coalition budget emphasises their desire to maintain an independent voice in parliament. While much has been made of the positive working relationships between individual Conservatives and Liberal Democrats at a ministerial level, it has been equally clear that both leaderships will have to work hard to keep their backbenchers on board. For the Liberal Democrats this was highlighted during the election for deputy leader of the party. Simon Hughes, generally seen as being on the left of the party, was duly elected following a campaign in which he pledged to ensure that a distinctive Liberal Democrat voice was heard in parliament.

Fears of the Liberal Democrats becoming subsumed within the Conservatives are a genuine concern for the party. This to a certain extent mirrors the aftermath of the 1997 general election when the party's close cooperation with the Blair government led to frequent accusations that the party was merely an 'adjunct' to Labour (Cowley and Stuart 2003). While the Liberal Democrats more frequently voted with than against Labour in the early sessions of the 1997–2001 parliament, the party shifted towards opposition over time and by the end of 2007 it was more often voting against than with the government (Cowley and Stuart 2003; 2007). In truth there has been little opportunity for the party to act independently of either of the two main parties (Cowley and Stuart 2007).

Of course high profile issues, for example the war in Iraq or issues concerned with civil liberties and tuition fees, have led to more of a consolidated and public separation between Labour and the Liberal Democrats. Changes in Liberal Democrat parliamentary voting behaviour have occurred incrementally and are directly linked to the changes in Liberal Democrat leadership (Cowley and Stuart 2007). In short, each new Liberal Democrat leader since Paddy Ashdown has moved the party further away from Labour in parliament, facilitating cooperation with the Conservatives in the new coalition. Nevertheless, the balancing act required by the Liberal Democrats initially created difficulties, as the next section explains.

The challenges of coalition

In the short term the party faced a number of interrelated challenges: to maintain their distinctive identity within a coalition government dominated by Conservatives; to negotiate the differences between the coalition government and the party's policy preferences; and, to ensure that Liberal Democrat members and activists remain willing to campaign on behalf of the party. These three challenges were irrevocably bound both to the legislative programme of the coalition government and the extent to which the wider party remains loyal to the party leadership. The tension between party policy and the realities of coalition were revealed immediately when, in his first outing at Prime Minister's Questions, deputising for

David Cameron, Nick Clegg immediately caused controversy when the Liberal Democrat leader denounced the war in Iraq as 'illegal'.[6] Some areas are clearly going to be difficult for the Liberal Democrats in government to negotiate, and speaking simultaneously for the government and their party may at times prove impossible. The coalition's approach to key Liberal Democrat policies such as opposition to university tuition fees and the referendum on electoral reform were particularly likely to prove decisive for both the Liberal Democrat leadership and also the coalition government.

Opposition to tuition fees has been a staple component of the party's electoral platform for the past two elections. It is this policy that generated significant student support, helping them to secure seats such as Cardiff Central and Manchester Withington. The coalition agreement stated that if the response of the government to the proposals included in Lord Browne's review of higher education is one that Liberal Democrat MPs 'cannot accept' then they would be allowed to abstain in any vote.

This dilemma proved particularly problematic for the Liberal Democrats when totemic issues such as tuition fees or electoral reform arose. The coalition government's decision to allow universities to increase tuition fees by up to 300 per cent, as recommended by the Browne Commission, flew in the face of the Liberal Democrats' high profile opposition to the existing system of tuition fees; many Liberal Democrat candidates had signed formal pledges to oppose tuition fee hikes as part of their election campaigns. In the event, Liberal Democrat MPs split over the issue, with twenty-one MPs, including two junior ministers, voting against the reform, and the remaining government ministers and backbenchers supporting it. The long-term electoral damage caused by this controversial policy is difficult to calculate, but it may have contributed to the Liberal Democrats dropping to around 10 per cent in opinion polls at the end of 2010. Furthermore, it is also clear that those MPs representing university towns and cities may face some sort of electoral penalty at the next election if Labour is able to mobilise effectively.

The party leadership was acutely aware of the critical importance of securing a 'yes' vote in the referendum to change the electoral system. The Conservatives' concession of a whipped vote in parliament in favour of holding a referendum on electoral reform was seen as key for many within the party uneasy at the coalition. While the alternative vote is far from proportional, some research has suggested that the Liberal Democrats would have increased their number of seats by 22 (Travis 2010). AV was presented by the party leadership to its members as being a vital stepping stone towards the introduction of full PR for Westminster elections. As a result, the overwhelming rejection by the electorate of the proposed change to the voting system had a devastating impact on the morale of the Liberal Democrats, who had long cherished the goal of electoral reform (Russell and Fieldhouse 2005). Another constitutional conundrum for the party is the House of Lords. Specifically, the combined numbers of Conservative and Liberal Democrat peers amount to an 'inbuilt majority' for the government in the Lords, undermining the revisory nature of the second chamber.[7] Indeed, while the Liberal Democrats have long been in favour of a wholly elected second chamber, they attracted criticism when it was announced that 100 new Conservative and Liberal Democrat peers would be appointed to better reflect the share of the vote that each party received at the general election.

Despite the observation that party activists have become increasingly loyal to the party leaders at conference (Grayson 2010), the twice yearly meetings, which will now attract a much greater degree of media scrutiny, offer disgruntled party activists a chance to inflict embarrassment upon the leadership. Indeed, rather than functioning as a rallying cry to the party faithful, party conferences may now act more as a safety valve for party activists. Furthermore, it is unclear what role conference, or indeed the FPC, will continue to play in the policy-making process given that the party is now in coalition government. Indeed, the democratic system of establishing working groups and allowing party members to vote on policy may prove unworkable. A reduced role for party activists in influencing the shape and direction of the party will inevitably cause resentment among the grassroots. The role of party activists is also likely to be sidelined at conference with an anticipated increase in the number of lobbyists and outside interests attending.

For the Liberal Democrats maintaining a distinct identity is paramount if they are to increase their number of seats at the next election. Part of their identity is irrevocably bound to their position on the centre-left of British politics, and how this will be maintained within a Lib Dem-Conservative coalition remains unclear. Despite frequent criticism, not least from the Liberal Democrats themselves, regarding the usefulness of the left-right scale as a way of gauging a political party's ideological temperature, it remains a key way of understanding party identity. Broadly speaking the Liberal Democrats continue to be a centre-left party as articulated by former leader Sir Menzies Campbell, 'I'm a politician in the centre-left, I joined a centre-left party, I'm leading a centre-left party, I make no secret of that' (Woodward and White 2007). Furthermore, research has shown that Liberal Democrat members also consider themselves to be on the centre-left or centre of British politics (Whiteley *et al.* 2006). Further to policy disagreements then, this psychological identification of the party as a centre-left party is important for the party's identity.

In addition to concerns regarding the party's identity, it also faces organisational challenges. To date the party has been able to professionalise in part due to the benefits of Short money, a government payment made to opposition parties to support their work in parliament. The payment is calculated using a combination of money per seat won and money per votes cast. Now that the party is in government it no longer qualifies for this money, which means it will lose around £2 million a year. The implications of this withdrawal of funding are significant considering the money was used to pay for the party's research department. While the Liberal Democrats have sought to argue that as the junior partner in the coalition government they should not lose out on all of the Short money, it is unlikely that the rules will change.

Conclusion

Since entering into coalition government the Liberal Democrats initially plummeted in public opinion while the Conservatives benefited. Indeed, during July 2010 voting intention polling data from YouGov saw the party average 14.5 per cent, compared with 42.5 per cent for the Conservatives, and by the end of the year this had dropped even further to around 10 per cent (YouGov 2010). Perhaps the most interesting poll, however, was about second preferences in an AV election: before the election two-thirds of Labour voters would transfer to the Liberal Democrats, but a month after the coalition was formed this was down to only one third; meanwhile about half of Conservative voters would give the Liberal Democrats their second preferences, a similar figure to before the election (Wells 2010). This proved to be troubling not only for the Lib Dem leadership, but also for Cameron himself who was keen to ensure that his coalition partners remained in place until 2015, the default date of the next general election. So worried was the Conservative leadership about the poor state of the Liberal Democrat polling figures that it led some to speculate that he could be prepared to concede more ground to the Liberal Democrats, particularly regarding the renewal of the UK's nuclear deterrent Trident, which the Liberal Democrats want scrapped (Hoskin 2010).

The threat to the Liberal Democrats is to become like Germany's Free Democrat Party (FDP) whose election campaigns often revolve around who they will seek to form a coalition with. Based upon his responses to questions of this sort during the 2010 election campaign, this is something that Nick Clegg will wish to avoid. While many within the party are clearly pleased with the coalition agreement and with the opportunity to implement some Liberal Democrat policies, whether or not they are able to convince the electorate, let alone their own activists, that they are sufficiently different from either main party will be key. While the party is in coalition with the Conservatives there are many within the party who would be keen to see an electoral cooperation with Labour. The key issue however, may well be whether the Liberal Democrat leadership will be tempted to pursue an electoral pact with the Conservatives, particularly in marginal seats.

The ties between Labour and the Liberal Democrats are, broadly speaking, rooted in an ideological commitment to progressive centre-left politics. Connections between the two have also been underpinned by a sense of shared history, for instance the Lib-Lab pact of the 1970s, and the close relationship between Tony Blair and Liberal Democrat leader Paddy Ashdown in the late 1990s. Notwithstanding these links the two parties are of course electoral competitors. Indeed, one of the strategic assumptions made during the formation of the Liberal Democrats was that the new party would come to replace Labour as the main opposition to the Conservatives (Russell and Fieldhouse 2005: 39), just as it had been Labour's intention to replace the Liberals at the beginning of the twentieth century. While recent years have seen the party try to position itself as the 'real alternative' to Labour, it is unclear how their role in the coalition government will affect this.

The Liberal Democrats are used to forming coalitions at sub-national level and their experiences at the local level, coupled with their time in coalition government with Labour in Scotland and Wales, signal that the party has been able to negotiate the difficulties associated with political partnerships. However, the extent to which the coalition with the Conservatives will inflict long lasting damage on the party's electoral prospects remains uncertain. Maintaining a distinctive identity while demonstrating to their activists that they have implemented Liberal Democrat policies will be key. Intra-party tension is perhaps inevitable, and the continued professionalisation of the party will likely exacerbate this further.

Notes

1 Members of the COG include senior parliamentarians, representatives from each of the federal committees and each of the three state parties, while the chief executive attends it in a non-voting capacity. It is also worth noting that the leader of the party is also chair of the Federal Policy Committee, while another MP is vice-chair, this means that no elected activists representing FPC are present on COG.

2 At the 2010 general election the party increased the number of seats in which it came second from 188 to 242.

3 Including the media-friendly MP Lembit Opik who lost Montgomery in Wales despite enjoying a very large majority.

4 Wells (in South-West England) is arguably the only seat in which the expenses scandal had any real benefit for the party. They were able to win the seat from the Conservatives who had held it since 1929 in part because David Heathcoat-Amory was badly affected by the expenses scandal, after it emerged that he had claimed the cost of 550 tons of manure for his garden.

5 The party does not have a record of the number of party members who supported or opposed the coalition agreement at the conference, although a senior party official described the decision as 'almost unanimous'.

6 *Hansard* 21 July 2010, Col: 346.

7 *Hansard* 12 July 2010, Col: 518.

References

BBC (2010). 'Hung Parliament: Labour Close to Conceding Defeat', 11 May. http://news.bbc.co.uk/1/hi/uk_politics/election_2010/8674103.stm (accessed 11 May 2010).

Bones, C., P. Burstow, K. Parmiter and D. Greenland (2008). *Report of the Party Reform Commission*. London: Liberal Democrats.

Brack, D., R. S. Grayson and D. Howarth (eds) (2007). *Reinventing the State: Social Liberalism for the 21st Century*. London: Politico's.

Clegg, N. (2009). *The Liberal Moment*. London: Demos.

Cole, M. (2009). 'Growing without Pains? Explaining Liberal Democrat MPs' Behaviour', *British Journal of Politics and International Relations*, 11 (2): 259–279.

Cowley, P. and M. Stuart (2003). 'Labour in Disguise? Liberal Democrat MPs, 1997–2001', *British Journal of Politics and International Relations*, 5 (3): 393–404.

Cowley, P. and M. Stuart (2007). 'A Long Way from Equidistance: Lib Dem Voting in Parliament, 1997–2007'. www.revolts.co.uk/A%20long%20way%20from%20equidistance.pdf (accessed 15 November 2009).

Curtice, J. (2007). 'New Labour, New Protest? How the Liberal Democrats Profited from Blair's Mistakes', *Political Quarterly*, 78 (1): 117–127.

Curtice, J. and M. Steed (1982). 'Electoral Choice and the Production of Government: The Changing Operation of the Electoral System in the United Kingdom since 1955', *British Journal of Political Science*, 12: 249–298.

Denver, D. (2007). *Elections and Voters in Britain*. Basingstoke: Palgrave Macmillan.

Evans, E. (2007). 'Grassroots Influence: Pressure Groups within the Liberal Democrats', *Political Quarterly*, 78 (1): 99–107.

Evans, E. and E. Sanderson-Nash (2011). 'From Sandals to Suits: Professionalization, Coalition and the Liberal Democrats', *British Journal of Politics and International Relations*, 13 (4): 459–475.

Grayson, R. S. (2010). 'The Liberal Democrat Journey to a Lib-Con Coalition – and Where Next'. www.compassonline.org.uk /publications/item.asp?d=2628 (accessed 14 June 2010).

Hoskin, P. (2010). 'The Coalition's Lib Dem Conundrum', *The Spectator*, 1 August. www.spectator.co.uk/coffeehouse/6180603/the-coalitions-lib -dem-conundrum.thtml (accessed 2 August 2010).

Hurst G. (2006). *Charles Kennedy – A Tragic Flaw*. London: Politico's.

Marshall, P. and D. Laws (eds) (2004). *The Orange Book: Reclaiming Liberalism*. London: Profile Books.

Nagel, J. H. and C. Wlezien (2010). 'Centre-Party Strength and Major-Party Divergence in Britain, 1945–2005', *British Journal of Political Science*, 40: 279–304.

Russell, A. (2005). 'The Liberal Democrat Campaign', in P. Norris and C. Wlezien (eds), *Britain Votes 2005*. Oxford: Oxford University Press.

Russell, A. and E. Fieldhouse (2005). *Neither Left nor Right? The Liberal Democrats and the Electorate*. Manchester: Manchester University Press.

Russell, A., E. Fieldhouse and D. Cutts (2007). 'De Facto Veto? The Parliamentary Liberal Democrats', *Political Quarterly*, 78 (1): 89–98.

The Scotsman (2010). 'Election 2010: Adonis in Plea to Lib Dems', 10 April. www.scotsman.com/politics/Election-2010–Adonis-in-.6217313.jp (accessed 12 April 2010).

Travis, A. (2010). 'Electoral Reform: Alternative Vote System Would Have Had Minimal Impact on Outcome of General Election', *The Guardian*, 15 July.

Walker, K. (2010). 'Vince Cable Admits Previously Opposing VAT Rise to "Score Points"', *Daily Mail*, 28 June. www.dailymail.co.uk/news/article -1290176/Vince-Cable-admits-previously-opposing-VAT-score-points.html#ixzz1Bg1oZWt8 (accessed 30 June 2010).

Webb, P. (2000). *The Modern British Party System*. London: Sage.

Wells, A. (2010). 'How Would an Election Look Tomorrow under the Alternative Vote System?'. http://today.yougov.co.uk/commentaries /guest/how-would-election-tomorrow-look-under-alternative-vote (accessed 31 July 2010).

Whiteley, P., P. Seyd and A. Billinghurst (2006). *Third Force Politics: Liberal Democrats at the Grassroots*. Oxford: Oxford University Press.

Woodward, W. and M. White (2007). 'Campbell Happy to Claim Centre-left Ground', *The Guardian*, 20 September.

YouGov (2010) http://ukpollingreport.co.uk/blog/archives/date/2010/07 (last accessed 1 October 2011).

6

The financial crisis and financial regulation in the UK[1]

Lucia Quaglia

Introduction

In 2008–2009 the world economy experienced financial turmoil on a scale that had not been witnessed since the Great Depression. What began as a localised phenomenon in the US sub-prime residential mortgage market in mid-2007 became a fully-fledged global financial crisis in late 2008. The United Kingdom was severely hit by the global financial crisis. Indeed, its financial system was one of the worst affected in Europe. This chapter examines how the crisis played out in the UK, the response of the British authorities and the ways in which the repercussions of the crisis affected the 2010 elections.

The first section provides an overview of the configuration of the British financial system and the regulatory and supervisory framework in the UK. It also outlines the specific features that the crisis assumed in this country, arguing that its high degree of exposure to the global financial crisis was determined by the size of its financial sector, the importance of the City of London for the British economy, the presence of many foreign owned banks in the City, including large US banks, and the banking model adopted by many British banks.

The second section examines the public authorities' response to the global financial crisis at the national and European levels. In the short term, on certain crisis management matters, such as the banking rescue plans that were adopted across Europe, British policy-makers acted as pace-setters for the adoption of concerted parallel national plans, which were however subject to considerable national variations. British policy-makers were the first to devise a feasible plan because the country was extremely exposed to the financial crisis and had the domestic policy capacity to elaborate a timely response.

The third section examines the broader political repercussions of the global financial crisis in the UK. It discusses the impact of the crisis on the public finances and on the electoral fortunes of the main political parties, first and foremost the Labour Party in office. Gordon Brown managed to regain some short-lived domestic and external popularity in the autumn of 2008, when the so-called 'Brown plan' for the rescue of distressed banks was devised and partly 'exported' across Europe. However, the ultimate failure of Labour to hold onto power can also be interpreted as a consequence of the crisis. This section also discusses how the election of a Conservative-Liberal coalition government might affect the prospects for institutional reforms concerning financial services regulation and supervision in the UK and the EU.

The financial system and the regulatory framework in the UK

The financial system is a key component of the Anglo-Saxon model of capitalism, which has been characterised in different ways (see Albert 1993; Hall and Soskice 2001; Rhodes and van Apeldoorn 1998). Prior to the global financial crisis, the main features of this model of capitalism were: mobility and flexibility in the labour market; limited social welfare provisions; a limited mediation role for trade unions; minimal public intervention in the economy; arms-length relations between the sources of finance and firms, promoting short-term financial profitability and short-term contracts; and the deregulation of the service sector, first and foremost financial services. The global financial crisis increased state intervention in the economy and some of the main British banks were de facto nationalised. However, it did not seem to substantially change the national variety of capitalism in the UK (Moschella 2011).

As far as the financial sector is concerned and taking a historical perspective, the Conservative government led by Margaret Thatcher began a process of deregulation and liberalisation – the so called 'Big Bang' in the City (Moran 1986; 1991) – which was designed to enable London to compete successfully with the main financial centres, especially in the US, making the City an attractive place for international financial companies to conduct business. Hence, in the 1980s, the City was transformed from a gentleman's club to an internationalised market place with many foreign investment firms operating therein (Reid 1988). By the end of the Conservative term in office, London had a leading edge as one of the main international financial centres.

The new Labour government elected in 1997 with Gordon Brown at the helm of the Treasury for more than a decade continued the policy initiated by the Conservative Party, prioritising the competitiveness of the financial industry in the UK and the attractiveness of London as a financial centre (Gamble 2009; Hodson and Mabbett 2009). Paraphrasing the motto often used with reference to the US and the General Motors corporation, the approach adopted by successive governments in the UK, regardless of political ideology, seems to have been that 'what is good for the City is good for the UK'.

In contrast to other EU countries, the financial sector in the UK rests on an extensive securities market, whereas continental financial systems are primarily bank-based (Allen and Gale 2000). Indeed, in the Anglo-American system securities traded in stock exchanges are the main source of corporate finance (Deeg and Perez 2000). In the UK, there is a high degree of non-banking intermediation, due to the presence of several institutional investors (e.g. pension funds), a result of the importance of private pension schemes in a country with a minimal welfare state. London also hosts the largest insurance market in Europe, which, together with a well-developed securities market and a modern banking sector, has promoted the creation of numerous financial conglomerates that took root in the UK at a relatively earlier stage than in other EU countries.

In the banking sector there are two bank circuits: retail banking, which consists of banks operating under British law and dealing with deposits and loans; and foreign banks dealing with wholesale investment and international banking. Both banking circuits are characterised by the presence of several large banks. Prior to the 2007–2009 financial crisis, there were no publicly owned banks in the UK and the majority of financial firms in the City were not British-owned. Indeed, many US financial companies have set up extensive operations in London, which contributes to explaining why the financial turmoil that originated in the US spread so quickly and extensively to the UK.

The presence of a large number of foreign financial companies in the City and the international nature of the business taking place in London account for the ongoing concern of the British authorities for maintaining the competitiveness of London as a financial centre and reconciling tensions between EU, US and international financial regulation (Quaglia 2010a). A very good example of this was the opposition of the UK government to the EU regulation on credit rating agencies, many of which are headquartered in the US, but whose ratings are used by issuers and intermediaries operating in the City of London (Quaglia 2009b). Another example is the UK's opposition to the proposed directive on hedge funds, related to the fact that Britain hosts three quarters of all hedge fund managers in the EU. In both cases, companies operating in the City would be strongly affected by new EU rules.

Given the importance of the financial sector for the British economy and the fact that the City of London is one of the main international financial centres, private financial interests and their associations tended to receive a sympathetic hearing in policy-making circles prior to the crisis. The global financial crisis partly changed these political dynamics in that the Labour government as well as the opposition took a somewhat less sympathetic stance towards the financial sector, adopting for example some cosmetic measures such as the 50 per cent one-off bonus tax.[2] Regulating the financial sector became an important political issue in the run-up to the 2010 election, with the main political parties competing to present their own regulatory responses to the crisis.

In order to explain how the crisis unfolded in the UK and how the public authorities reacted to it, it is useful to outline the main features of the national framework for financial regulation and supervision. Prior to the financial crisis, the 'deep core' of the regulatory philosophy of British policy-makers was rooted in 'market trust'. This philosophy prioritised market liberalisation, mainly through market-making measures that defined conditions for market access and operation, stimulating competition and market efficiency. It favoured light-touch regulation, principle-based and competition-friendly regulation, and it promoted private sector governance, based on the involvement of industry through consultation, drafting and implementing soft law (Quaglia 2010a; 2010b). This regulatory approach came under strain when the financial crisis erupted because it was seen as having failed to prevent the crisis. Nonetheless, it was not abandoned by the British authorities, even though somewhat different views were expressed by the main policy-makers in the post-crisis period of reflection, as shown in an influential document produced by the FSA, the so-called Turner review discussed below, as well as in several speeches of the Governor of the Bank of England.

Until 2010, the institutional framework for financial services supervision in the UK was based on a single agency, the FSA, which had responsibility for micro-stability, prudential supervision, conduct of business and transparency of the entire financial sector.[3] These arrangements required cooperation between the FSA, the Bank of England (given enhanced responsibility for financial stability after the financial turmoil) and the Treasury, based on a memorandum of understanding. Cooperation between these institutions, as well as the modus operandi of the Bank of England and the FSA, were challenged by the unsatisfactory handling of the Northern Rock episode. The severity of the crisis in the UK triggered an overarching political debate about the allocation of the responsibilities for financial stability and the distribution of supervisory tasks between the existing institutions, as discussed in the penultimate section. The future of this tripartite arrangement was a key area of dispute between Labour and the opposition parties during the election campaign.

The unfolding of the crisis and the response of the British authorities

The UK was particularly severely hit by the global financial turmoil because of the size of its financial sector, the importance of the City of London for the British economy and the presence of many foreign owned banks in the City, including large US banks. Furthermore the banking model adopted by many British banks, based on high levels of leverage, low levels of depositor funding, reliance on short-term financing on the wholesale markets, exposure to subprime lending, and extensive quantities of mortgages in a declining housing market made British banks extremely vulnerable to the global financial crisis.

Given the fact that many banks and financial institutions in the UK relied heavily on refinancing on the wholesale market, they were among the first and the most heavily hit by the credit crunch in Europe. At the outset of the crisis in the summer–autumn of 2007, Northern Rock (and subsequently Bradford and Bingley) had to be rescued by the public author-ities, having failed to avoid a run on the bank. During the height of the financial turmoil, increasing loan defaults and decreasing asset prices reduced the capital of financial institutions worldwide – and the UK banks were badly affected. In October 2008, the Bank of England estimated that capital losses for six of the largest UK banks were likely to be in excess of £100bn (Bank of England 2008: Box 4), threatening the solvency of indi-vidual institutions and the collapse of the entire banking system. Persistent problems of illiquidity and maturity mismatch froze interbank lending, jeopardising the capacity of the banking system as a whole to resume lending – hence, the 'credit crunch' (Quaglia *et al.* 2009).

Equity markets were in disarray, with British bank shares plummeting. For example, on 7 October 2008, the day preceding the unveiling of the British banking rescue plan, shares in the Royal Bank of Scotland went down by 39 per cent.[4] In the autumn of 2008, when the second and most powerful wave of financial instability unfolded, four British banks had to receive substantial capital injections from the British government, which become the owner of up to 70 per cent of one of these banks, making them de facto part-nationalised. Furthermore, at the same time, the British authorities had to grapple with the domestic effects of the failures of Icelandic banks, which had large amounts of British savings invested in them, and the fleeing of funding to Irish banks, protected by a state deposit guarantee issued by the Irish authorities.

The economic recession that followed the financial crisis also hit the British economy particularly hard, given the importance of the financial sector for the British economy: economic growth fell, unemployment soared and the state of public finances deteriorated. The soaring public deficit and debt levels were due to the considerable amount of public funding invested in rescuing distressed banks, the reduced revenues collected on financial activities, and the public spending undertaken in order to deal with the recession with a view to stabilise the economy. This dismal economic scenario was a clear threat to Labour's future as governing party, as an election was due in less than two years and Gordon Brown's leadership was already under intense pressure by late 2007.

However, when the crisis intensified in the autumn of 2008, the initial response to the crisis reinforced Brown's authority as Prime Minister. The British authorities were the 'first movers', namely the first to come up with a comprehensive, 'fit for purpose' banking rescue plan when the financial crisis erupted with full force in October 2008 because of the interaction of two factors: the national degree of exposure to the financial crisis, explained above, and domestic policy capacity to deal with the crisis. Indeed, British policy-makers – first and foremost, the Prime Minister's office and the Treasury – could rely on a considerable level of expertise on financial matters, largely as a result of the experience accumulated by regulating the largest financial centre in the EU and the second largest financial centre worldwide. Moreover, the Prime Minister himself had been a generally well-regarded Chancellor of the Exchequer for more than a decade, prior to the financial crisis. A number of Gordon Brown's advisors at the Treasury had joined his staff in the Prime Minister's office and some of them had previously worked in the banking sector. The policy-makers most involved in devising the British plan were the Prime Minister's office, the Treasury (ministerial level and high-ranking civil servants) and the Bank of England, which, together with the FSA, were all involved in the adoption of the rescue plan (Quaglia 2009b).

It should also be noted that the institutional setting in the UK, characterised by majoritarian political institutions, confers a considerable amount of power to the executive, most of all the Prime Minister's office. This also reduces the potential veto points and the need for political compromises associated with the development of new policies. The relatively swift adoption of the British plan contrasts starkly with the delayed and politically contested adoption of the US banking rescue plan, which was slowed down by the federal institutional setting in the US and the system of checks and balances between the executive and the legislature (Quaglia 2009a).

The key features of the British scheme began to take shape at a confidential meeting held on 2 October 2008 by a restricted number of participants, including current and former Treasury officials close to the Prime Minister and banks representatives (Thal Larsson *et al.* 2008). On 7 October, financial markets in the UK were in disarray and after an inconclusive Economic and Financial Affairs Council (EcoFin) Council meeting, Chancellor Alistair Darling and Gordon Brown agreed to adopt the far reaching banking rescue plan that was announced the following day. There was concern that one large UK bank would struggle to fund itself unless the plan went into effect quickly. The British plan was articulated on three key points: liquidity provision to the financial system, through the special liquidity scheme operated by the Bank of England; banks' recapitalisation, whereby the government would buy bank shares; and government guarantees of new debt issued by banks. The government established a facility to make available capital in an appropriate form (mainly preference shares) to 'eligible institutions', namely UK incorporated banks, including UK subsidiaries of foreign institutions. The Bank of England for its part committed itself to take all actions necessary to ensure that the banking system had access to sufficient liquidity. The amounts of money involved were unprecedented: £50bn for bank recapitalisation, £250bn for the state guarantee of bank debt and £200bn made available by the Bank of England under the special liquidity scheme (Her Majesty's Treasury 2008).

The European response was much less swift and decisive. Several meetings of the largest EU member states (France, Germany, the UK and sometimes Italy) had resulted in vague joint statements and the response of the EU authorities was also feeble. On the same day the British rescue plan was announced in the UK, the British Prime Minister telephoned the French President (France held the rotating presidency of the EU) to 'explain why if the UK had not acted, British banks faced the real risk of collapse within hours. It was the first of several conversations that helped to shape a European rescue initiative on a largely UK model' (*Financial Times* 2008). The French President Sarkozy was persuaded that Brown's approach was right for Europe and called a special Eurogroup meeting, to the first part of which the British Prime Minister was invited to outline the British approach. As the *Financial Times* commented, Gordon Brown 'emerged as an unlikely European "superhero" for his effort' (Parker 2008).

The Eurogroup, acting in agreement with the European Commission and the ECB, approved a concerted action plan and urged the other EU countries to adopt its principles. By and large, this plan followed the template set by the plan announced by the British government a few days before the Eurogroup meeting. On 16 October the European Council welcomed and endorsed the concerted action plan of the euro area countries. In sum, Gordon Brown's response to the financial crisis won him an enhanced international profile and briefly boosted his popularity at home. However, the medium-term repercussions were far less favourable to his Labour government.

The repercussions of the financial crisis: political change in the UK

The global financial crisis had far reaching consequences in the UK, economically and politically. In the aftermath of the crisis, a severe recession hit the British economy, which was heavily reliant on financial services. Other parts of the service sector providing services to the City of London were the first to be affected by the slow down in the financial sector, followed by the manufacturing sector, for example car manufacturing. While the government's response to the financial crisis led to the de facto part-nationalisation of some of the main British banks, nothing similar happened in the manufacturing sector. This was a significant change for a country that had led the wave of privatisations in Europe in the 1980s and that did not have one single publicly owned bank prior to the crisis. The 2010 UK election therefore took place against the backdrop of crisis: not only a short-term crisis in the form of a deep recession, but also a more fundamental crisis of sustainability of the economic model that had been broadly accepted by the British political elite ever since the late 1980s.

In terms of the immediate effects of the crisis, the drop in output blew a deep hole in the government's budget. The public finances experienced a major shock due to the soaring public deficit and public debt resulting from the slump in economic activity and the counter-cyclical measures adopted by the government to tackle the recession, such as the increase in public spending and the reduction of taxes (for example, the VAT rate was reduced). Bank recapitalisation and other measures designed to secure market liquidity posed additional demands on the public purse. The explosive growth in the deficit led to a transformation in the debate about taxing and spending, from concern for how to distribute the fruits of growth to deep concern over the government's ability to finance its activities. In response, the Labour government allowed automatic stabilisers to function and rejected Conservative demands for action to reduce the deficit. The revenue raising one-off bonus taxes of 50 per cent introduced in December 2009, besides being designed to improve the state budget, was also adopted to appease public opinion with a view to the forthcoming elections. In the same period, Gordon Brown's call for an international tax on short-term financial transactions similar to the so-called Tobin tax seemed to serve the same purpose.

The opposition parties were also wrong-footed by the financial crisis.

David Cameron's approach to economic policy had been forged during the years of expansion and he had committed the Conservative Party to maintaining high levels of public spending in areas such as health and education, while curbing his party's instincts to cut taxes. Faced with the collapse of Britain's economic model, Cameron and his Shadow Chancellor George Osborne struggled to offer a coherent response to the crisis, while Gordon Brown briefly recovered strongly in opinion polls. However, by the beginning of the election campaign the Conservatives had settled on a more fiscally stringent approach than Labour, promising to reduce the deficit more quickly, while safeguarding spending on key services, notably healthcare.

The Liberal Democrats were initially the main losers from Gordon Brown's political recovery, but as the election campaign approached, they were able to build support around a more robust rhetoric of reform of the banking system than that offered by the other parties. In particular, their Treasury spokesperson Vince Cable was one of the few British politicians who had criticised Britain's over-leveraged economic model before the financial collapse, and he was able to articulate proposals for reform from a position of greater credibility than either of the rival parties. He called for the break-up of big banks, forcing them to separate their riskier investment banking activities from their safer retail banking operations, and advocated the virtual elimination of bankers' bonuses (Parker 2010).

As well as provoking a recession, the financial crisis called into question the regulatory framework and institutional arrangements to maintain financial stability in the UK. It also questioned the regulatory philosophy that had underpinned the financial bubble in the previous period. Similar discussions took place in other countries, in the EU and at the international level. Hence, it was a multi-level regulatory debate that often cut across different levels of governance. Two main sets of legislative measures were adopted in the UK as part of the regulatory response to the global financial crisis: the Banking Act of 2009 and the Financial Services bill, as yet still under discussion.

The global financial crisis brought into the spotlight the absence of an adequate regime to deal with ailing banks in the UK. The Banking Act, proposed in October 2008, was passed on an accelerated timetable in February 2009, due to cross-party support and cooperation. The centrepiece of this legislation was a new permanent Special Resolution Regime, providing the competent authorities with a range of tools to deal with failing banks and building societies. Such a regime built on the temporary tools introduced by the Banking (Special Provisions) Act 2008, used to deal with Northern Rock. The bill also increased the monitoring powers of the Bank of England, although not as much as the Governor of the Bank of England would have liked. Indeed, the setting in place of the new regime was preceded and surrounded by some disagreement between the Treasury, the FSA and the Bank of England about the power that each of the three authorities should have and its role in the new regime (Treasury Committee 2008a; 2008b). The Governor of the Bank was particularly concerned about the responsibilities allocated to the Bank not being matched by adequate powers (King 2009). The new regime was regarded by many observers as state of the art in Europe with its provision to request living wills from banks.

Political dynamics also seemed to enter the debate about the framework for financial supervision in the UK. Indeed, in July 2009, the Conservatives hinted at the possibility of transferring supervisory powers back from the FSA to the Bank of England, as it was the case before the 1997 reform implemented by the then Chancellor of the Exchequer Gordon Brown. It also contemplated abolishing the FSA. On more than one occasion, the Governor of the Bank of England was critical of the government's borrowing plan in 2009, which set him on a collision course with Chancellor Alistair Darling (Stewart and Seager 2009). According to some commentators, these unusual statements, which broke the convention that the Governor does not comment on fiscal policy, were hints that he favoured a Conservative government.

The effectiveness of the tripartite agreement between the Treasury, the FSA and the Bank of England to safeguard financial stability was challenged by the Northern Rock episode, in which the cooperation between the three authorities had been less than satisfactory. In that episode the (inadequate) supervision provided by the FSA was also criticised (FSA 2008), as was the belated decision of the Bank of England to provide liquidity support to the bank. However, the tripartite agreement was basically left unchanged, even though there were changes of personnel at the top of the FSA in early 2008. Following the consultations on the government's paper 'Reforming Financial Markets' issued in July 2009, the British government put forward the Financial Services Bill in November 2009. The cornerstone of the bill was the establishment of the Council for Financial Stability, chaired by the Chancellor of the Exchequer and comprising the Governor of the Bank of England and the Chairman of the Financial Services Authority. Although the Bill was still under discussion in parliament, the Council was set up and held its first meeting in January 2010. It is responsible for considering emerging risks to the financial stability of the UK and the global financial system, and coordinating an appropriate response by the UK's authorities. The coming into office of the Liberal-Conservative coalition following the general election was followed by government proposals for the overhaul of the supervisory framework in the UK, as discussed below.

Besides these key legislative measures, two influential public documents that partly informed the debate on the regulatory and institutional reforms should be mentioned: the Turner review and the Walker report. The Turner review, named after the chairperson of the FSA who commissioned the report, represented the first sign of a rethink of the existing approach to financial services regulation in the UK. The review acknowledged (FSA 2009: 38–39) that the global financial crisis robustly challenged on 'both theoretical and empirical grounds' the existing 'regulatory philosophy' and the 'intellectual assumptions' of 'efficient', 'rational' and 'self correcting markets' on which it was based. Yet, the government response to it was much more cautious (Her Majesty's Treasury 2009). The Walker report, which was named after the person who presented it, was an independent review of corporate governance in the UK banking industry (Walker 2009). The review also discussed remuneration practices. The preliminary conclusions and recommendations of the review were issued as a consultation paper in July 2009 and the revised final conclusions were presented in November 2009. It should be noted that the Walker review was not followed by binding rules on bonuses and banks governance.

At the EU level, the British government had to fight a rearguard battle to prevent a regulatory backlash (or in their words 'over-regulation') after the outbreak of the financial crisis. On the one hand, the UK had to compromise on several issues, given its weakened negotiating position following the crisis – the light touch regulatory paradigm promoted by the British authorities was very much in disrepute in EU policy-making circles. On the other hand, in 2009 the financial industry based in the UK began to strike back, warning against regulatory excesses in the EU, arguing that this would make European financial centres less competitive worldwide and business would relocate outside the EU. As the UK based financial industry and some policy-makers put it, they opposed 'an attempt of continental Europe to regulate the City'.[5]

Furthermore the issue was complicated by some disagreements among the British authorities. Indeed, the Bank of England seemed to support tougher regulation and called for greater power for the Bank in the supervisory field (King 2009). For example, the Governor of the Bank of England went on the record saying that 'if a bank is too big to fail, it is simply too big' (Conway 2009), implicitly calling for a cap on bank size, a suggestion that was opposed by the government. In their annual Mansion House speeches to the City in June 2009, the Bank of England Governor and the Chancellor openly displayed different ideas on what needed to be done to control banks and prevent a repeat of the financial crisis. This was indeed an important theme of the electoral campaign, as was the Labour and Conservative rivalry about the reform of the supervisory framework in the

UK. The FSA in the so-called Turner report (2009) partly questioned the market friendly regulatory approach that had informed policy-making in the previous decade. Moreover, the FSA seemed to take a rather positive attitude towards engagement with the EU, endorsing the strengthening of the EU supervisory regime. The Chancellor Alistair Darling warned against the danger of over regulation, especially coming from the EU (Darling 2009), but at the same time it was unable to prevent some EU regulatory initiatives from going ahead, such as the proposed regulation on hedge funds. Hence, between the FSA and the Bank of England on the one side and the financial industry on the other, and facing pressure for further integration in financial regulation and supervision coming from other member states in the EU, the British political authorities, first and foremost the Treasury, found themselves between a rock and a hard place.

In the domestic regulatory debate, Conservatives and Liberal Democrats also tried to differentiate themselves somewhat from the Labour government and its regulatory approach that was seen as having failed to prevent the crisis. Consequently, the arcane subject of financial regulation and supervision became the subject of a relatively heated political debate. When the Conservatives were still in opposition, they could afford to be more populist against banks. Indeed, at one point the Conservative Party seemed to advocate tougher rules than those proposed by the Labour government in office, which was quite a turn around given the fact that Conservative deregulation and the Big Bang in the City of London (Moran 1986; 1991) had set in motion most of the financial phenomena that subsequently led to the crisis. However, the party was wary of proposing specific measures that could harm the competitiveness of the City of London as a leading financial centre (Gamble 2009). By contrast, the Liberal Democrats, in particular their spokesperson on financial issue Vincent Cable, were more enthusiastic about regulatory reform and the need for more restrictive rules.

The political effects of the global financial crisis were also far reaching. After the Northern Rock debacle the Labour government, first and foremost the Prime Minister, shelved the idea of calling an early general election, as some political advisors to the Prime Minister had initially suggested. The run on the Northern Rock severely damaged the reputation for economic competence that the Labour government had built under the leadership of Gordon Brown at the Treasury, and when the crisis erupted with full force in the autumn of 2008, this reputation was in tatters. The Prime Minister and his Chancellor Alistair Darling regained some short-lived domestic political popularity after the successful implementation of the British plan, also called the 'Brown plan', which was to some extent copied across Europe. As Gordon Brown put it in a memorable slip of the tongue, he had 'saved the world'. But by the time of the election, this effect had worn off and what remained was the deepest recession since the 1930s, triggered under a Labour government.

Conclusion

The global financial crisis has left a lasting economic and political legacy in the UK. Economically, the partial public ownership of banks represented a major change in the Anglo-Saxon variety of financial capitalism, while the rapid deterioration of the public finances will also have lasting effects. Politically, the near meltdown of the British financial system and the deep economic recession that followed obscured the relative success of Gordon Brown's emergency measures and represented the final nail in the coffin of the Labour government.

After the general election, the new Conservative Chancellor George Osborne proposed a major overhaul of the supervisory framework in the UK, following up on David Cameron's pledge in July 2009 to abolish the FSA and return supervisory powers to the Bank of England. According to the Treasury proposal (Osborne 2010), the FSA would be abolished and supervisory powers split between the Bank of England and a newly created Consumer Protection and Markets Agency. It remains to be seen how this institutional reform will be implemented.

As far as the scope and content of financial regulation is concerned, after the election both the Conservatives and the Liberal Democrats softened their stance on issues that substantially affect the competitiveness of London as an international financial centre, first and foremost the breaking up of big banks, to be examined by an independent commission set up by the new administration. The outcome rides on the relationship between the Conservative Chancellor, George Osborne, who has the ultimate responsibility for banking regulation, and the Liberal Democrat Business Secretary, Vincent Cable, who has the lead on issues such as bank lending to business and consumer credit.

On the fiscal side, the Liberal-Conservative government has announced draconian plans for fiscal restraints, which were endorsed by the Governor of the Bank of England. The plans are designed to bring the public debt on a downward path and to reassure financial markets, though they are likely to dampen economic growth over the next few years. The debate over the pace of deficit reduction emerged in 2010–2011 as the key battleground between the parties. The outcome of the next election may well depend on the success or otherwise of the coalition government's programme of spending cuts.

Notes

1 Financial support from the European Research Council (204398 FINGOVEU) is gratefully acknowledged. This chapter was written while I was visiting fellow at the Robert Schuman Centre for Advanced Studies, European University Institute. I wish to thank the editors for their perceptive comments on an earlier draft of this chapter.

2 In 2009, the Labour government introduced a 50 per cent tax rate on bank bonuses of more than £25,000.

3 Prior to the institutional reform introduced by the then newly appointed Chancellor of the Exchequer Gordon Brown, the FSA did not exist and the Bank of England was responsible for banking supervision. The reform transferred banking supervision from the central bank to the newly established FSA, and the Bank of England was given operational independence (Quaglia 2008, Westrup 2007).

4 ITV (2008). I wish to thank Rob Eastwood for pointing this out to me.

5 Author interview, London, August 2009.

References

Albert, M. (1993). *Capitalism Versus Capitalism*. New York: Three Windows, Four Walls Press.

Allen, F. and D. Gale (2000). *Comparing Financial Systems*. Cambridge, MA: MIT Press.

Bank of England (2008). 'Financial Stability Report'. October.

BBC (2009). 'King and Darling Clash on Banks', *BBC News*, 18 June.

Conway, E. (2009). 'Mervyn King: Banks Cannot Be Too Big to Fail', *Daily Telegraph*, 17 June.

Darling, A. (2009). Speech by the Chancellor of the Exchequer at Mansion House, 17 June.

Deeg, R. and S. Perez (2000). 'International Capital Mobility and Domestic Institutions: Corporate Finance and Governance in Four European Cases', *Governance* 13 (2): 119–153.

Financial Times (2008). 'Whatever it Took', *Financial Times*, 15 October.

FSA (2008). 'The Internal Audit Review', London. www.fsa.gov.uk /pages/Library/Communication/PR/2008/028.shtml (last accessed 1 October 2011).

FSA (2009). 'The Turner Review, A Regulatory Response to the Global Banking Crisis', March, London.

Gamble, A. (2009). 'British Politics and the Financial Crisis', *British Politics*, 4 (4): 450–462.

Hall, P. and D. Soskice (eds) (2001). *Varieties of Capitalism: The Institutional Foundations of Comparative Advantage*. Oxford: Oxford University Press.

Her Majesty's Treasury (2008). 'Government Statement on Financial Support', 8 October, London.

Her Majesty's Treasury (2009). 'Reforming Financial Markets', 8 July, London.

Hodson, D. and D. Mabbett (2009). 'Paradigm Lost? UK Economic Policy and the Global Economic Crisis', special issue of the *Journal of Common Market Studies*, 47 (4): 1041–1061.

ITV (2008). 'Cash Crisis Talk Batters Banks'. www.itv.com/News /Articles/RBS-shares-tumble-on-bailout-fears-165173924.html (last accessed 1 October 2011).

King, M. (2009). Speech by the Governor of the Bank of England at Mansion House, 17 June.

Moran, M. (1986). *The Politics of Banking*. London: Macmillan.

Moran, M. (1991). *The Politics of the Financial Services Revolution: The USA, UK and Japan*. Basingstoke: Macmillan.

Moschella, M. (2011). 'Different Varieties of Capitalism? British and Italian Recapitalization Policies in Response to the Subprime Crisis', *Comparative European Politics*, 9: 76–99.Osborne, G. (2010). Speech by the Chancellor of the Exchequer at Mansion House, 16 June.

Parker, G. (2008). '"Super-hero" Looks to Next Stage', *Financial Times*, 15 October.

Parker, G. (2010). 'UK Banks Are Warned to Expect Restructuring', *Financial Times*, 15 May.

Quaglia, L. (2008). 'Explaining the Reform of Banking Supervision in Europe: An Integrative Approach', *Governance*, 21 (3): 439–463.

Quaglia, L. (2009a). 'The 'British Plan' as a Pace-setter: The Europeanisation of Banking Rescue Plans in the EU?', special issue of *Journal of Common Market Studies*, 47 (4): 1059–1079.

Quaglia, L. (2009b). 'The Politics of Regulating Credit Rating Agencies in the European Union'. Working paper of the Centre for Global Political Economy at the University of Sussex, No. 5, June.

Quaglia, L. (2010a). *Governing Financial Services in the European Union*. London: Routledge.

Quaglia, L. (2010b). 'Completing the Single Market in Financial Services: The Politics of Competing Advocacy Coalitions', *Journal of European Public Policy*, 17 (7): 1007–1022.

Quaglia, L., R. Eastwood and P. Holmes (2009). 'The Financial Turmoil and EU Policy Cooperation 2007–8', *Journal of Common Market Studies Annual Review*, 47 (1): 1–25.

Reid, M. (1988). *All-Change In The City: The Revolution In Britain's Financial Sector*. Basingstoke: Macmillan.

Rhodes, M. and B. van Apeldoorn (1998). 'Capital Unbound? The

Transformation of European Corporate Governance', *Journal of European Public Policy*, 5 (3): 406–427.

Stewart, H. and A. Seager (2009). 'Bank of England Governor Attacks Darling's Borrowing Policy', *The Guardian*, 24 June.

Thal Larsen, P., G. Parker and L. Saigol (2008). 'Salvage Mission that Became Global Template', *Financial Times*, 17 October. www.ft.com/cms /s/0/7d77dd7a-9c87–11dd-a42e-000077b07658.html#ixzz1BgxArtWz (last accessed 1 October 2011).

Treasury Committee, House of Commons (2008a). 'The Run on the Rock, Fifth Report of Session 2007–08'. The Stationery Office, London.

Treasury Committee, House of Commons (2008b). 'Financial Stability and Transparency'. The Stationery Office, London.

Walker, D. (2009). 'A Review of Corporate Governance in UK Banks and Other Financial Industry Entities, Final Recommendations' (Walker Report), 26 November.

Westrup, J. (2007). 'The Politics of Financial Regulatory Reforms in Britain and Germany', *West European Politics*, 30 (5): 1096–1119.

7

Inequality, poverty and the 2010 election

Jonathan Hopkin and Martina Viarengo

Introduction

Inequality and poverty have been core themes in recent British political debates. One of the most politically influential books of 2009, *The Spirit Level* (Wilkinson and Pickett 2009), presented an array of statistical evidence of the damaging effects of income inequality on health, mortality, crime and mental well-being. A lively debate ensued as to the validity of some of the causal claims made in the book, but the book initially received a warm welcome from politicians and commentators across the political spectrum. In early 2010, the government's National Equality Panel presented its own report on the nature and consequences of the unequal distribution of wealth in Britain (Hills *et al.* 2010), and came to similar conclusions about the corrosive effects of inequality and poverty. In the aftermath of the financial crisis and resulting recession, national soul-searching about the economic and social costs of the UK's credit-fuelled boom was deeply fashionable.

As a result, the 2010 election campaign exhibited a curious degree of consensus among the main political parties about the nature of the UK's social and economic difficulties. All parties were quick to blame 'greedy bankers' for the financial crisis (the Liberal Democrat leader Nick Clegg proving particularly vociferous), while concern about poverty ran across the political spectrum, with the Conservatives launching a campaign poster deriding Gordon Brown (with the words 'I increased the gap between rich and poor' beneath the Prime Minister's grinning face). Labour, in turn, responded by warning that the Conservatives planned to 'take Britain back to the 1980s', an era of mass unemployment and dramatic increases in poverty.

The tone of the campaign suggested a heightened concern for

distributional politics, and an awareness of popular disquiet over the rising gap between rich and poor, exemplified by the stratospheric bonuses enjoyed by top bankers, despite the government having to bail out their bankrupt institutions. At the same time, however, there was very little in the way of serious discussion of how inequality and distributional fairness might be achieved, and beneath the surface, partisan divisions over how, or indeed whether, to address inequality could be clearly perceived. This chapter will provide an assessment of economic and social inequalities in the UK and of the way in which concerns about inequality feed into the political debate. It places the issue in historical and comparative context, by showing how inequality in the UK compares with other similar countries and by looking at how it has changed over time. We then assess the impact of measures taken by the Labour governments from 1997 to 2010 to reduce poverty and social exclusion, and end by speculating about the prospects for social policy under the Conservative-Liberal coalition formed after the 2010 elections.

Poverty and inequality in the UK: comparative and historical considerations

Why has inequality become an issue in British politics? The main reason for the growing attention to income distribution in the UK is that inequality is actually rather high compared to most similar advanced democracies. A variety of measures are used by economists and political scientists to gauge income inequality. Among the most widely used indicators, the Gini coefficient measures the degree of inequality of an income distribution, producing values varying between 0, which represents total equality (an equal share for all) and 1, which represents maximum inequality (all income allocated to just one individual). Table 7.1 presents the Gini coefficient of income inequality for a selected number of OECD countries from 1975 to 2005. For much of this period the United Kingdom has had higher levels of inequality than most other OECD countries, being closer to the United States than to the more egalitarian countries of Western Europe. Of the European countries listed in Table 7.1, only Italy comes close to the UK's inequality score, while the other large economies – France and Germany – have significantly lower inequality, and the smaller Western European states are far more egalitarian.

Table 7.1 also reveals that there is a broad trend towards higher inequality across the advanced states in this period, with Gini coefficients higher in 2005 than in 1985 in all cases except France and Spain. However, the United Kingdom is the country that has experienced by far the greatest increase in income inequality: approximately +36 per cent, against +19 per cent in the United States, and +10 per cent in Sweden and Canada. The fastest increase appears to have occurred in the 1980s and then to a smaller extent in the 2000s. So, not only does Britain have comparatively high levels of income inequality, it has also suffered the sharpest increase in inequality of any major democracy over the past few decades. To illustrate the change in comparative terms, Britain moved from being slightly more equal than Canada in 1975, to being considerably more unequal than Canada in 2005 (even though Canada's Gini coefficient also rose!).

Of course, this general picture of inequality does not tell the whole story. One way in which we can get a clearer idea of the phenomenon is to assess how inequality has changed along the earnings distribution, since labour income represents the main source of earnings for most individuals. The 90–10 wage ratio provides an indicator of the difference between the earnings of workers near the top of the wage distribution (90th percentile) with respect to those near the bottom of the distribution (10th percentile). Again, from Table 7.2 it seems that pay gaps have increased everywhere but in France. Inequality has increased more in Anglo-Saxon countries than in Nordic and Continental European countries. The United Kingdom has the second highest inequality level after the United States at the end of the

Table 7.1 Gini coefficient across OECD countries, 1975–2005

	1975	1985	1995	2000	2005
Australia	...	...	0.31	0.32	0.30
Canada	0.29	0.29	0.28	0.30	0.32
Finland	0.23	0.21	0.23	0.26	0.27
France	...	0.31	0.28	0.28	0.28
Germany	...	0.26	0.27	0.27	0.30
Italy	...	0.31	0.35	0.34	0.35
Japan	...	0.30	0.32	0.34	0.32
Netherlands	0.25	0.26	0.28	0.28	0.27
New Zealand	...	0.27	0.34	0.34	0.34
Spain	...	0.37	0.34	0.34	0.32
Sweden	0.21	0.20	0.21	0.24	0.23
United Kingdom	0.28	0.33	0.36	0.36	0.38
United States	0.32	0.34	0.36	0.36	0.38

Note: data refer to the total population. A similar pattern is observed when the working-age population is examined.

...: not available

Source: OECD Stat Extracts on income distribution and inequality

Table 7.2 90–10 wage ratios across OECD countries, 1975–2005

	1975	1985	1995	2000	2005
Australia	2.57	2.72	2.91	3.01	3.12
Canada	...	...	...	3.61	3.74
Finland	...	...	2.34	2.41	2.49
France	3.5	3.12	3.08	3.04	2.91
Germany	...	2.89	2.79	2.93	3.26
Italy	...	...	...	...	...
Japan	3.11	3.12	3.01	2.98	3.12
Netherlands	...	2.50	2.77	2.90	2.91
New Zealand	...	...	2.27	2.62	2.79
Spain	...	...	4.22	...	...
Sweden	2.24	2.06	2.2	2.35	...
United Kingdom	3.01	3.20	3.48	3.46	3.60
United States	3.75	4.13	4.59	4.49	4.86

Note: data refer to the total population.

...: not available

Source: OECD Stat Extracts on income distribution and inequality

period considered. In 2005, a worker on the 90th percentile earned around 3.6 times more than a worker on the 10th percentile, while in Finland, the most egalitarian case here, the former earned just two and a half times more than the latter. Moreover, these numbers, by failing to consider dynamics at the very top of the income scale, may even understate the extent of the problem. As Machin and Van Reenen (2010) suggest, the top half of the wage distribution has become more unequal and the top 1 per cent of the population has earned significantly more than the rest of the population, and this has had a significant effect on the concentration of income; one only has to look at the vast earnings of bankers, company executives and even professional footballers to see how overall wage inequality could be much greater than suggested by a 90/10 ratio.

Of course, wages are only a part of the story, since government measures to tax earnings and redistribute income through social transfers and services have large effects on the incomes individuals and families ultimately receive. Moreover, interventions through the tax and benefits system are the main way in which governments can influence the distribution of income. Figure 7.1 shows how household income inequality has changed over time in the United Kingdom. These figures are extracted from the Expenditure and Food Survey, which provides four measures of

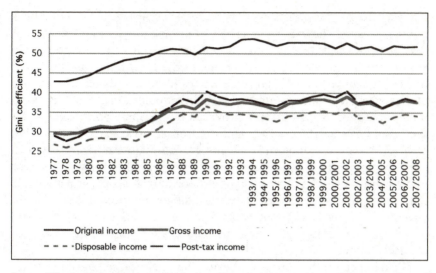

Source: Office for National Statistics, Distribution of household income, House of Commons Library

Figure 7.1 Gini coefficient for household income in the UK, 1977–2008

household income (i.e. original income, gross income, post-tax income and disposable income[1]). The overall trend is revealing of an increase in the concentration of income around the wealthiest. Since 1977 inequality of original income and post-tax income has increased by nearly 9 per cent; inequality of gross income has risen by 8 per cent and the Gini coefficient of disposable income has grown by 7.3 per cent. The two variables of interest in our assessment of the policy implications of inequality are original (or market) income and post-tax income, which reflect the distribution of market income and income after tax and benefits have been paid respectively. Overall, inequality in these different measures of incomes has followed an upward trend. This trend was particularly sharp in the 1980s under the Thatcher government. Inequality of original income reached its highest levels in the early 1990s (Gini coefficients of 53.5 per cent in 1993 and 53.7 per cent in 1993/94) whereas inequality of post-tax income reached its highest values in 1990 (40.3 per cent) and 2001/02 (40.4 per cent). Since 1996/97 there has been a decrease in the inequality of original income (-1 per cent) and post-tax income (-0.3 per cent). Taxation and benefit policies, which will be more closely examined in the next section, kept post-tax income inequality lower than original income inequality. So changes in inequality are at least to an extent the result of policy choices, and changes in government feed into changes in the distribution of income.

The Gini coefficient is a good measure of overall inequality, but it does not tell us exactly how much of a share of income different groups get, nor does it necessarily tell us much about how specific income groups do relative to each other. Figure 7.2 examines the growth in real income for the low, the middle and high income groups (the 1st, 3rd and 5th quintiles of the income distribution) under the different political parties. It is worth noting that median real income increased by the same percentage under the Labour Party (1997–2009) and the Conservative Party (over 1979– 1997).[2] Moreover average real income growth is little different between the two periods (2.1 per cent under the Conservative Party, 2 per cent under Labour). On the other hand, if we look at real income growth across the income distribution we can observe a different pattern under different governments, suggesting that policy made a difference to how rich and poor fared even under quite similar conditions for those in the middle of the distribution.

Real income at the bottom of the distribution increased the most under Labour (particularly over 2001–2005), suggesting that Labour policies were – as would be expected – more redistributive and favourable to the poorest. But there were also different patterns of income growth for the more disadvantaged within the periods in office of the two parties. Income at the low end of the distribution grew barely at all under the Thatcher government, but grew slightly more under John Major. Income growth for the poor was much higher in the first two terms of Tony Blair's Labour government, but during Labour's third term real income growth for the more disadvantaged was actually negative. Moreover, if we examine the annualised rate of the overall real income growth under the Labour Party we can observe that the highest growth rate has been experienced by those at the 30th percentile group and not by those at the very bottom of the distribution (10th percentile group).[3] If we look at the other end of the income scale, real income at the top of the distribution increased the most under the Conservatives, particularly under Margaret Thatcher (+3.6 per cent), and to a limited extent under the Major government (+0.7 per cent). Interestingly, on average, real income also grew at a significant rate at the high end of the income distribution during the first term of the Labour Party (+2.7 per cent). Part of the reason for Labour failing to reduce overall inequality by very much was due to the continued high growth at the top of the income distribution during the Blair and Brown governments.

So interesting patterns of change in income inequality can clearly be observed in the British data. Changes in economic and social policy, particularly during the period of Conservative government in the 1980s, led to a sharp increase in inequality, which then stabilised by the 1990s. Labour came to power in 1997, with a manifesto committing it to addressing some

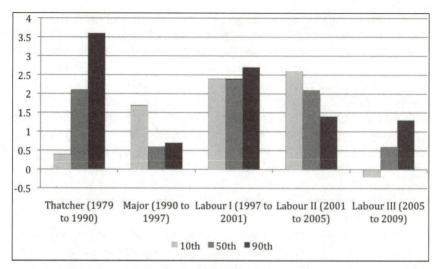

Source: Family Expenditure Survey and Family Resources Survey, Joyce et al. (2010)

Figure 7.2 Real income growth by decile group under different governments

of the problems associated with inequality, notably crime, inequality of educational opportunities and entrenched poverty, problems that were referred to generically in the New Labour lexicon as 'social exclusion'. Yet we can see from the data presented in this section that Labour broadly failed to reverse the trend to higher inequality. The next section asks why.

Labour's record: did Britain become fairer?

The previous section showed that over the past three decades, the UK became one of the most unequal societies in Western Europe. It also showed that this increase in inequality was not linear; instead inequality did not increase at the same rate, with some governments presiding over rapid increases, while under others the situation remained stable. This suggests that policy interventions have an impact on income growth and inequality, and that political parties do have some influence over income distribution, although clearly broader structural factors are also at work. Labour did not come to office promising an equal society, but they did commit to tackling poverty and social exclusion, and the electorate in 2010 was also casting judgement on Labour's success in fulfilling this commitment. Here we are going to examine the policies and interventions aimed at reducing poverty and economic inequality undertaken by Labour over the period 1997–2010.[4] Did Labour make a concerted effort to tackle inequality? If so, how successful was this effort?

Certainly, Labour made resources available to the state to address poverty and inequality. A recent report of the Institute for Fiscal Studies (IFS) (Chote *et al.* 2010) shows that the UK had the largest increase in public spending as a share of national income among OECD countries[5] between 1997 and 2010. In comparative terms this means that the UK shifted from being the 22nd biggest spending government among OECD countries to being the 6th in 2010 (Chote *et al.* 2010: 1). However, this apparently dramatic change should be nuanced a little, since part of the reason for the UK's high level of spending as a proportion of GDP in the late 2000s is that the contraction in GDP resulting from the financial crisis was more severe here than elsewhere. Still, the UK had the second largest increase in spending between 1997 and 2007 (and the largest increase over the period 2007–2010).

Levels of public spending have a strong relationship with inequality in comparative studies, with high spending governments mostly presiding over more egalitarian distributions of income. Overall, total public spending[6] increased more under Labour than under the preceding Conservative governments (although significant increases began only from 2000[7]), providing the government with resources to address some of the social concerns of Labour voters. Spending on public services has increased faster than total spending under Labour, in contrast to what happened under the previous Conservative governments: 4.4 per cent per year in real terms against 0.7 per cent per year (Chote *et al.* 2010: Table 3.2). However, aggregate spending levels are not necessarily a good predictor of inequality, since a lot depends on how the money is raised and how it is spent. If we disaggregate spending we see that the NHS, education and transport have increased faster than other areas, and although they have distributional implications, it is not entirely clear how growth in spending on services available notionally to all could reduce the gaps between income groups. However, there is evidence that inequality and poverty would have been even higher without the government interventions of the Labour period (Mirrlees Review 2010; Machin and Van Reenen 2010). A number of policies, some of which were directly redistributive, had an important impact on poverty and inequality.

Dealing with inequality: the 'New Labour' approach

To understand Labour's policies to address poverty and inequality it is necessary to understand the logic of Tony Blair's 'New Labour' political strategy. Tony Blair became party leader in 1994, shortly after Labour had suffered a demoralising fourth consecutive electoral defeat at the hands of the Conservatives. Blair's diagnosis of Labour's electoral failures was that many of Labour's traditional working-class supporters felt that the Conservatives, with their stress on property ownership and low personal taxation, offered them greater opportunities to improve their living standards. He illustrated his argument by evoking his encounter with a voter while on the campaign trail in 1992: the voter, a self-employed electrician and former Labour supporter, had switched to the Conservatives since buying his own home and setting up his own business. Blair felt that 'his instincts were to get on in life. And he thought our instincts were to stop him' (Fielding 1997: 25).

This analysis of the British electorate had important implications for Labour's anti-poverty strategy. In order to win an election Labour needed to convince the aspirant middle-income groups that the party was on their side, while at the same time offering something to its supporters at the bottom of the income scale. The acuteness of the political dilemma resided in the hostility of many middle income voters towards the kinds of redistributive policies that would imply higher taxes in order to help the poor. In terms of political discourse, Labour's answer to the dilemma was to stress 'social inclusion' rather than equality, and to use measures to promote employment to achieve poverty targets. By attacking social exclusion rather than inequality, Labour hoped to keep both middle and low income groups happy, evading any trade-off between their interests. By focusing on employment rather than straight fiscal transfers, Labour hoped to achieve a virtuous circle of declining poverty and lower social expenditure, freeing up resources for public services that appealed to the wider electorate, such as health and education.

How precisely did Labour seek to achieve this? The key to reducing poverty would be an 'employment friendly' combination of measures to incentivise work and reform features of the welfare system which 'trapped' recipients in poverty. Low-paid work was subsidised through a variety of 'tax credits', which topped up income for low-skilled workers with family responsibilities, in order to ensure that they would be made better off by taking paid employment. A legal minimum wage was established, in order to help push wages up to levels higher than welfare benefits, again to incentivise work over unemployment. Significant government investment in childcare and family services – most notably the 'SureStart' initiative – sought to provide support for lone parents to facilitate their taking up jobs. And in order to ensure that the unemployed took advantage of these incentives, a series of 'activation' measures under the 'New Deal' programme (partly financed by a levy on privatised utility companies) sought to encourage welfare recipients to take up subsidised work or training opportunities (Hopkin and van Wijnbergen 2011).

Did this approach succeed in defeating poverty while reconciling the interests of lower and higher income groups? The picture is rather mixed. First, Labour can claim some success in addressing the problem of poverty resulting from the large number of workless households: unemployment fell consistently during the first decade of Labour rule, and even after the downturn caused by the 2008 financial crisis unemployment remained lower than in previous recessions. Although broader structural factors outside the control of governments are important, Labour's employment policies can claim some of the credit for the decline in unemployment up to 2008 (Petrongolo and van Reenen 2010), and measures such as the tax credits succeeded in removing some of the perverse incentives inherent in the welfare system. However, some of the tax and benefit changes also had the effect of reducing work incentives for certain groups, notably as a result of the high marginal effective tax rates facing second earners in low income households with children (Brewer *et al.* 2010). The dilemma of tax credits was that as the credits were withdrawn at higher levels of earnings, some workers quickly lost tax advantages when their income increased, and some of the difficulties in calculating tax credit entitlements – which could only be accurately established retrospectively – also ended up damaging some recipients.

Labour could claim more confidently to have improved the incomes of children and elderly citizens at risk of poverty. Measures such as the Minimum Income Guarantee for pensioners lacking adequate private pension arrangements, the tax credits focused on families with children, and the encouragement to lone parents to enter the labour market, made significant impacts on these particular groups. The IFS's analysis found that the numbers in these two groups below the poverty level declined between 1996–1997 and 2007–2008, reflecting a policy of income transfers in their favour (Brewer *et al.* 2010). The Labour commitment to reducing child poverty, consisting in the setting of quantitative targets and, ultimately, the ambitious (and probably implausible) target of total eradication by 2020, tied the government to policies that transferred resources to families with dependent children at the bottom of the income scale. This amounted to a major commitment to redistribution, since the most effective way to achieve reductions in the child poverty rate was to increase the welfare benefits available to poor families. Similarly, pensioner poverty, to an even greater extent, could only be addressed by cash transfers, since the 'welfare to work' approach was inappropriate by definition for this group. Added to income supplements for the poorest pensioners, Labour also instituted the Winter Fuel Allowance, which gave all pensioners a non-means tested cash allowance to meet their heating bills and help to pay TV licences. All in all this panoply of measures significantly reduced poverty for some of the most vulnerable groups.

However, the headline remained, slightly misleadingly, that Labour failed in its aspiration to reduce inequalities in Britain. In part, the measures taken could only address part of the problem, given the political constraints Labour had accepted. Helping poor children and pensioners – the 'deserving poor' – gave the government political cover, but it was much more difficult to justify transfers to other groups that lacked public sympathy, notably the unemployed or low waged poor of working age without dependants, whose poverty rate actually increased during the Labour years (Brewer *et al.* 2010). Moreover, Labour also boxed itself in by promising not to raise income tax rates and even reducing the basic rate from 23 per cent to 20 per cent by 2007. This had clear redistributive consequences. First, refusal to increase income tax reduced the scope for increased government spending on public services and redistributive transfers, hindering Labour's attempts to address the problem of entrenched poverty. Countries with lower levels of inequality than the UK mostly have higher income tax rates, so the evidence is that by accepting the existing tax arrangements as an upper limit Labour was effectively putting a ceiling on its redistributive ambitions. Second, leaving existing income tax rates intact, and even lowering the standard rate, allowed the real disposable income of the highest earners, which was growing at a far faster rate than average incomes, to continue soaring above the rest of the income distribution, exacerbating the gap between rich and poor. Although the trend towards continually increasing overall income inequality was the result of a complex set of factors, many beyond government's control, Labour's tax policy amounted to abandoning any aspiration to rein in the increasing gap between the most advantaged groups and the rest. Although the financial crisis pushed the Brown government into raising income tax to 50 per cent for the very highest earners (above £150,000 per year), the redistributive effect of this measure was small and overwhelmed by the powerful trend towards expanding incomes at the top of the distribution. Labour's redistributive strategy was therefore inherently limited in its ambition, due to the self-imposed constraints the party leadership considered essential to electoral success.

Public service expansion: bringing the middle classes into the New Labour coalition

Another important constraint on Labour's redistributive ambition was its determination to appeal to middle income voters by increasing spending on public services used by the vast majority of Britons, notably education and healthcare. Poverty, although high by comparative standards, affected a minority of the electorate, many of whom were either reliable Labour supporters or non-voters. Labour could not defeat the Conservatives in an election on the back of redistribution to the poorest in society. Instead, Blair and Brown needed to find a way to tailor their appeal to middle income voters while maintaining Labour's commitment to government activism to resolve poverty and inequality. Expansion of the key public sector activities directed at middle as well as low income voters was key to this political strategy. In particular, healthcare and education were targeted by Labour as areas for increased government spending.

Education was perhaps the area Labour emphasised most: 'education, education, education' was Tony Blair's response when asked of his main priorities on coming to office. In the UK, education is the third largest area of government spending, and spending on schools has the largest share of this spending (Holmlund *et al.* 2010). During the 2000s government expenditure on primary and secondary schools increased by 40 per cent in real terms. However, despite this significant step change in government's financial commitment to education, public spending in this area remained only just above the OECD average (McNally 2010), confirming that the UK had fallen a long way behind its major competitors. Labour's education spending was concentrated on early years education and primary and secondary schooling, with spending on higher education growing more slowly (Chowdry *et al.* 2010).

How did Labour spend this growing education budget? Labour's education policy was in fact an interesting mix of continuity and innovation. On the one hand, Labour implemented some policies conceived under the Thatcher and Major governments, including some Labour had opposed; on the other hand, these policies were adapted with the aim of improving educational opportunity for students at the low end of the educational and income distributions. On the continuity side, Labour embraced Conservative reforms such as the national curriculum, the introduction of externally marked exams at the end of each key stage and the increases in school autonomy and financial delegation (Smithers 2007), and also enthusiastically adopted the Conservative practice of setting targets for outcomes, accompanied by intensive monitoring and inspection. Moreover, choice and competition have been extended to different areas with little or no effect on students' performance (Gibbons *et al.* 2006; 2009). However, the focus on targeted outcomes was given a redistributive edge, with the adoption of specific programmes to improve the performance at the bottom of the distribution. Examples include the 'Literacy Hour' in primary schools, focused at improving core reading skills, the establishment of Academies in poor areas of cities, and targeted initiatives directing funds at specific areas of educational under-achievement (e.g. the Excellence in Cities programme or the Ethnic Minority Achievement Grant).

The degree of success of educational policy is a controversial area. Between 1997 and 2008 there was an improvement in educational outcomes at both primary and secondary levels with an increase in the share of students achieving the standard defined by the National Curriculum at the end of key stage 2 and the share of students achieving five or more GCSEs at grades A*–C. Opponents of Labour's approach – such as Conservative Education Secretary Michael Gove – dismissed this progress as a product of grade inflation or accounting tricks, but the improvement is confirmed by comparative research; for example, England's performance improved relative to the other countries that participated in the Trends in International Mathematics and Science Study (TIMSS)[8] in 1999 and 2007 (Freeman *et al.* 2010). Overall the existing evidence shows a modest increase in educational attainment (but a greater improvement for students from more disadvantaged backgrounds) (McNally 2010). The increased spending also included a significant investment in the physical infrastructure of the educational system, with large amounts of expenditure on school buildings and equipment, while teacher salaries were also increased, helping overcome some of the skills shortages that dogged the sector in the 1990s.

The focus of the Labour education policy has most certainly been on schools and far less priority was accorded to higher education. The most significant and controversial policy that was undertaken in higher education was the introduction of undergraduate tuition fees, which meant the abandonment of the principle of free higher education established in the 1960s. This unpopular policy required a heavy expenditure of political capital, since the party had been coy about its intentions in this area prior to the 1997 election. The initial legislation, passed in 1998, established a fixed tuition fee for all higher education institutions, which students had to pay up front, although they could request a student loan for this. A second reform in 2004 liberalised the tuition fees regime, freeing universities to charge variable fees, but establishing a maximum fee, then of just over £3000 per year. This reform also introduced a system of loans and grants to help students from less affluent backgrounds face the costs of going to university. Although the government increased investment in research quite sharply and, partly through the fees regime, relaxed the squeeze on university funding, universities were not big winners in Labour's educational expansion. This reflects the pattern of centre-left parties focusing resources on early years and compulsory level schooling, which tends to have redistributive effects, while public spending on higher education generally benefits the higher income groups.

Healthcare was another big priority for Labour, to such an extent that a slogan the party used before the 1997 election was '24 hours to save the

NHS'. From 1999, public spending on the National Health Service was rapidly increased, and the first decade of the twenty-first century proved the largest ever sustained increase in the history of the NHS, reaching an average of 7 per cent a year in real terms (Cooper and McGuire 2010). While Britain had one of the lowest levels of spending on health in the 1990s, by the end of the 2000s, total expenditure on health was higher than the European average and public sector spending has become among the highest in the world (Bosanquet 2007).

As in education, the increase in resources went alongside the introduction of a set of market-oriented reforms aimed at increasing the overall productivity of the NHS. Specifically, Labour presided over an increase in government-set targets, quality-related targets (e.g. a new general practitioner contract that enables providers to earn additional revenue by achieving various clinical and service related quality targets), as well as an increase in competition between hospitals by increasing patient choice (Cooper and McGuire 2010). Some performance indicators reveal an improvement in the quality of the health system. Access for care has improved; waiting times have decreased (Bosanquet 2007). However, the NHS still lags behind other European countries on several quality indicators (e.g., health outcomes such as cancer, strokes and heart attacks, OECD 2004; 2007); moreover there has been a lack of progress in reducing childhood health inequality (Department of Health 2006) and health inequalities more generally. By 2010, the gap in life expectancy between the richest and poorest social groups had grown compared with the 1990s, largely because the improvements in longevity enjoyed across the social spectrum were much larger among the most prosperous sectors of the population. As in other policy areas, despite huge investment over the Labour years, acute inequality remained and even increased.

Back to the future? Inequality in Britain after the 2010 election

Although inequality as a substantive issue in itself was not central to the election campaign and surrounding debates, the issues of income distribution and poverty were underlying themes in the discussions around how to resolve Britain's fiscal problems. All the main parties were committed to a programme of fiscal consolidation combining tax rises and spending cuts to eliminate the budget deficit by the end of the parliament, and all stressed the importance of 'fairness' in the distribution of pain. However, there were significant differences in emphasis and substance between the parties. While the Conservatives advocated early and extensive spending cuts to bring down the deficit as quickly as possible, Labour and the Liberal Democrats argued for a gentler pace of consolidation, on the grounds that too brutal a fiscal tightening could derail the fragile economic recovery. There were also differences between the parties in the extent to which fiscal readjustment would be achieved through spending cuts as opposed to tax rises, with Labour and the Liberal Democrats arguing for a higher share of the burden to fall on taxpayers while the Conservatives pushed for greater spending reductions. These differences reflected the left–right divide on economic policy between the Conservatives, traditionally committed to fiscal solidity and low taxes, and Labour and the Liberal Democrats, more concerned with maintaining public services and getting the wealthy to pay a greater share to sustain state activities.

In view of these dividing lines, the result of the general election threw economic and social policy in Britain into flux. On the one hand, Labour and the Liberal Democrats were closer on economic issues, with the Liberal Democrats appearing more radical in their tax policy with proposals such as a 'mansion tax' to be paid by owners of expensive prop-erties and increases in corporate taxation. On the other, Labour's undeniable defeat in the election, falling over sixty seats short of a majority and polling its second lowest share of the vote since 1918, made a Labour-Liberal Democrat coalition implausible, particularly since Nick Clegg had explicitly ruled out the possibility of supporting a government led by Gordon Brown. As a result, the only workable parliamentary majorities would have to consist of the Conservatives and either the Liberal Democrats or a group of nationalist parties from Scotland, Wales and Northern Ireland. Cameron opted for the former and was able to convince Nick Clegg to bring the Liberal Democrats fully into the govern-ment.

This coalitional arrangement was, in the face of it, riven with internal tensions over key economic and social issues. The Liberal Democrats had to make important concessions in order to join the government, including signing up to what was effectively the original Conservative deficit reduction plan, with no significant new rises in personal taxation and a battery of cuts to social and welfare spending which, according to the analysis of the Institute for Fiscal Studies (2010), would have regressive redistributive effects. Government policies supported by the Liberal Democrats included substantial housing benefit cuts, a 2.5 per cent increase in VAT, cuts to tax credits for low earners and reductions in capital spending on schools, all of which conflicted with prior Liberal Democrat positions. Although some of the measures to be introduced over the fiscal year would increase tax for high earners, most of them were already in the Labour government's spring budget: the new measures contained in the new government's emergency budget had the broad effect of cutting spending more quickly than planned by Labour and shifting the burden for deficit reduction more heavily onto the recipients of welfare payments and social services.

The economic strategy adopted by the coalition clearly placed the Liberal Democrats under pressure to explain sharp policy reversals to their electorate, and the initial signs at the end of 2010 were that the party was struggling to do this: autumn polls consistently showed the Liberal Democrats to have lost around 50 per cent of their electorate as a result of joining the coalition. Nick Clegg's initial response was to reposition the party in a more economically liberal position, while attempting to reconcile its support for spending cuts with Liberal Democrat concerns for inequality. In a speech in November 2010 he sought to draw a dividing line between 'old progressives' focused only on income inequality and 'new progressives' more interested in improving equality of opportunity.[9] Clegg sought to justify the government's plans on progressive grounds, arguing that 'there is nothing progressive about saddling the next generation with our debt' and derided Labour's use of cash transfers to hit poverty targets as 'huge amounts of money being devoted to changing the financial position of these households by fairly small amounts – just enough, in many cases, to get them above the line'. Instead, Liberal Democrats, through policies such as the 'pupil premium' (higher spending on state school pupils from deprived backgrounds) would be able to enhance equality of opportunity even in the context of drastic reductions in state spending.

This Liberal Democrat position was consistent with Conservative rhetoric about the 'Big Society' (Kisby 2010), which emphasised the limitations of government interventionism for resolving social problems. The Big Society was David Cameron's key idea for addressing what he described as 'broken Britain', an allusion to problems of entrenched poverty, crime and anti-social behaviour in areas with traditionally high unemployment. Cameron's interpretation of social problems suggested that government interventionism could aggravate social problems by discouraging community activism and volunteering, and that government should encourage communities to take a more active role in policies that affect them. The Big Society, however, was not defined in terms of detailed policy choices before the 2010 election, with a handful of exceptions (such as the policy to allow community groups to set up schools free of local authority control with government money, a policy ostensibly imported from Sweden). The concrete policies took shape after the formation of the coalition government, with proposals to decentralise decision-making in the health service and the education sector, as well as a range of reforms to the welfare state that are likely to create a vacuum of public provision in some areas.

Whether or not the Big Society project proves successful on its own terms, it is improbable that it would achieve any improvement in Britain's poor record on income inequality, given the likely economic context of high unemployment and cuts in redistributive public spending. However, the political debate on the question of inequality does seem to be undergoing a kind of transformation. The election of Ed Miliband as Labour leader represented a move away from the New Labour strategy of the previous sixteen years, and his campaign for the leadership placed greater emphasis on equality as a defining value of the centre-left than previous leaders had been comfortable with. If Miliband continues to associate Labour with a more egalitarian discourse, this creates a greater space for Nick Clegg to redefine centre politics. However, the risks of the Clegg strategy are also significant, and any increase in poverty resulting from the coalition's cuts in public spending will be hard to reconcile with 'new progressive' politics. The Conservatives' firm embrace of welfare reform and voluntarism leaves the Liberal Democrats in an uncomfortable dilemma on the income distribution question, and the durability of the coalition depends in part on how this dilemma is resolved.

Conclusion

In 2010 Britain remained one of the most unequal societies in the advanced world in terms of the distribution of income and wealth. Although thirteen years of Labour government brought a range of policies designed to deal with poverty and social exclusion, many other factors were acting to push inequality higher. The end result was that despite the gains for certain vulnerable groups and the rise in living standards for most of the income distribution, the New Labour era ended with overall economic inequality barely any lower than when it started.

Inequality as such was not one of the main themes of the election campaign, but the likely distributional implications of government policies to address Britain's economic crisis did take centre-stage. All parties argued for deficit reduction over the medium term, but the Conservative position of faster retrenchment was electorally most successful. It is improbable that a deficit reduction plan based overwhelmingly on spending cuts can reduce inequality; the main question remains whether or not inequality and poverty will increase significantly or not. The Conservatives have moved towards a hard-line attitude to high government spending, evoking the mood of the Thatcher era, while Ed Miliband has emphasised the consequences of excessive inequality in his early statements as Labour leader. Should these trends continue, they would suggest a polarisation of British politics around distributive issues. The question of economic inequality could well be at the centre of election campaigns in the future.

Notes

1 Original income is the income received directly from employment, self-employment, savings and investment; gross income is defined as original income plus direct cash benefits; disposable income is calculated as gross income less direct payroll taxes, local taxes and tax credits; post-tax income is equal to disposable income less indirect and intermediate taxes.

2 That is 1.6 per cent annualised real income growth. These figures refer to annualised real income growth, as derived by Joyce *et al.* (2010, table 3.1) using Family Expenditure Survey and Family Resources Survey.

3 That is, average annualised real income growth rate is equal to 1.9 per cent for the 30th quintile group and to 1.6 per cent for the 10th quintile group (Joyce *et al.* 2010, table 3.1).

4 We acknowledge the importance of examining other aspects related to income inequality, such as for example how inequality varies across different demographic groups or how gaps have changed between and within groups (by age, gender, ethnic group or area). However, these issues go beyond the purpose of this chapter – the interested reader can refer to the Report of the National Equality Panel (Hills *et al.* 2010).

5 That is, among the twenty-eight OECD countries for which comparable data are available.

6 Total public spending is defined as the sum of current spending and public sector net investment (Chote *et al.* 2010).

7 Public spending was 39.9 per cent of national income in 1997, 36.3 per cent in 2000 and reached 47.9 per cent in 2010 (Chote *et al.* 2010).

8 TIMSS is a curriculum-based test administered to students in 4th and 8th grades. The same test is taken by students in participating countries and this allows for cross-country comparisons. Fifty-nine countries participated in TIMSS 2007.

9 The Hugo Young Lecture 2010: www.guardian.co.uk/politics/2010/nov/23/nick-clegg-hugo-young-text (last accessed 1 October 2011).

References

Bosanquet, N. (2007). 'The Health and Welfare Legacy', in A. Seldon (ed.), *Blair's Britain 1997–2007*. Cambridge: Cambridge University Press, pp. 385–407.

Brewer, M., D. Phillips and L. Sibieta (2010). *Living Standards, Inequality and Poverty: New Labour's Record*. Institute for Fiscal Studies: Election Briefing Note No.2 (IFS BN89).

Chote, R., R. Crawford, C. Emmerson and G. Tetlow (2010), 'Public Spending under Labour', Institute for Fiscal Studies: 2010 Election Briefing Note No. 5.

Chowdry, H., A. Muriel and L. Sibieta (2010). 'Education Policy', Institute for Fiscal Studies: Briefing Note BN98.

Cooper, Z. and A. McGuire (2010). 'Health: Higher Spending Has

Improved Quality But Productivity Must Increase', in *CEP Election Analysis 2010*. London School of Economics and Political Science: Centre for Economic Performance, pp. 41–54.

Department of Health (2006). *Annual Report*. London: Department of Health. www.dh.gov.uk/en/Publicationsandstatistics/Publications /AnnualReports/DH_4134613 (last accessed 1 October 2011).

Fielding, S. (1997). *The Labour Party Since 1951: 'Socialism' and Society*. Manchester: Manchester University Press.

Freeman R. B., S. Machin and M. Viarengo (2010). 'Variation in Educational Outcomes and Policies across Countries and of Schools within Countries', NBER Working Paper No. 16293.

Gibbons, S., S. Machin and O. Silva (2006). 'Choice, Competition and Pupil Achievement', IZA Discussion Papers 2214, Institute for the Study of Labor (IZA).

Gibbons, S., S. Machin and O. Silva (2009). 'Valuing School Quality Using Boundary Discontinuities', SERC Discussion Papers 0018, Spatial Economics Research Centre, LSE.

Hills, J. *et al.* (2010). *An Anatomy of Economic Inequality in The UK: Report of the National Equality Panel*. London: Government Equalities Office/Centre for Analysis of Social Exclusion (LSE). http://sticerd.lse .ac.uk/dps/case/cr/CASEreport60.pdf (last accessed 1 October 2011).

Holmlund H., S. McNally and M. Viarengo (2010). 'Does Money Matter for Schools?', *Economics of Education Review*, 29: 1154–1164.

Hopkin, J. and C. van Wijnbergen (2011). 'Europeanization and Welfare State Change in Britain: Another Case of "Fog Over the Channel"?', in P. Graziano and B. Palier (eds), *Europeanization and Welfare State Change*. Basingstoke: Palgrave.

Institute for Fiscal Studies (2010). 'The Distributional Effect of Tax and Benefit Reforms to be Introduced Between June 2010 and April 2014: A Revised Assessment', IFS Briefing Note, August.

Joyce, R., A. Muriel, D. Phillips and L. Sibieta (2010). 'Poverty and Inequality in the UK', Institute for Fiscal Studies, May.

Kisby, B. (2010). 'The Big Society: Power to the People?', *Political Quarterly*, 81 (4): 484–91.

Machin, S. and J. Van Reenen (2010). 'Inequality: Still Higher But Labour's Policies Kept it Down', in *CEP Election Analysis 2010*. London School of Economics and Political Science: Centre for Economic Performance, pp. 108–117.

Mirrlees Review (2010). *Reforming the Tax System for the Twentieth Century*. Institute for Fiscal Studies. www.ifs.org.uk/mirrleesReview (last accessed 1 October 2011).

McNally, S. (2010). 'Evaluating Education Policies: The Evidence From

Economic Research', in *CEP Election Analysis 2010*. London School of Economics and Political Science: Centre for Economic Performance, pp. 23–39.

OECD (2004). *OECD Health Data 2004*. Paris: OECD.

OECD (2007). *OECD Health Data 2007*. Paris: OECD.

Petrongolo, B. and J. Van Reenen (2010). 'Jobs and Unemployment. It's Bad But Not as Bad as You Might Think', in *CEP Election Analysis 2010*. London School of Economics and Political Science: Centre for Economic Performance, pp. 73–85.

Smithers, A. (2007). 'Schools', in A. Seldon (ed.), *Blair's Britain 1997–2007*. Cambridge: Cambridge University Press, pp. 361–384.

Wilkinson, R. and K. Pickett (2009). *The Spirit Level: Why More Equal Societies Almost Always Do Better*. London: Allen Lane.

8

Immigration and multiculturalism: controversies and policies

Roberto Bertinetti

Introduction

For over half a century the issue of immigration has divided Britain, periodically sparking heated debate between those who perceive immigration as an economic necessity and those who experience it as a threat to national identity. The first violent clashes over race and immigration were triggered by migratory flows from the Caribbean, South Asia and Africa in the immediate post-war period. In the late 1940s rental advertisements could be seen in London and other cities warning 'No blacks, no dogs'. Riots were recorded in Liverpool as early as 1948, and in Deptford the following year. At the same time, the British authorities were desperately seeking workers from the former colonies to meet the labour shortages that were compromising the country's reconstruction. The recurring social and political scripts were already clearly drafted: in times of necessity or economic prosperity governments encourage immigration, which is often reluctantly accepted by public opinion. Hostility against immigrants then tends to grow, often indulged by opportunistic politicians, in times of increasing unemployment rates.

The 2010 election campaign reflected these tensions, as demonstrated by the opening lines of the first TV debate, broadcast in mid-April from Manchester. As soon as presenter Alastair Stewart allowed questions from the studio audience, the three leaders were asked what they intended to do, if elected, to introduce restrictions on immigration. Gordon Brown, David Cameron and Nick Clegg all gave predictable and rhetorical answers. However, the dominant view among the audience was evident: borders should be better guarded and further immigration, far from representing an opportunity, was seen as a threat.

This chapter looks at the way immigration politics has played out in

Britain over the post-war period, both in formal party political debate and in the cultural sphere, through an assessment of post-colonial fiction and divergent ideas on multiculturalism. The objective is to frame immigration within a coherent historical perspective, to move beyond the instrumental use of immigration by politicians for headline-grabbing stunts and to analyse the many political, social and cultural issues it raises.

The political use of immigration in electoral programmes

Riding the moods of public opinion to win voter support is hardly uncommon in electoral campaigning. Polls have long signalled popular fear of immigration in Britain, accentuated in the current period of acute economic crisis. Playing up the supposed risks linked to immigration for political advantage is, after all, an ancient practice. The best known example dates from April 1968, when Enoch Powell made his apocalyptic speech about 'the River Tiber foaming with much blood', which earned him headlines and contributed to the Tories' strong electoral performance in the Midlands in the 1970 elections. According to historian Peter Clarke, Powell 'was applying a political torch to a highly combustible heap of social grievances which others had swept into a corner' (1996: 324).

Milder variants of Powell's rhetorical strategy have since been deployed several times, particularly by the right and especially by the press, often engendering an inaccurate public perception of the phenomenon of migration. Robert Winder (2005) demonstrates this by quoting a 2001 survey published in *Reader's Digest*, which found that two thirds of British citizens believed that the overall number of immigrants was above 20 per cent of the population, when it was in fact only 4 per cent. The general belief was that the UK hosted at least one fourth of all political refugees in the world, while the actual figure was less than 2 per cent, and that central government gave refugees a weekly pay of over £100, when in fact they only received £36 per week. Given the degree of confusion it is not surprising that the vast majority of those surveyed favoured restrictions on new arrivals and judged the choices of all previous administrations as 'too permissive'.

Clarke (1996) highlights a paradox: the theme of immigration first gained significant media coverage at precisely the point when, in the early 1960s, parliament passed legislation limiting the right of Commonwealth citizens to settle in the UK. The origin of this paradox resides in the emergence of a generation of British-born children of black or Asian-origin migrants, making the phenomenon of immigration increasingly apparent in the UK's streets and in the country's schools. Since then, the debate on immigration has frequently become intertwined with the phenomenon of racist prejudice, directed at both migrants and their descendants. An insightful interpretation of this pattern can be found in the work of writer Hanif Kureishi:

> Frequently during my childhood, I met my Pakistani uncles when they came to London on business. They were important, confident people who took me to hotels, restaurants and cricket matches, often in taxis. But I had no idea of what the Indian sub-continent was like or how my numerous uncles, aunts and cousins lived there. When I was nine or ten a teacher placed some pictures of Indian farmers in old crowded houses in front of me and said to the class: Hanif comes from India. I wondered: did my uncles ride on camels? Surely not in their suits. Did my cousins, so like me in other ways, squat down in the sand like little Mowglis, half-naked and eating with their fingers? (1986: 9)

Kureishi's case was hardly an isolated one, and post-colonial writing, which will later play a major role in altering the hierarchies of English literature, became a powerful artistic form, as well as contributing to our understanding of the political and social dimensions of immigration.

Immigration in post-war Britain: between culture and politics

Historians, sociologists and other writers have offered a clear picture of what happened in the United Kingdom – and particularly in London – following the migratory flows that began in the post-war period. They were able to capture the reactions to migrant workers, generally coming from other Commonwealth countries, often in response to recruiting campaigns to help to reconstruct Britain. Robert Winder (2005) reports that by the end of the war the Foreign Labour Committee estimated that about one million jobs were available for foreign workers in agriculture, hospitals and factories. Because few Europeans had chosen to cross the Channel, in 1948 the Commons passed the Nationality Act to grant resident permits to citizens from other Commonwealth countries. This bill was seen as necessary to fill vacancies in vital economic sectors.

The numbers of new immigrants at this early stage were still low, a few thousands every year, but racial tensions quickly developed. As well as the riots in Liverpool and Deptford mentioned above, in several parts of the capital intolerance towards immigrants, though ignored by the press, was growing. Hostility was not necessarily fostered only by the political right, and as documented by Winder (2005), trade unions also rallied against the employment of foreign workers, exacerbating prejudices against those who 'stole' jobs from the white British workforce. Within a decade, immigration had grown and tensions worsened. In this respect, the riots that shook the then very poor area of Notting Hill in 1958 are emblematic. By the end of the 1950s the dynamics and the perverse logic that later fed into populist debates on immigration, encouraging xenophobic movements and politicians playing the 'race card', was well established. Clarke (1996) describes the relationship between British citizens of different ethnicities as 'the perennial problem', accentuated in the 1980s by economic problems and then in the 1990s and later by the emergence of fringes of Islamic fundamentalists, particularly from Pakistan.

For Tariq Modood (2009), the 1980s represented a turning point in terms of race relations and marked the emergence of profound changes that would later have crucial implications. If initially the debate on racism – and the legislative measures to punish it – focused on the division between 'whites' and 'blacks', in this new phase a 'non-white' identity developed, based around ethnic belonging or religious belief. Modood argues that this was partly a consequence of post-1968 ideological battles combined with the emergence of a multicultural model. The mix of demands for recognition on the part of ethnic minorities clashed with the unease towards immigration of many white Britons, stoking further popular fear of immigration. The developing tension in the 1980s was starkly described by Salman Rushdie:

> At first, we were told, the goal was 'integration'. Now this word rapidly came to mean 'assimilation': a black man could only become integrated when he started behaving like a white man. After 'integration' came the concept of 'racial harmony.' Now once again, this sounded virtuous and desirable, but what it meant in practice was that blacks should be persuaded to live peaceably with whites, in spite of all the injustices done to them every day. The call for racial harmony was simply an invitation to shut up and smile while nothing was done about our grievances. And now there's a new catchword: 'multiculturalism'. In our schools, this means little more than teaching the kids a few bongo rhythms, how to tie a sari and so forth. [...] Multiculturalism is the latest token gesture towards Britain's blacks, and it ought to be exposed, like 'integration' and 'racial harmony' for the sham it is. (1992: 137)

The emerging concept of multiculturalism – that is, the idea of the 'politics of recognition' celebrated in 1992 by Charles Taylor's influential book – while not always as crudely dismissed, did lay bare some of the social tensions described by Rushdie. Ironically, the city of Bradford, an industrial city in West Yorkshire with a large Muslim Asian population, was to emerge as a stage on which these tensions were played out, with Rushdie as a prominent victim.

An early sign of tension in Bradford came with the so-called 'Honeyford Affair'. The head teacher of a secondary school, Ray Honeyford, wrote a newspaper article denouncing the risks of having increasing numbers of

Asian students in his school. Honeyford was accused of racism by some parents and politicians, but was supported by the Conservatives and several right-wing academics and the issue played out in the national media. Honeyford was eventually removed from his post. Hanif Kureishi (1985; 1986) gave an account of the affair in which he noted that several people from Bradford were clearly racist, but he also emphasised that many residents of Pakistani origins tended to isolate themselves, contributing to the problem. In some ways, Kureishi's contribution anticipates a question that will be later raised in 2004 by David Goodhart, in an article published in *Prospect*: could too much diversity exacerbate social fractures and encourage racism?

A series of key events that deeply impacted the debate on immigration occurred between the beginning of autumn 1988 and February 1989, shortly after the release of Rushdie's *The Satanic Verses*, when the Ayatollah Khomeini's fatwa forced the writer into exile (Modood 2009). In Bradford copies of the novel were burned in public and tensions rapidly spread to other areas of the UK and to other western countries. These events raised a series of questions that began to be debated publicly: should freedom of speech always have priority? Or should religious teachings always be respected? Such questions tended to divide progressive thinking and not only in the UK; they fomented xenophobic tensions and they also compromised the debate on how best to manage relationships between communities, halting some of the progress that had been made.

The negative implications of the Rushdie case highlight the challenges posed to British multiculturalism and the ways in which the debate on immigration can easily become conditioned by the cultural and social tensions that multiculturalism seeks to address. The same challenges reappeared (with nuances) in commentaries on the 2005 London bombings, and again in the party manifestos for the 2010 elections. One major weakness of Britain's peculiar variant of multiculturalism is that it is interpreted as a patchwork of allegedly fixed identities shaped by ethnic or religious belonging. This often means consigning representation and leadership of those identities to restricted, and often self-referential, groups who are indifferent if not outright hostile to the spontaneous dynamics that emerge in society through processes of social mixing.

Gerd Baumann offers an insightful analysis of the pitfalls of the strategies employed by successive administrations in Britain, which have heavily affected immigration policies. In his cross-country comparative study, Baumann writes that:

> The British example of conflating civil rights and community rights is remarkable because it is largely unnecessary. Britain is unique in Western

comparison in that almost all its minority citizens are entitled to the status of nationals and thus share the same right to equal civil rights. Yet strangely and paradoxically it is Britain that has gone furthest on the path away from a civil rights approach. While this has historical reasons, it is nonetheless an astonishing example of what happens when civil rights give way to ethnic or religious rights. Britain has an institution called 'The Muslim Parliament,' as if Muslims were not represented at Westminster, the famed 'Mother of Parliaments'; its governing Labour Party has a special 'Black Section,' as if there were a white and a nonwhite version of social democracy; and Britain has local authorities that involve temples and mosques in administering the naturalization of overseas migrants into British citizens. None of these things are bad by themselves [...] Yet all these details show is the opposite of a color-blind, or religion-blind – and thus secular – modern state. (1999: 12–13)

The limitations of the British approach and its consequences, as argued by Baumann, can be summarised in two main points: first, the (often violent) conflict among British citizens based on religion and skin colour; second, persisting popular hostility towards immigration, which, regardless of the actual number of new immigrants, is always perceived as a threat. Paul Gilroy (1992), cited by Baumann (1999: 104), dwelled on the consequences of both these negative dynamics. He highlighted the peculiar (and worrying) convergence between the anti-racist left and the racist right: both understand cultures of origin as an inescapable and fixed ethnic legacy. The rigidity of this interpretive matrix has fomented tensions rather than diluted them, contributing to strengthening those 'identity cages' that exacerbate continuous conflicts.

Is too much diversity a danger? The difficult search for a common culture

The debate on the British left over the pitfalls of multiculturalism heated up following the publication in David Goodhart's *Prospect* article in 2004. In this article, later extended into a much discussed book (2006), Goodhart brought into focus what he defined as 'the progressive dilemma', or how to reconcile what many perceived as excessive diversity with social cohesion. Goodhart did not emphasise migration as such – although he often referred to 'ethnic minorities' – but it seemed clear that multiculturalism and the growing presence of immigrants represented two sides of the same coin. Amid such growing diversity, wrote Goodhart, Britain was losing a precious good: a shared culture. Economic development required foreign labour, but by the same token the ethnic diversity generated fear for part of public opinion. Such sentiments were exacerbated by the memory of the race riots

sparked in northern England in the early 2000s and by the negative repercussions of the US terror attacks in 2001. Goodhart argued that the UK
needed to rebuild a common social fabric based around shared and
accepted values, a 'third way on identity that can be distinguished from the
coercive assimilationism of the nationalist right, which rejects any element
of foreign culture, and from multiculturalism, which rejects a common
culture' (2004).

The questions raised by Goodhart acquired dramatic relevance just
over a year after publication, when more than fifty people died and 700
were wounded in the 2005 London bombings. The country discovered with
horror that the fundamentalists that carried out the attack were British
citizens of Asian origin, born and bred in the UK. The immediate effect of
this shocking attack was an increase in hate crimes, strengthening a preju-
diced hostility towards Muslim people and heating up the debate on the
risks of liberal immigration policies and on the 'natural' challenges of
creating a shared culture. The question of British 'identity' dominated the
public discussion in the months following the attacks. The far right and
part of the Conservative Party invoked a 'white' identity that should be
protected and recovered at all costs, while Labour put emphasis on the
pressing need to define a 'mixed and shared' identity. At the same time, the
Labour administration passed measures to restrict migrants' entry into the
UK and introduced anti-terror laws aimed at monitoring individuals
suspected of links with fundamentalist groups, measures that were widely
perceived as draconian and criticised by human rights advocates.

From the 'Britishness test' to the immigration cap

In the course of the 2000s, the Blair and Brown governments introduced
several pieces of new legislation regulating immigration, finally implementing a points system for non-EU citizens and a compulsory 'Britishness
test' (officially, the 'Life in the UK' test) for residents applying for citizenship. A range of other proposals were aired, though ultimately abandoned,
such as compulsory modules on 'Britishness' in schools and Gordon
Brown's idea to encourage Britons to fly the Union Jack flag in their
backyards, like the many US citizens who fly the Stars and Stripes. David
Cameron, then leader of the opposition, rejected this invitation to patriotic
display.

Following the 2005 bombings, the issue of immigration, particularly
Muslim immigration, became a frequently debated issue in the press, on
television and in even within the staid institution of parliament. A parliamentary report released in spring 2008 stated that immigration could
negatively affect citizens' well-being and recommended to limit new

arrivals. Chaired by former Energy Secretary Lord Wakeman, the committee concluded that immigrants represented fierce competition for unemployed teenagers and other workers at the bottom of the earnings scale.

In this context it is perhaps not surprising why immigration acquired such significance during the 2010 electoral campaign. The fact that in the run-up to the election the numbers of new arrivals decreased (a predictable response to an economic crisis) had little effect on public perceptions. One survey found that by the end of 2009 over 70 per cent of the population claimed to be unhappy about the way things are in the UK, compared with only 40 per cent in 1997; according to Ben Page, chief executive of the market research company Ipsos-Mori, these figures reflected 'growing nostalgia for the good old days' (*The Economist* 2010).

Real numbers have made little difference to the perception of the phenomenon. According to data from the last census (2001) British citizens belonging to 'ethnic minorities' represented only 7.9 per cent of the total population, although the early 2000s saw around 150,000 new arrivals every year and just above 100,000 political asylum seekers. The government's most recent estimates (ONS 2009) indicate 356,000 overseas arrivals (of which 273,000 were students) and smaller numbers of asylum seekers. Within EU countries, the UK is third for yearly arrivals, after Spain (498,000) and Germany (237,000), yet the perception fuelled by the tabloids and some politicians was that Britain was uniquely overwhelmed by immigration, a perception someway distant from reality.

Party politics and immigration in 2010

The 2010 election was by no means the first election to see a focus on immigration. During the 1980s, immigration once again emerged as a prominent political issue. The Conservative government led by Margaret Thatcher had published detailed plans to restrict immigration in its manifesto, while Labour had largely ignored the issue. The rhetoric under-pinning Thatcher's strategy on the topic would later be widely employed, normalising political proposals to reduce immigration. The new norms protected those who were full British citizens, 'regardless of race, colour, or religious belief', but strict controls of incoming migration flows serve 'to guarantee the possibility of maintaining good relationships within the national community' (Conservative Party 1979).

Since then, commitments to intervention in both directions have multi-plied, earning increasing space within electoral manifestos, and gaining unprecedented limelight during the 2005 election and again in the 2010 campaign. It is significant that in the 2010 Labour manifesto proposals on immigration controls are contained in the same chapter that covers tackling crime, implicitly linking the two issues in voters' minds. Gordon Brown insisted on the positive results secured by Tony Blair and his own administration, clarifying that, with regard to asylum applications, 'decisive' action had translated into lower numbers of applications and residence permits awarded, compared to alleged 'laxity' of Tory governments. 'In this new world, people need to know that the rules for immigration are fair and that coming to Britain is a privilege, not a right', says the 2010 Labour manifesto. This approach conflicts with the positions of the 1970s and 1980s 'old' left as well as with reformist ideas of the 1990s, summarised by Anthony Giddens in his book, *The Third Way* (1998). Giddens, a close advisor to Tony Blair, stressed that 'immigration has long been fertile soil for racism, in spite of the fact that studies from around the world show that immigration usually proves advantageous for the host country' and advocated a 'benign, cosmopolitan nationalism' as the obvious response to globalisation (1998: 135–137).

This position (largely reiterated by Giddens in 2007) completely disappeared from the 2010 Labour manifesto, which was characterised by a 'law and order' narrative that stresses how one of Labour priorities was to manage migration flows, so as 'to promote and defend British values'. The UK of the future, as imagined by Gordon Brown and presented to the electorate, would be a nation anxious to protect its own borders, but also obliged to maintain an open channel for quality immigration (for instance, the 2010 Labour manifesto praises the results achieved through the new entry requirements). However, Brown's vision of Britain implied suspicions towards citizenship applicants, seeing them as a potential burden on public services, to the detriment of British citizens. Thus, in the few paragraphs dedicated to the issue, Labour takes a hard-line towards immigration by stating the intent to prevent breaches, 'saving taxpayers hundreds of million of pounds every year' (Labour 2010).

There was no direct mention of immigration in the Tory manifesto, but Cameron's ideas on this point were well known and were reiterated during the TV debate: the number of immigrants was too high and the number of new arrivals should be reduced. The Conservative leader avoided precise figures, but did not refrain from rhetoric when referring to the 'healthy' (though ill-defined) traditions of the past: in the debate Cameron stated that immigration 'has been too high in the past few years and I would dearly love to get it down to the levels it was in the past so it is no longer an issue in our politics as it wasn't in the past' (BBC 2010). Some historical memory would have sufficed to remember that the Tories were in power in 1962 when the Commonwealth Immigration Act, which restricted the right of Commonwealth citizens to settle in the UK, was passed. In fact, in the few months immediately preceding the implementation of the new bill over 200,000 people were allowed into the UK, under previous legislation. Cameron's stance would seem to be part of a precise communication strategy with two main objectives: to evoke the alleged splendours of the good old days – an argument to which, according to polls, rural England of conservative traditions is very responsive – and to avoid explicit commitments. The proposal Cameron offered was an immigration cap, but the Tory leader remained vague on the details and refrained from giving figures, stressing instead his policy differences with Labour.

As for the Liberal Democrats, their role as the third party forced them to put forward alternative policies to the two main parties. In the Lib Dem manifesto and on television, Nick Clegg sought a distinctive message by emphasising the consistent failure of both Tory and Labour immigration policies, which had forced immigrants underground. For Clegg, an amnesty was now necessary. The Lib Dems were strongly against Cameron's cap and proposed their own policy solution: a points system on a regional basis to help direct immigrants towards areas where they were needed. Clegg struggled to explain during the debate exactly how this system would be implemented, but he was more effective at highlighting the problems with the Conservative capping policy, asking Cameron, 'What if you have a cap run out mid-summer and somebody wants to come and play for Manchester City or Manchester United?' (BBC 2010). However Clegg's decision to enter coalition with the Conservatives after the election saw him subsequently having to defend the policy he had ridiculed in the debate.

The rise of the xenophobes?

The British National Party was not allowed to take part in the debates, although this xenophobic and racist movement has gained increasing support over recent years for its open hostility against any form of immigration. The BNP's unabashed racism, summarised in its idea of a 'battle against immigration in defence of British identity', prompted the exclusion from most television coverage of its leader, Nick Griffin, although the party was allowed an election broadcast. The BNP manifesto (BNP 2010) put forward an apocalyptic thesis of the UK's future if immigration is not halted: within less than half a century, they warned, 'true British people' (understood to mean white British, although the colour of the skin is not openly mentioned) would have become a minority. To prevent this scenario from becoming reality, the BNP called for drastic measures, such as immediately closing borders and deporting all illegal immigrants and all foreigners sentenced for crimes committed in the UK. Other proposed measures included the abrogation of legislation in favour of racial integration and the elimination of all anti-racist organisations such as the Equalities and Human Rights Commission, whose aim, it is argued, is to promote a dangerous multiculturalism that will threaten 'true British identity'.

Notwithstanding the ostracism of all the main television channels, the BNP was still able to win over half a million votes (564,331), amounting to 1.9 per cent of votes cast. This compared with 192,850 votes, equal to 0.7 per cent of the total, in 2005. However, these numbers are misleading: the party put up only 119 candidates in 2005, but almost tripled that number to 338 in 2010, so its performance in relative terms was rather worse than five years earlier. Moreover, the BNP leader Nick Griffin suffered a high profile defeat in the East London constituency of Barking, where the party poured resources into an attempt to unseat long-serving Labour MP Margaret Hodge. Not only was Griffin roundly beaten by Hodge, finishing in a distant third place behind the Conservatives, but his party also lost all four of its local councillors in the area. The Barking debacle, added to the loss of further council seats in other areas of the country, made the 2010 election a serious reverse for the British extreme right.

The BNP's halted progress should not, however, be seen as the end of the problem. The fact that the BNP could have been seen as a serious threat in such a safe Labour seat showed how, in less than a decade, a marginal political force with serious public image problems had been able to thrust itself into the national limelight. Its success, based on a single-issue appeal directed at the white working class, attracted unprecedented support from disgruntled former Labour voters, winning two European Parliament seats (and 6.2 per cent of the vote) in the European elections of 2009. Moreover, another party hostile to immigration, the UK Independence Party (UKIP), beat Labour into third place in the 2009 European elections, winning 16.5 per cent of the vote. Although UKIP is not overtly racist and campaigns largely about European Union issues rather than immigration per se, the growth of these two parties suggests an emerging constituency of nationalist right or extreme right political preferences in Britain, potentially reaching beyond the traditionally marginal presence accorded to such views in mainstream politics.

In the context of an economic crisis that has caused high rates of unemployment, politicians have greater than even opportunity to exploit voter fears about immigration. UK politics has not been immune to the demagogic and xenophobic contagion that has marked the political debate in continental Europe in the past few years. The fact that Labour tried to present their policies as the strictest also marks a new course taken by the party, whose main weakness has been to let other parties influence its own priorities. In the end Labour faced unfavourable circumstances and suffered a serious defeat. However, the success of anti-immigration rhetoric suggests that the hard right may have a bright future (Goodwin 2010), since immigration controls are likely to be debated for a long time, to the benefit of those who continue to act as the champions of an alleged 'white British identity' endangered by new immigrants.

Conclusion

In a climate of economic pessimism and disquiet about the growth in immigration during the first decade of Labour's period of government, the Tory proposal of restricting immigration was unsurprisingly welcomed by the electorate, to the detriment of those, like Brown and his party, who were viewed as 'soft' on immigration. Once elected, David Cameron kept his promise and announced that between July 2010 and April 2011 the UK would welcome no more than 24,000 non-EU workers. The new Prime Minister omitted to mention that the economic crisis has dramatically reduced the number of jobs available for both immigrants and British citizens, and that the austerity measures recently adopted by the coalition government would be likely to increase unemployment further, at least in the short run.

In these circumstances, the emphasis on the need to control immigration could prove an effective diversion strategy, distracting from other problems. After all, over half a century of public debate on controlling immigration shows that in times of crisis there is a tendency to scapegoat those who come from abroad. In the absence of an economic recovery, mistrust towards immigration is unlikely to fade quickly and in this respect the UK is no different from the rest of Europe. Thus, support will grow for those who – albeit with varying tones – have made the defence of insularity their political flagship during the last electoral campaign.

References

Baumann, G. (1999). *The Multicultural Riddle*. London: Routledge.

BBC (2010). 'The First Election Debate'. http://news.bbc.co.uk/1/shared /bsp/hi/pdfs/16_04_10_firstdebate.pdf (last accessed 1 October 2011).

BNP (2010). *BNP Election Manifesto. Democracy, Freedom, Culture and Identity*. http://communications.bnp.org.uk/ge2010manifesto.pdf (last accessed 1 October 2011).

Clarke, P. (1996). *Hope and Glory: Britain 1900–1990*. London: Penguin.

Conservative Party (1979). *1979 Conservative Party General Election Manifesto*. www.conservative-party.net/manifestos/1979/1979-

conservative-manifesto.shtml (last accessed 1 October 2011).

The Economist (2010). 'Through a Glass Darkly: Britain's "Broken Society"', *The Economist*, 4 February.

Giddens, A. (1998). *The Third Way*. Cambridge: Polity.

Giddens, A. (2007). *Over To You, Mr Brown*. Cambridge: Polity.

Gilroy, P. (1992). *The Black Atlantic: Modernity and Double Consciousness*. Cambridge, MA: Harvard University Press.

Goodhart, D. (2004) 'Too Diverse?', *Prospect*, 95, February.

Goodhart, D. (2006). *Progressive Nationalism. Citizenship and the Left*. London: Demos.

Goodwin, M. (2010). 'Life after Griffin', *Prospect*, 172, June.

Kureishi, H. (1985). 'Dirty Washing', *Time Out*, 14–20 November: 26.

Kureishi, H. (1986). *My Beautiful Laundrette* and *The Rainbow Sign*. London: Faber.

Labour (2010). *Labour's Manifesto. A Future Fair for All*. www.labour .org.uk/labours-manifesto-for-a-future-fair-for-all (last accessed 1 October 2011).

Modood, T. (2009). 'Ethnicity and Religion', in M. Flinders, A. Gamble, C. Hay and M. Kenny (eds), *The Oxford Handbook of British Politics*. Oxford: Oxford University Press, pp. 484–497.

ONS (2009). 'Ethnicity and Identity'. Office for National Statistics. www.ons.gov.uk/ons/taxonomy/index.html?nscl=Ethnicity+and+Identity (last accessed 1 October 2011).

Rushdie, S. (1992). *Imaginary Homelands*. London: Granta.

Taylor, C. (1992). *Multiculturalism and the Politics of Recognition: An Essay by Charles Taylor*. Princeton, NJ: Princeton University Press.

Winder, R. (2005). *Bloody Foreigners. The Story of Immigration to Britain*. London: Abacus.

9

Devolution and the 2010 UK election in Scotland, Wales and Northern Ireland

Alan Trench

Introduction

Viewed in territorial terms, the 2010 election was an odd one. Voters in England were electing their only legislature; those in Scotland, Wales and Northern Ireland were sending representatives to Westminster, but this did not affect the large areas of government activity devolved in those parts of the UK. The territorial effects of the election therefore varied widely according to where one voted. Whoever took office at Westminster would have to manage complex constitutional and political relationships with the devolved governments and legislatures in Scotland, Wales and Northern Ireland, and deal with a number of difficult issues that needed immediate attention. The outcome of the election also produced substantial political change. At the time of Labour's victory in the 2005 election, devolution had not been a source of significant political contestation; not only did Labour govern in Westminster, but it was the (minority) administration in Wales and the dominant partner in coalition in Scotland, while devolution remained suspended in Northern Ireland. With the formation of the Labour-Plaid Cymru coalition in Wales and the SNP minority government in Scotland after the devolved elections of May 2007, all that changed – particularly once Gordon Brown succeeded Tony Blair as UK Prime Minister and devolved government was restored in Northern Ireland. With the arrival of the Conservative-Liberal Democrat government, the UK moved from having a high degree of political cohesion between different levels of government to the highest degree of variation possible. Each party held office somewhere, but none in more than one jurisdiction.

This chapter will assess the impact of devolution on the 2010 election, and of the 2010 election on the practice of devolved government, by looking at four issues. First, it will survey the key political and institutional developments that had taken place since 2005, to map out the context in which the May 2010 elections took place. Second, it will look at developments in how the political parties had responded to devolution and their campaigns and territorial strategies for the election, including the various policies and programmes set out in their manifestos. Finally, it will look at the formation of the Conservative-Liberal Democrat government and the early steps it took in office.

Background: the state of play in 2010

Between the 2005 and 2010 elections, the politics of devolution changed considerably. Important changes resulted from the political alternation that took place after the 2007 devolved elections, bringing the SNP and Plaid Cymru into government for the first time, leading Labour (in Wales) to share power with a nationalist party, and in Northern Ireland forcing Sinn Fein and the Democratic Unionists to share office.

In Northern Ireland, the UK government had suspended devolution in 2002 and reintroduced direct rule from London. The restoration of devolved government was a major undertaking, for the UK and Irish governments as well as the political parties in Northern Ireland. Key to this was the St Andrews Agreement of October 2006, which provided for a statutory ministerial code and a clearer basis for operation of the Northern Ireland Executive, provided for the devolution of justice and policing, and abolished the UK government's power to suspend devolution. That created sufficient trust for devolved elections to take place in March 2007 and the restoration of devolved government shortly afterwards. This led to Sinn Fein (formerly the political wing of the IRA) and the Democratic Unionist Party, the most intransigent of the unionist parties, sharing leading roles in government. This worked better than anyone had expected; the evident bonhomie between the First and Deputy First Ministers, Ian Paisley and Martin McGuinness, led to them being known as 'the chuckle brothers'. Making the new arrangements work proved rather harder in practice, though, especially after Ian Paisley retired and was succeeded as DUP leader by Peter Robinson, who brought a more 'businesslike' approach to the relationship. One problem was the sheer difficulty of getting any sort of agreement within the Executive; another, the tendency of the DUP and SF ministers to form an 'inner executive' and marginalise ministers from the other parties. Devolution of justice and policing was held up by mutual suspicion between the various parties and sectarian groups and by disagreements over how to finance the measures and over the choice of a

Justice Minister. After David Ford (leader of the non-sectarian Alliance Party) was chosen as Justice Minister, devolution of justice and policing eventually took place in April 2010.

In Wales and Scotland, the changes of government in 2007 triggered renewed debates about both the constitutional and the financial aspects of devolution. A new government of Wales Act had been passed in 2006, barely eight years after the legislation creating the National Assembly for Wales. The new Act created two separate mechanisms to confer legislative powers on the National Assembly. In the short term, under Part Three of the Act, these would be conferred piecemeal by Westminster; in the longer term, under Part Four, the Assembly would have 'primary legislative powers' over a range of fields including health, education, local government, culture and the environment. That would, however, need the assent of the public in a referendum. These arrangements may have been intended to end debates about Wales's devolved conditions or at least damp them down. But instead, they fuelled them.

Following the 'One Wales' coalition agreement between Labour and Plaid Cymru, two separate bodies were set up. The All Wales Convention was charged with considering public understanding of the arrangements under Part Three of the Government of Wales Act 2006 for conferring legislative powers, and with assessing support for moving to the 'primary legislative powers' set out in Part Four of the Act. In November 2009 it reported largely in favour of moving to Part Four; the present system was unduly complex, defective and poorly understood, and there was public support for a clearer devolution settlement (All Wales Convention 2009). Indeed, public opinion in 2009–2010 on the question of legislative powers seemed emphatically in favour of the 'Part Four' powers, in contrast to the caution displayed by politicians in the National Assembly. With the report and sustained opinion polling in favour of primary legislative powers, the Assembly voted to trigger a referendum in February 2010. However, given the timing of the UK election, the ultimate decision on the vote would fall on the incoming UK government and the new Secretary of State for Wales.

On the financial side, the Independent Commission on Funding and Finance for Wales was not set up until the summer of 2008. Unlike the All Wales Convention, the Commission was a small expert body composed of just three professional economists. Its first report was published in July 2009 and confirmed a point that had long been argued by Plaid Cymru: that, in relation to Wales's needs, the National Assembly was 'underfunded' and received less to provide public services than other parts of the UK with similar needs. The amount of underfunding was small, however: Holtham gave the figure of £300 million a year, or 2.1 per cent of the National Assembly's budget (Independent Commission on Funding and

Finance for Wales 2009). Its second report (Independent Commission on Funding and Finance for Wales 2010) amplified these figures, suggested how a 'fair' (needs-related) grant could be calculated, and proposed a model for giving the National Assembly a form of fiscal accountability similar to that recommended by the Calman Commission for Scotland, based on devolving control of 10 points of income tax (discussed in more detail below). This model both adjusted the Calman recommendations to Welsh conditions and made a number of improvements to those recommendations that would materially improve its operation.

The Scottish debates were more complex and more disjointed. There were two rival processes, each covering both constitutional and financial issues. Shortly after coming to office, the SNP initiated what it called a 'National Conversation' about Scotland's constitutional position. It indicated from the outset that its preferred option was independence, though it would respect the wishes of the Scottish people in any case. The SNP programme envisaged a referendum on independence, which it committed to holding before the 2011 Scottish elections (though it finally abandoned the idea in the summer of 2010 after it became clear that such a bill would make little progress). The National Conversation therefore mutated into a forum for holding a variety of events – ministerial speeches, public meetings and so forth – and a website to absorb the views of the public. It culminated in November 2009 with the publication of a white paper on constitutional options for Scotland's future, setting out four broad options:

- the status quo,
- a form of 'devolution plus' along the lines of the recommendations of the Calman Commission,
- what it called 'full devolution', and others have called 'devolution max', under which Scotland would remain part of the Union but with complete domestic self-government, and with the UK level responsible only for defence, foreign affairs and macro-economic matters such as the currency and interest rates, and
- outright independence, with Scotland becoming a separate state though forming a 'social union' with the remainder of the UK, allowing for free movement of persons (Scottish Government 2009).

While the white paper expressed a preference for independence, its detailed scheme for 'full devolution' was widely interpreted as constituting the SNP's willingness to accept that approach instead.

The Calman Commission was the response of the unionist parties – Labour, the Liberal Democrats and the Conservatives – to the constitutional debate initiated by the SNP government. That it took place at all reflected a significant change of view on the part of the Labour and Conservative parties. The Liberal Democrats had published their own recommendations for extending devolution in March 2006, in the form of the report by an internal party commission chaired by Lord Steel of Aikwood, former UK Liberal Party leader and Scottish Parliament Presiding Officer (Steel Commission 2006). The Conservatives' acceptance of devolution as a *fait accompli* did not suggest any great wish to see it extended, while Labour had fought the 2007 elections claiming that no change in the institutional arrangements for devolution was needed, and that such a debate was a distraction from more important policy issues. Within months of the election, however, it was clear that refusal to take part in the debate was politically risky, and Labour's new leader, Wendy Alexander, proposed a cross-party commission to review the working of devolution, the division of powers between devolved and UK levels, and financial arrangements. The Commission was chaired by Sir Kenneth Calman (formerly chief medical officer in both the Scottish and UK governments) and reported not only to the Scottish Parliament but also to the UK government. It also developed close links with the Scottish leaders of the Conservative, Labour and Liberal Democrat parties at Westminster.

Its first report published in December 2008 indicated general principles more than any firm conclusions. Its final report in June 2009 (Commission on Scottish Devolution 2009) suggested modest changes to the institutional framework of devolution, recommending among other things that some extra powers regarding driving offences be devolved and that greater use be made of the Joint Ministerial Committee in managing intergovernmental relations. The most important and eye-catching recommendations related to finance, where it found the parliament's responsibilities for policy and spending were not accompanied by adequate financial accountability. It recommended that the Scottish Parliament should become responsible for raising about one-third of its spending, mostly through devolving part of personal income tax. UK income tax rates would be reduced by 10 pence in the pound for Scottish tax-payers, and the block grant from the UK government would also be reduced 'commensurately'. The Scottish Parliament would be free to set its own rate of income tax, whether the 10 pence by which it had been reduced, or more, or less. The idea behind this mechanism was to force the Scottish Parliament to make a choice about its tax rate, rather than allowing it to maintain the same rate as in other parts of the UK by default (as has happened in Spain). Control of tax rates, allowances and so forth would not be devolved; the parliament would simply control a portion of the tax, and its revenue, but have no involvement in the overall fiscal structure of the UK.

Although this approach was regarded in immediate press and political reaction as radical, in fact it was a highly conservative approach to the issue (Trench 2009). The powers it devolved were strictly limited and much control would remain at Westminster. (That in turn would prove problematic if the UK government were to make significant changes to the tax system.) Moreover, it arose from a *political* concern on the part of the Calman Commission: what it saw as a lack of financial accountability to go with the Scottish government's political accountability to the parliament, and then through the ballot box to the wider public. This limited measure of fiscal autonomy was meant to transform the Scottish government from a spending agency into something that also had a measure of fiscal responsibility.

The UK government's response to Calman appeared in a November 2009 White Paper that seemed to agree to implement the Calman recommendations, but in reality rejected several of them (Secretary of State for Scotland 2009). The most important was that the revenues that would come to the Scottish Parliament from the use of the Scottish rate of tax would be based on Treasury estimates of tax paid by Scottish taxpayers, not a share of the actual taxes they paid. These estimates would be reviewed at each spending review (every three years or so), and the amount of reduction in the Scottish block grant adjusted accordingly. This system would not introduce a hard budget constraint of any sort for Scotland, and so it would also fail to introduce meaningful fiscal accountability. Rather, it would emphasise the ongoing role of the Treasury and leave the whole of the Scottish government's finances under the control of the Treasury. This traded administrative practicality and maintaining the status quo for the limited measure of political and financial autonomy that Calman offered.

It is notable that the UK government's role in all these developments was limited and reactive. Since 1999, it has never taken the view that devolution or territorial relations across the UK require active management from the centre. It has seemed most comfortable when the devolved parts of the UK have been quiescent and caused it no bother. While it beefed up its capacity in response to the SNP's election in 2007, even that change was limited. It has also preferred to handle such matters as need its involvement bilaterally, without building any administrative framework to address the UK-wide implications of devolution. The chief arms of UK government concerned with devolution have therefore been the separate Scotland, Wales and Northern Ireland Offices, with a very limited role for a 'central' team based in Cabinet Office or the Ministry of Justice (Trench 2007; also Trench 2005). Such an approach may reflect the historic structure of the UK as a 'state of unions' (Mitchell 2007), but it also prevents any more synoptic approach to the issues arising from the UK's territorial constitution. It is an acute form of path dependency in which the past is allowed to determine the future, not merely set the direction of travel.

Manifestos, programmes and campaigns

The period between 2005 and 2010 saw little change in the various parties' attitudes towards devolution. Among the Britain-wide parties, Labour initially resisted the constitutional debates that devolution had unleashed, then reluctantly moved towards accepting limited measures of incremental change. It remained protective of the Union as such, but reluctant to artic-ulate what this meant. It was sporadically keen to talk about 'Britishness', though this debate was much more about relations between different ethnic groups and the place of immigrants in the UK than about articulat-ing shared interests. Attempts to develop a concept of shared UK-wide social citizenship were largely confined to academic debate (e.g. Greer 2009). Although this term and the related one of a 'social union' were used in various documents such as the Calman report, the use appeared to be little more than a device to avoid any reconsideration of the framework of devolution, rather than a genuine attempt to rethink the nature of the Union.

The Conservatives' most important shift arose from the election of David Cameron as leader. Between 1999 and 2005, the Conservatives appeared uneasy with the new arrangements. Their votes lay largely in England, particularly southern England, and their policies had little appeal outside there. With strong policies on 'English votes for English laws', at the 2001 and 2005 elections they looked rather like an English nationalist party. Although speeches and party policy documents often asserted the importance of the Union, it was far from clear why they were so attached to it – or what a Conservative UK government might be able to offer those who did not share that sentimental attachment. This approach changed considerably after Cameron became leader. He identified a rationale for the Union that included habit and tradition, but went beyond that, high-lighting the role that a United Kingdom was able to play in the wider world. He also emphasised that the Conservatives accepted devolution and would treat the Scottish government with 'respect' and seek a more coop-erative relationship (e.g. Cameron 2009). While this changed the general atmosphere, it still did not involve any concrete proposals.

The nationalist parties spent much of the period from 2005 focused on government in their own nations. In Scotland, that meant trying to prove competence in government, while lacking a parliamentary majority. The result was a slim legislative programme, a difficult annual budget round with enough concessions to ensure support from at least one other party (more often than not, the Conservatives), and the defeat of several flagship SNP policies including reform of local council funding. Despite these obstacles, they succeeded in at least proving themselves a viable alternative to Labour. In Wales, Plaid Cymru found a number of difficulties in their relationship with Labour, notably over progress towards a referendum on legislative powers, arising largely because Labour did not take the terms of the 'One Wales' coalition agreement seriously. Despite setbacks, particularly relating to culture and the Welsh language (key areas for Plaid Cymru), it succeeded in making a significant impact on policy as well as on extending devolution.

Despite these successes, nationalist parties could only approach the UK elections with limited expectations. It is clear that the nationalist parties do better in devolved elections than UK ones. This appears to be a structural phenomenon, relating to voters' understanding of the roles of the parties in the various electoral arenas (Wyn Jones and Scully 2006). The Britain-wide parties would enter the UK elections in a much stronger position and would be helped by the effects of the 'first past the post' electoral system. For Labour, this was expected to help maintain their advantage in both Scotland and Wales; for the Conservatives, while they hoped to make advances in Scotland (and committed considerable resources there), Wales was the key battleground. Indeed, Conservative politicians took the view that they needed to win twelve seats there if they were to secure a majority at Westminster.

The distinctive features of devolved politics were not, however, very well reflected in the election campaigns. Labour's campaign in Scotland was highly defensive, attacking both the Conservatives and the SNP (Mitchell and van der Zwet 2010). In Wales, it was little better (Bradbury 2010). Issues of devolution figured very little in most of the campaign in the media, which largely followed traditional (pre-devolution) lines in talking about policy as it related to England. Moreover, attempts by the nationalist parties to participate in the three televised leaders' debates came to little, despite various threats and denunciations by both and (unsuccessful) legal action by the SNP. Their leaders were able to take part in separate Scottish and Welsh leaders' debates, but these had nothing like the prominence of the ones involving Nick Clegg, David Cameron and Gordon Brown.

Perhaps the most significant intervention by the nationalist parties was their joint attempt to set out the terms on which they might deal with other parties in the event of a hung parliament. At a joint press conference, the two leaders identified four key requirements: protecting frontline public services, reform of the way devolved governments were funded, investment in green transport and more help for businesses. This was as much a campaign move, intended to emphasise the valuable role nationalist MPs could play if elected. In the case of the SNP, they also highlighted the slogan 'more Nats less cuts'. However, they then undermined this approach by each adding different issues to that agreed list – undermining arguments about 'Celtic solidarity' and inviting deals to be done with one party but not another, parliamentary arithmetic permitting.

The three Britain-wide unionist parties adapted their programmes and electoral platforms to devolution in rather similar ways.[1] Each party issued three manifestos: one, usually describing itself as 'British', intended to apply only in England, and separate ones for Scotland and Wales. The Scottish and Welsh versions in principle provided scope for each party to tailor its message to the particular conditions of those countries, as well as providing additional opportunities for media exposure at launch events. In contrast, and less surprisingly, the nationalist parties and the unionist parties in Northern Ireland (which operate in only one part of the UK) each issued a single manifesto concerned only with Northern Ireland.

The manifestos reveal how the parties currently understand the role of a UK general election in a devolved United Kingdom. Many functions are devolved in Scotland, Wales and Northern Ireland, and many of these functions are in areas such as health, education or law and order, which voters care deeply about and which constitute the major electoral battle-grounds. Political debate about what sort of drugs or hospital treatment are available on the NHS, or the quality of schools, are matters of great concern to voters in England, and a UK election is the only opportunity for English voters to express a meaningful view about them. That is not so outside England; these are matters for the devolved governments, and constitu-tionally speaking the proper place to debate them is a devolved election, not one for Westminster.

Not that one would know that from the manifestos themselves. Those of the Britain-wide parties do their utmost to mask the nature of devolution from the voters, particularly those in England. Eight of the nine manifestos (all three from the Labour and Conservative parties, and the Scottish and British ones from the Lib Dems) are concerned with both UK and devolved-level matters, even though devolved ones were not at stake. The parties evidently regarded a UK election as an appropriate place to discuss the full range of party policy, regardless of whether decisions about policies would be determined by votes at the election.

The only manifesto to set out a programme clearly and specify which tier of government was responsible for a particular policy was the Liberal Democrats' manifesto in Wales. The Lib Dems, in their other manifestos, included a sentence on the inside back cover noting that the manifesto was concerned only with matters that could be decided at Westminster and that many functions were devolved in Scotland and Wales (although it did not specify what those were, leaving it to readers and voters to work this out for themselves). The Scottish Labour manifesto, and the Conservatives' Welsh and Scottish ones, similarly noted that devolved matters were not at stake in the election, but failed to spell out which matters were devolved. The Labour and Conservative 'British' manifestos made no mention of the impact of devolution at all, so readers in England would perhaps have been surprised to learn that the promises made had no bearing whatever outside England. Only the Welsh Labour manifesto spelled out the specifically Welsh implications of UK-level policies – a task for which such separate Scottish and Welsh manifestos would appear ideally suited.

When it came to substantive commitments about devolution, there was a remarkable degree of common ground among the unionist parties. All three parties committed to implement the recommendations of the Calman Commission in Scotland (in Labour's case, along the lines it had already adopted), and to hold a referendum on primary legislative powers for Wales. The Conservatives also made further commitments to review the 'West Lothian question' (the ability of MPs from Scotland and Wales to vote on matters affecting England that are devolved in those countries). The Liberal Democrats agreed to review the retention by the UK government of the Scottish proceeds from the fossil fuel levy, a long-standing Scottish grievance. There was some variation in specific manifestos: for example, the Scottish Lib Dem manifesto made it clear that they saw implementation of Calman as a first stage to further fiscal devolution, not a final settlement, while the Welsh Labour manifesto committed Labour to ensuring 'fair funding' for Wales, as recommended by the Holtham Commission. But this was largely identifying and emphasising issues with particular local resonance. The overall messages, as well as the content of the manifestos generally, remained highly uniform.

In this setting, the greatest concern with constitutional propriety came from the Scottish National Party and Plaid Cymru. These parties only contest elections in Scotland or Wales, and therefore do not have to worry about their messages in one part of the UK spilling over across the border and affecting their campaign in another territory. Both nationalist parties are also much more accustomed to constitutional debates, given that constitutional issues are a key part of their wider political mission. Moreover, as parties of government since 2007, one would expect them to be keen to ensure they are not blamed for decisions over which they have no control, while taking maximum credit for those they can shape. That may explain their care in framing manifestos that scrupulously distinguished between devolved and non-devolved matters and made policy commitments that were only relevant to the UK level. This approach makes much political sense, but is notable for departing from the approach the SNP (more than Plaid Cymru) has taken in the past. Thus, Plaid Cymru's manifesto took care to talk about UK-level changes in devolved powers, both generally and for specific areas like mental health, about the need to alter the financial basis of the Assembly, and about other UK-level matters such as banking regulation or treatment of the armed forces.

Ultimately, the framing of the manifestos and more general conduct of the election campaign effectively masked the constitutional nature of the UK as it now is from voters. In many ways, the 2010 campaign was difficult to distinguish from that of any pre-1997 election. While methods of communication and campaigning may have moved on since 1997, the content of the various territorial campaigns had not palpably changed in the eyes of the Britain-wide parties. Unlike the nationalist parties, they seemed to see no significant electoral advantage in drawing attention to the implications of devolution, particularly to voters in England.

The outcome: devolution and the coalition

The outcome of the election – a UK parliament with no overall majority and a full-blown coalition between the Conservatives and Liberal Democrats – had not been widely expected before the election, although the prospect of a hung parliament had been the subject of considerable attention. This was, of course, a government with a limited mandate outside England (and particularly southern England). Scotland largely rejected the 'British' pattern of increasing Conservative votes, as did Wales to a lesser extent. The Conservatives had picked up a few seats in suburbs of the larger cities of northern England, but these were islands of blue in a generally red electoral map. The Conservatives also remained stuck at just a single MP from Scotland. In Wales, they picked up five more seats (giving them a total of eight) – but as plans for a Conservative majority at Westminster implied winning at least twelve, that was a poorer performance than expected. The Lib Dems kept their Scottish seats, but lost one in Wales (won by the Tories).

Perhaps the most important area where the Conservatives' electoral strategy had failed, however, was in Northern Ireland. Many observers had questioned the logic of the alliance between the Conservatives and the Ulster Unionists there to form the Ulster Conservatives and Unionists – New Force alliance (known as UCUNF). The weak performance of the UUP at successive elections meant they were eager to secure some electoral advantage. However, it was unclear what the Conservatives were hoping to gain from this alliance. It would entangle them firmly in the internecine conflicts of Northern Ireland politics, while offering just a handful of

Table 9.1 The 2010 UK election results in Great Britain

	UK	England	Scotland	Wales
Total number of MPs	650	533	59	40
Labour (no. of seats)	258	191	41	26
Percentage of vote		*28.1*	*42.0*	*36.2*
Conservative (no. of seats)	307	298	1	8
Percentage of vote		*39.6*	*16.7*	*26.1*
Liberal Democrats (no. of seats)	57	43	11	3
Percentage of vote		*24.2*	*18.9*	*20.1*
Scottish National Party (no. of seats)	6	–	6	–
Percentage of vote		–	*19.0*	–
Plaid Cymru (no. of seats)	3	–	–	3
Percentage of vote		–	–	*11.3*

Westminster seats at most. More compelling as a rationale was the idea of helping reintegrate Northern Ireland into the mainstream of UK politics and of creating a prospect that votes in Northern Ireland could affect the composition of a government at Westminster. From that perspective, the tie-up between the Conservatives and the UUP could make a measure of sense, in supporting a (small 'u') unionist project. But the disadvantages of this strategy were considerable and worsened in the run-up to the election. Many members of the Conservatives in Northern Ireland (where it had branches and members even though it did not contest elections) were unionists but not Protestants, and they left in response to the link because of its sectarian associations. The UUP's sole MP, Sylvia Hermon, was a unionist but not a Conservative (she was regarded as close to the Blairite section of the Labour Party), and refused to campaign under its banner. Running as an independent, she kept her seat; but no candidate running for UCUNF won. The only unionist party with MPs in the new parliament would be the Democratic Unionists.

Neither partner in the new coalition could claim to have 'won' outside England. But while the Lib Dems had largely maintained their position, neither gaining nor losing seats, the Conservatives' strategy had clearly failed. For all the resources put into Scotland, they had gained no seats there, nor even made much headway in terms of votes. Their gains in Wales were substantially less than had been hoped or expected, and their performance was a little less strong than in parts of northern England. This aspect of the Conservatives' performance was largely missed in discussions

Table 9.2 The Northern Ireland election results, 2010

	Number of seats	Percentage of vote
UCUNF	0	15.2
Democratic Unionist Party	8	25.0
Alliance	1	6.3
Social Democratic & Labour Party	3	16.5
Sinn Fein	5*	25.5
Independent**	1	3.1
Total	18	

* Sinn Fein's MPs decline to take to take an oath of loyalty to the Sovereign and therefore do not take their seats at Westminster.

** Sylvia Hermon, elected as an independent Unionist in North Down. Numerous other candidates stood unsuccessfully, including an independent unionist in Fermanagh and South Tyrone who lost to Sinn Fein by four votes.

of the election outcome at the time, however, mainly because it was overtaken by the question of government formation.

Beyond that, the election results show the effects of the disproportionality of the 'first past the post' electoral system. This clearly worked most to the advantage of Labour, which gained 69 per cent of Scottish MPs and 65 per cent of Welsh ones with 42 and 36 per cent of the vote respectively. The Conservatives' sole Scottish seat amounted to 1.7 per cent of Scotland's parliamentary representation – but they won nearly ten times that share of the vote. The Liberal Democrats may have won fewer seats than their share of the votes in Wales (7.5 per cent of seats on 20 per cent of the vote) but they were less penalised in Scotland, where they won 18.6 per cent of the votes and 18.9 per cent of seats. While the nationalist parties perform less well in general elections than in devolved elections, which are seen as their 'natural' arena, they too may have lost out from tactical voting, as voters recognised the biases in the electoral system. The SNP received 19 per cent of Scottish votes but only 10 per cent of the seats; Plaid Cymru, 11.3 per cent of votes and 7.5 per cent of seats.

Given the speed with which the coalition was put together, it is not surprising that relatively little thought was given to devolution issues in the coalition deal. Indeed, the surprise is that any thought was given to these at all. Few of the members of the negotiating team had much knowledge of politics in Scotland or Wales, though Oliver Letwin (for the Conservatives) had been involved in general internal debates about the Conservatives' electoral strategy and Danny Alexander of the Lib Dems sat for a Scottish seat and was reputedly close to Jim Wallace, former Deputy First Minister in Scotland. The first draft agreement (issued on 11 May) contained three devolution-related commitments: to implement the recommendations of the Calman Commission for Scotland, to hold a referendum on primary legislative powers in Wales (already requested by the National Assembly), and to establish a commission to look at the West Lothian question. By the time the full *Programme for Government* was issued a few days later, some further commitments were added to these: a review of the rate of corporation tax in Northern Ireland, a commission on finance for Wales similar to the Calman Commission in Scotland, and a review of the operation of the fossil fuel levy for Scotland (HM Government 2010).

Most of these promises were taken from the Conservative manifesto: the commitments regarding implementing the Calman recommendations, the referendum in Wales and reviews of the West Lothian question and corporation tax in Northern Ireland. Several had also appeared in the Lib Dems' manifesto – notably the commitments regarding Calman and a Welsh referendum. In each case, the Lib Dems had made stronger commitments than the Conservatives; their Scottish manifesto made it clear that Calman was a first step towards more extensive fiscal devolution for Scotland, for example. Nonetheless, the *Programme for Government* reflected the narrower commitments made by the Conservatives. The policy on the fossil fuel levy was a Lib Dem commitment, while reviewing the West Lothian question and corporation tax were Conservative policies. On that basis, the Conservatives could be regarded as 'winners' from the coalition negotiations so far as the devolution commitments were concerned.

Several of the proposed policies made little sense. The review of corporation tax in Northern Ireland was an evident concession in the manifesto to the Ulster Unionists, having become a major issue in Northern Ireland politics over the last few years. Rightly or wrongly, corporate tax competition because of lower rates in the Republic of Ireland is seen in Northern Ireland as a key factor in weak economic performance there. The case had, however, been examined for the Treasury under Labour by Sir David Varney and rejected emphatically. The problems of devolving corporation tax – both fiscal and practical – had been considered in the Scottish context by the Calman Commission and also rejected. The commitment to establish the West Lothian Commission has no practical bearing on the coalition government's ability to get its business through parliament, and could be interpreted as an attempt to kick the issue into the long grass. In any event, it involves revisiting work carried out by the Conservatives' Democracy Task Force, chaired by Ken Clarke. Whether the new review incorporates views from other political parties remains unclear.

The commitment regarding a financial commission for Wales had appeared in neither manifesto and puzzled many observers. It failed to respond to existing Welsh demands (for putting the block grant from the UK government on a needs-related basis, as recommended by the Holtham Commission's first report of June 2009); it overlooked the fact that the final report of Holtham addressing fiscal issues and borrowing powers was due within a few weeks; it disregarded the fact that the Calman Commission was set up by the Scottish Parliament not the UK government, and that Holtham (set up by the Welsh Assembly government) was its Welsh parallel; and any change was linked both to a 'yes' vote in a referendum on legislative powers (irrelevant to the issue of underfunding of public services) and to restoration of health to the UK's public finances (deferring it into the indefinite future).

The most substantial and far-reaching commitment remains the implementation of the Calman Commission's findings. Even this policy has its contradictions, however. The economic impact of the Calman recommendations has been questioned not only by the nationalist government in Scotland, but also by a number of economists and business people there. During 2009–2010, a significant swathe of Scottish opinion had moved against the Calman recommendations as not only insufficient for Scottish needs, but also economically damaging. This gains greater significance (although the UK government has not publicly acknowledged it) as any bill conferring tax powers on the Scottish Parliament would need the consent of the parliament, given the way the Sewel Convention is applied.[2] A significant groundswell of opinion in Scotland against the Calman plans could leave the UK government with a choice of either dropping its plans and reopening the issue, or imposing these on the Scottish Parliament (which inter alia would open up a range of wider constitutional issues about the extent to which devolved government was subordinate government).

Beyond this, the new government made few changes to the arrangements for dealing with devolution within government. The separate posts of Secretary of State for Scotland, Wales and Northern Ireland were maintained, though it was questionable whether they fulfilled any useful function. None of the roles now needed a full-time minister, but the new government resisted calls to merge them. Two of the ministers were Conservatives: Cheryl Gillan at the Wales Office and Owen Paterson at Northern Ireland, both taking posts which they had shadowed for some time in opposition. The Lib Dems got the Scotland Office, but the first Scottish Secretary was clearly only going to devote part of his time to the portfolio; Danny Alexander had been one of the coalition negotiators and his role was also to give 'policy support' to Nick Clegg as Deputy Prime Minister. However, following the speedy resignation of David Laws as Chief

Secretary to the Treasury, Alexander was moved to that post and replaced as Scottish Secretary by Michael Moore. In his new role, in charge of public spending and therefore the cuts programme, Alexander would nonetheless retain an interest in devolution. These arrangements left intact those that Labour had operated since 1999; the new government generally avoided making any changes to the machinery of government that were not strictly necessitated by the peculiarities of a coalition administration.

On the civil service side, the new government made slightly greater changes. These largely followed the realisation that while Nick Clegg had assumed responsibility for the coalition's programme of political and constitutional reform, the officials dealing with this area were located in the Ministry of Justice. Their transfer from this Ministry to the Cabinet Office to work more directly for Clegg included the relocation of the team dealing with devolution strategy there; but the senior post of Director General for Devolution vanished in the restructuring in the summer of 2010. Thus, despite the importance of the issues and the fact that part of the new government's problem was a fragmented and ad hoc approach to complex, inter-related policy matters, the new arrangements undermined government's capacity to look at the devolution issue as a whole.

The other side of the new government's approach was the emergence of the 'respect' agenda, as it was called. There was little new about the Conservatives, in particular, emphasising their 'respect' for the devolved governments. As noted above, this had been a consistent theme of Conservative policy under Cameron's leadership. What was notable was the action taken to give form to these words. Within a week of taking office, Cameron had made visits to all the devolved capitals and paid courtesy visits to their governments and legislatures. A plenary meeting of the Joint Ministerial Committee (with the UK Prime Minister and devolved first ministers) took place on 8 June, barely a month after the election. This helped introduce a generally helpful tone to relations at the outset. However, commentators and devolved politicians were quick to pick up on potential problems, including finance and the impact of cuts set out in the new government's emergency budget, and the effect of holding the promised referendum on the electoral system for Westminster elections on the same day as devolved elections in May 2011. Part of the problem here may have been caused by the UK government's failure to consult devolved governments and its desire to make a rapid progress on both its constitution and economic agendas, at the cost of overriding devolved concerns. Nonetheless, it had the effect of undermining the climate of 'respect' very quickly.

Conclusion

The new coalition government initially sought to sweep under the carpet the serious issues devolution raised. It secured limited electoral support in Scotland and Wales and had little political common ground with the devolved governments in those nations. At the same time, it embarked on a radical policy agenda, seeking not just to cut the UK's fiscal deficit and national debt, but to reshape the state in a very different image from Labour's social democracy. If that agenda had limited support in England, it had far less in Scotland, Wales or Northern Ireland. Indeed, the tensions that arose between UK and devolved government before 2007 mainly arose from the desire of devolved governments to pursue more traditionally social democratic policies than did Labour at the centre.

The new situation was much more complex. The SNP in Scotland aimed to advance Scottish independence and to use more day-to-day concerns to support its constitutional arguments. Plaid Cymru's ambitions were less clear and its strategy more gradualist, but a London coalition that imposed cuts would be an adversary, not an ally – and that would spill over into Welsh politics as well, affecting possible choices of coalition partners there. For Labour, the new scenario posed a huge challenge. Devolution now afforded it the chance of retaining a government platform, even when out of office in London. However, the constitutional design of devolution would not allow it to protect the welfare state in Scotland or Wales, if London wished to weaken it. Moreover, maintaining a sustained opposition to the UK government without allowing the debate to spill over into talk of 'independence' would be difficult.

At the same time, the coalition appeared to have a narrow view of politics after devolution. Its strategy included a number of specific policies addressed to particular parts of the UK and the deployment of rhetorical 'respect', but no overall vision for what the UK should be or how it should function, and no apparatus for providing any coordinated management from the centre. It is far from clear if that will prove sufficient to cope with the strains likely to arise during the term of the new parliament.

Notes

1 This section draws on a more detailed constitutional analysis of the various British parties' election manifestos, reported at: http://devolutionmatters .wordpress.com/2010/05/05/%E2%80%98devolution-literacy%E2%80%99 -and-the-2010-manifestoes (last accessed 1 October 2011).

2 The Sewel Convention is an important aspect of the devolution settlement, reflected in the Memorandum of Understanding between the UK government and the Scottish government, which establishes that 'Westminster would not

normally legislate with regard to devolved matters in Scotland without the consent of the Scottish Parliament'.

References

All Wales Convention (2009). *Report*. Cardiff: Welsh Assembly Government.

Bradbury, J. (2010). 'Wales and the 2010 General Election', in A. Geddes and J. Tonge (eds), *Britain Votes 2010*. Oxford: Oxford University Press.

Cameron, D. (2009). 'I Would Govern Scots with Respect', *Scotland on Sunday*, 8 February.

Commission on Scottish Devolution (2009). *Serving Scotland Better: Scotland and the United Kingdom in the 21st Century. Final Report – June 2009*. Edinburgh: Commission on Scottish Devolution.

Greer, S. L. (ed.) (2009). *Devolution and Citizenship Rights in the United Kingdom*. Bristol: Policy Press.

HM Government (2010). *The Coalition: Our Programme for Government*. London: The Cabinet Office.

Independent Commission on Funding and Finance for Wales (2009). *Funding Devolved Government in Wales: Barnett and Beyond, First Report to the Welsh Assembly Government*. Cardiff: Welsh Assembly Government.

Independent Commission on Funding and Finance for Wales (2010). *Final Report: Fairness and Accountability: A New Funding Settlement for Wales*. Cardiff: Welsh Assembly Government.

Mitchell, J. (2007). 'The United Kingdom as a State of Unions: Unity of Government, Equality of Political Rights and Diversity of Institutions', in A. Trench (ed.), *Devolution and Power in the United Kingdom*. Manchester: Manchester University Press, pp. 24–47.

Mitchell, J. and A. van der Zwet (2010). '"A Catenaccio Game": The 2010 Election in Scotland', in A. Geddes and J. Tonge (eds), *Britain Votes 2010*. Oxford: Oxford University Press.

Scottish Government (2009). *A National Conversation – Your Nation, Your Voice*. Edinburgh: Scottish Government.

Secretary of State for Scotland (2009). *White Paper. Scotland's Future in the United Kingdom*. www.scotlandoffice.gov.uk/scotlandoffice/files /Scotland's%20Future%20in%20the%20United%20Kingdom.pdf (last accessed 1 October 2011).

Steel Commission (2006). *Moving to Federalism – A New Settlement for Scotland*. Edinburgh: Scottish Liberal Democrats.

Trench, A. (2005). 'Whitehall and the Process of Legislation after Devolution', in R. Hazell and R. Rawlings (eds), *Devolution, Law-making and the Constitution*. Exeter: Imprint Academic, pp. 165–192.

Trench, A. (2007). 'Washing Dirty Linen in Private: The Processes of Intergovernmental Relations and the Resolution of Disputes', in A. Trench (ed.), *Devolution and Power in the United Kingdom*. Manchester: Manchester University Press, pp. 160–197.

Trench, A. (2009). 'The Calman Commission and Scotland's Disjointed Constitutional Debates', *Public Law*, October: 686–696.

Wyn Jones, R. and R. Scully (2006). 'Devolution and Electoral Politics in Scotland and Wales', *Publius: The Journal of Federalism*, 36 (1): 115–134.

10

Between Europe and America: the coalition and Britain's changing international role

Gianfranco Baldini

Introduction

In 1946, Winston Churchill described the complex and multiform British identity and international role by using the metaphor of the three circles: the British Empire, the Anglo-Saxon sphere and Europe. Although the Empire has gone, the tension between Britain's relationship with the English-speaking world and its involvement in the process of European integration has become the defining feature of British foreign policy. This chapter assesses Britain's changing international role, by looking at the first steps undertaken by the Cameron government in the international arena. I will argue that the coalition government has been generally successful – in its first few months in office – in drawing a delicate balance between the traditionally very different approaches displayed by the two parties on European and international issues. However, this has implied many compromises, especially in Europe, and policy has been affected by the serious cuts in the resources available for foreign and defence policy, as a result of the deficit reduction strategy. The chapter starts with a short description of the peculiar international profile that the coalition has inherited from previous governments, and then assesses the coalition's approach to international affairs in its first few months of office.

Legacies of empire: Britain as a bridge over the Atlantic

Britain's place in the world today remains in part defined by its past as the centre of one of the biggest empires in history, which, by the end of the nineteenth century, dominated a vast territory well beyond the confines of

Europe (Gamble 2003). Over the last few decades Britain has struggled to redefine its role in the international arena, in the context of a relative economic and military decline. In 1962, Secretary of State Dean Acheson famously declared that 'Great Britain ha[d] lost an Empire and ha[d] not yet found a role'. Since the end of the Second World War Britain has prided itself – given its strong political links and the many cultural and economic similarities in the Anglo-Saxon sphere – on enjoying a 'special relationship' with the United States. Although this delayed its membership of the European Economic Community, Britain has never ceased to aspire to a key role as a 'bridge' between Europe and America. Twenty years after Churchill identified the three arenas defining British foreign policy, one US observer noted that 'Britain, by not choosing one path or another, has been gradually forced to let down all three' (Calleo 1968, quoted in Hood 2008: 186). Despite Margaret Thatcher's attempts to revive memories of Britain's former imperial status with the Falklands war, Britain's overall importance as a global power had already declined significantly by the 1980s. By the end of the Cold War, Britain was clearly just one of the major European powers, and the tension between Atlanticism and Europeanism has meant that successive British governments have been viewed with suspicion by Brussels, especially once Tony Blair made clear that he was perfectly comfortable with the neo-liberal and pro-American policies bequeathed by Thatcherism.

New Labour's foreign policy in the 1997–2005 period was marked by a distinctive commitment to four main principles: multilateralism, Atlanticism, neo-liberalism and moralism (Williams 2005). These principles did not follow any particular hierarchical order, and one took precedence over the others according to the issues involved in any specific policy decision. Britain's controversial participation in the Iraq war was by many standards a logical consequence of the principles expressed by Blair as early as 1999 in his famous Chicago speech, when he set the stage for an active commitment to intervene against dictatorships and use military action on humanitarian grounds. But Blair was also committed to placing Britain 'at the heart of Europe'. The echoes of the Iraq conflict meant that New Labour obtained only a narrow victory in the 2005 election, when the party struggled to contain the debate about a war that had divided European powers to an unprecedented degree. Iraq brought the UK's multilateralism and European commitments on the one hand, and its loyalty to the United States on the other, into head-on collision. The rest of this chapter assesses the tension between these relationships in recent British history, and discusses how the new coalition government has sought to manage them.

Britain: the awkward partner in Europe

It has been half a century since French President Charles De Gaulle first vetoed Britain's accession to the EEC, delaying British entry for a decade. Ever since, Britain has been regarded as a 'reluctant' or 'awkward' partner in Europe (George 1998), rarely showing any enthusiasm for the European project. Both the Labour and Conservative parties have always contained Eurosceptical elements within their ranks. Now both parties display more cohesive positions: on the one side the Tories' 'soft Euroscepticism' with occasional concessions to tough talk (Baker *et al.* 2008); on the other Labour's half-hearted Europeanism. Among the main political forces, only the Liberal Democrats are traditionally pro-European, while the fourth most voted party in the 2010 elections, the United Kingdom Independence Party (UKIP), bases its political identity on hostility towards the EU.

Given the scope of this chapter, it is not possible to analyse in detail the ways in which Britain's suspicion of Europe has influenced the behaviour of the most recent British governments. However, this instinctive Euroscepticism is a key structural feature of British foreign policy. Charles Grant (2008) explained the peculiarities of British Euroscepticism in terms of four central factors: history, geography, economy and the press. Great Britain, a multinational state (see Alan Trench's chapter in this volume), was born out of several wars against France (Colley 1992), the country's nearest neighbour and a key initiator of the European project. Britain's historic linguistic and cultural ties to the rest of the English-speaking world, and particularly the 'special relationship' with the US, make the Atlantic Ocean seem at times narrower than the English Channel (Garton Ash 2006). But the reality of European economic development has modified Britain's global economic reach; in 1960 only 23 per cent of British exports went to Europe, but this figure had tripled by 2005 (Hay 2009: 864). The competing influences of geography, history and economics have created tensions in Britain's geopolitical identity. Grant's fourth factor, the press, is well known: barely any comment can be found in the mainstream press that acknowledges the successes of integration.[1]

A further factor that can help explain Britain's traditional detachment from the EU is the nature of the UK's political system. The Westminster model, based on direct confrontation between government and opposition, is diametrically opposed to the EU's consensual institutional arrangements, and despite many transformations over the past fifteen years (such as the UK's adoption of an independent central bank, devolution and the partial reform of the House of Lords) the broad patterns of British politics remain very different (Flinders 2010; Lijphart 1999). The new coalition government, of course, represents a dramatic, though not necessarily durable, transformation of this model. It also brings together in the same administration two parties that over the past few years, and even as recently as during the 2010 electoral campaign, have taken the most radically different stances on the European issue.

Party positions on the EU today must be understood from a historical perspective. In 1975, when Labour Prime Minister Harold Wilson called a referendum, anxious to keep his party together and his country in the EEC (Gowland and Turner 2000), only the Liberals unambiguously supported continued membership. The other main parties were divided, with significant factions of both Labour (led by Tony Benn) and the Conservatives (led by Enoch Powell) campaigning against it. By the early 1980s, patterns were shifting. In 1983, the year both Blair and Brown were first elected to parliament, the Labour Party manifesto advocated Britain's exit from the EEC. Thatcher, while initially taking a relatively pragmatic line on Europe, aggressively argued for a large reduction in Britain's contribution to the European Community budget, famously demanding 'I want my money back!' at the Fontainebleu summit in 1984. However, Thatcher also embraced the European project to the extent that it fitted her own neo-liberal agenda, supporting her former minister Arthur Cockfield in his decisive contribution to the 1986 Single European Act (SEA) (Buller 2009: 556). But the push for greater integration under the Delors Commission provoked a hostile reaction, with the British Prime Minister complaining: 'we have not successfully rolled back the frontiers of the state in Britain, only to see them re-imposed at a European level with a European super-state exercising a new dominance from Brussels'. Under John Major, just months after winning the 1992 election, the pound was forced out of the European Exchange Rate Mechanism and the Conservative Party became irrevocably split over Europe (Norton 1998), to the extent that the fractious internal politics generated by the issue contributed to their crushing electoral defeat in 1997, after four terms of office.

Depoliticising Europe

Given this background and the magnitude of his electoral success, it could be argued that Blair wasted an important opportunity to reconcile the country with Europe (Smith 2005). Certainly, the strongly pro-European position adopted in the 1997 Labour manifesto, which advocated 'UK leadership in Europe' translated into limited, though significant, real change. The two most important measures were the adoption of the European Social Charter and the launch of common foreign and security policies, marked by a symbolic meeting between Blair and Jacques Chirac in the Breton town of Saint-Malo in 1998. However, many critics accused Blair of not doing enough to promote pro-European sentiment after the positive start to his premiership. There is some evidence to support this view: in 1998 fully 46 per cent of British voters favoured adopting the single currency (Riddell 2005: 379), a percentage that progressively declined to less than half that by 2010.

The Labour government's position on the Euro was ambiguous. Labour was in favour of Euro entry in principle, but the ultimate decision to join the Euro would require five strict criteria of economic sustainability to be met (which according to some were impossible to assess: Rollo 2002). This was the first key element in the strategy of depoliticisation of Europe that would be common to both Labour leaders (Buller 2009): by transforming the decision of Euro entry into a technocratic judgement on purely economic criteria, the government was able to avoid a debate on the broader political question of Britain's role in the EU. It also gave the government the option of postponing the decision indefinitely, if public opinion could not be brought around. By indulging the mood of an increasingly Eurosceptic electorate, Blair effectively abdicated the leadership role in Europe promised in the Labour manifesto.

By the time of Brown's arrival at Number 10, any ambition to join the Euro had been abandoned and the government's approach to Europe became entirely defensive. Labour's 2005 electoral manifesto had promised a referendum on the constitutional treaty signed in Rome in 2004. But just a few weeks after Labour had won a third term in government the French and Dutch referenda rejected the Treaty, triggering a period of institutional crisis in the European Union. When Brown took office in 2007, the constitutional treaty was under revision. The new version recovered most of the earlier treaty, but gave up on the ambition of having constitutional status and dropped the most controversial symbolic elements, such as the hymn and the flag. The Lisbon Treaty was signed at the end of the year, with Brown seeking to assuage hostility at home by ostentatiously turning up late. Even so, he faced criticism from the Conservatives and the Eurosceptic press for his decision to renege on the referendum on the grounds that the treaty was not a European constitution, yet another attempt to depoliticise a delicate situation and sideline the European issue. Opinion surveys at the time confirmed the British electorate's hostility towards the Lisbon Treaty and support for a referendum.

Labour's strategy in both of the key European issues facing them was to transform political decisions into technical ones in an attempt to protect the government from political fallout. This was successful to some degree, in that the relevance of the European issue for voter behaviour declined during Labour's period in office: in early 1997, around 30 per cent of voters considered Europe an important issue; in the two years prior to the 2010 elections, this figure had dropped to only 5 per cent.[2] The Conservatives initially failed to adapt to this trend, and William Hague, the first in a succession of electorally unsuccessful Tory leaders, made the mistake of basing his ill-fated 2001 campaign on Euroscepticism (Baker *et al.* 2008). David Cameron learnt this lesson and avoided drawing too much attention to what was for the Conservatives a divisive issue.

The coalition and Europe: Cameron's Europragmatism

The 2009 European elections were an important test for Cameron's leadership credentials and had repercussions for the 2010 general election and for the government that emerged from it. Although the Conservatives came out winners in the European Parliament election, beating Labour by a comfortable 12 per cent, the big winner in the poll was the UK Independence Party (UKIP), which won 16.5 per cent of the vote, beating Labour into a humiliating third place. The UKIP's strong electoral performance in European elections, although not matched in parliamentary elections (where it is hampered by the plurality electoral system), posed a difficult dilemma for the Conservatives, whose soft Euroscepticism (Baker *et al.* 2008) was not enough for many hardliner voters.

The European elections also produced perhaps the most controversial move in Cameron's career as leader of the opposition: the decision to remove the Conservative MEPs from the mainstream centre-right grouping in the European Parliament, the European People's Party (EPP). As well as cutting the party off from its obvious partners in Europe, it also left them with little choice but to form a new and heterogeneous parliamentary group with a handful of Eastern European Eurosceptic parties, some of which had dubious reputations. This won Cameron harsh criticism not only within the UK but also from the leaders of the main European member states, first and foremost Nicolas Sarkozy and Angela Merkel. Why did Cameron choose to exit the EPP? It must be emphasised that the union between the Tories and the EPP was always 'a loveless marriage' (Lynch and Whitaker 2008). The Conservatives' positions are historically quite different from other European centre-right parties, as can be observed in voting data from the European Parliament. In the past legislature, which ended in 2009, the Tories held the record of dissenting votes from other members of their group: 25 per cent, compared with 8 per cent for Labour, affiliated with the Party of European Socialists (PES). The Conservative parliamentary party in Westminster, a more important support base for the party leader, is considerably more Eurosceptic than the party's MEPs in Strasbourg. When Cameron first floated the idea, during his campaign for the party leadership in 2005, only a minority of MEPs (seven out of twenty-seven) supported him (in a letter to the *Daily Telegraph*), with thirteen opposed (Lynch 2009: 207). Among Westminster MPs, the proposed 'divorce' had much more support.[3]

The European Conservatives and Reformists, the new parliamentary group created by Cameron, quickly attracted criticism. Much of this criticism focused on the questionable past of the two future main partners of the Tories, the Polish Order and Justice and the Czech Civic Platform.[4] However, the group showed quite high voting cohesion (0.86, on a scale in which 1.00 indicates unanimity, up to July 2010[5]), although the group's MEPs also have the lowest attendance rates at plenary assemblies (83.3 per cent) against an average of above 88 per cent. The divorce from the EPP was intended to bring the increasingly strong Eurosceptic wing of the party over to Cameron's side. Some observers have argued that the move was also intended to provide him with political cover to adopt 'softer' policies on tax and welfare.[6]

Once in office, Cameron embraced a new strategy based on compromise and pragmatism. But even before the election, a first step in this direction was taken with the abandonment of the promised referendum on the Lisbon Treaty, announced the day after the signature of Czech president Vaclav Klaus concluded the ratification of the Treaty by all the member states. In a speech on 4 November 2009, Cameron acknowledged the unavoidability of the institutional process, but also reiterated some key Conservative policies: opposition to the Euro, hostility towards any further integration, the aim to claw back some powers, and greater scrutiny of the process of legislative conversion of EU laws. The slogan Cameron offered on European issues was 'we will not let the matter rest'. This was not enough for many on the Eurosceptic fringes of the party, who were deeply unhappy about dropping the referendum commitment: the day after his speech the *Daily Mail* published a letter of protest signed by David Davis, his former rival for the party leadership (Davis 2009).

How did the parties handle the European issue during the 2010 elections? The party manifestos make interesting reading in the light of what happened after the vote. Unsurprisingly, the Labour manifesto offered continuity with the positions of the incumbent government. But the two future coalition partners published manifestos that adopted diametrically opposite approaches, most obviously with regard to the Euro, which the Conservatives unambiguously opposed and the Liberal Democrats equally fervently supported (although Nick Clegg admitted during the campaign that Euro membership would have damaged Britain in the context of the economic crisis). The two parties differed on other aspects of European policy too, with the Conservatives promising to reclaim some powers by opting out of some social and defence policies and the Lib Dems supporting further integration on precisely these policy areas, as well as others.

If we compare these proposals with the coalition agreement reached between the two parties after the 2010 vote, the Tories seem to have prevailed. Conservative positions won out over the Euro (and on any preparatory policy for its introduction), over transfers of sovereignty, over referenda on future treaties and over the defence of national interests in negotiations for the European budget (as well as the proposal to end the wasteful division of European Parliament activities between Strasbourg and Brussels). However, the Lib Dems were able to water down the proposed UK Sovereignty Act, which the Conservatives hoped would be an important symbolic gesture halting further integration. Tangible agreement already existed on two crucial and interconnected issues: the reform of the Common Agricultural Policy and the reform of the community budget. The first signs from the new government showed a (unavoidable) moderation of policies distant from the aggressive tones the Conservatives adopted from the opposition benches. But it was also clear that the Tories would not adopt Clegg's most pro-European positions, some of which, especially the Euro, were already becoming increasingly unpopular even among the Lib Dems.

Evidence of Cameron's newfound pragmatism came with his debut in Brussels on 17 June 2010. The appointment of David Lidington (one-time advisor of former Foreign Secretary Douglas Hurd and a rare pro-European Tory) as Europe Minister in place of the shadow minister, the Eurosceptic Mark Francois, sent an early signal that moderation and pragmatism would be the order of the day. Cameron's conciliatory approach was made possible by three key factors.

First, even before the economic crisis, Europe had reached an institutional impasse, meaning that the British would not have to face any significant advances in the integration process. In 2010 only Germany was pushing for new rules and greater economic and financial coordination, largely because of its own problems managing domestic opposition to the Greek bailout. It was highly unlikely that problems of an institutional nature would re-emerge in the short term, as member states were largely relieved to have completed the tortuous ratification process of the Lisbon Treaty and keen to avoid further political challenges. Europe in 2010 could not have been further away from the federal design feared by the British Conservatives. Second, the mediating role played by the Lib Dems, who had to step back from their traditional Euro-enthusiasm after the development of the Euro crisis, proved quite useful to Cameron, by offering him a pretext for marginalising the most Eurosceptical tendencies within his party and softening the traditional mechanisms of accountability. Finally the crisis of the financial sector (see Lucia Quaglia's chapter in this volume) facilitates Cameron's task in a sector traditionally considered as 'sacred' to British Conservatives. The discrediting of finance means that the new government can have more freedom in passing European measures such as the tax on the banking sector or the regulation of hedge funds, to which a more Eurosceptical executive would have been unremittingly hostile. In short, political conditions favoured Cameron's charm offensive in the initial phase of the coalition government (Grant 2010).

For some observers, Cameron's own personal abilities have also facilitated good relations with the main world leaders (Anderson 2010). The Prime Minister displayed his diplomatic skills on his first trips to continental Europe, smoothing relations with Sarkozy and partly with Merkel, notwithstanding the significant political differences between them. In the context of a Europe where the very survival of the Euro has been questioned and where divergences between France and Germany have dominated in recent years, the Conservative Prime Minister has been able to sideline the issue of the EPP exit.

Between Washington and Paris

Since 1997, Britain has been one of the west's most active military powers. In Iraq and Afghanistan, it has been Washington's closest ally, after being at the forefront in the toppling of Slobodan Milošević in Serbia. However, foreign and defence policies were not relevant issues during the 2010 electoral campaign (Whitman 2010). All the main parties agreed that the current level of defence expenditure could not be sustained for the future, but no party manifesto contained specific commitments as to where cuts should be made. The independent nuclear deterrent – and more specifically the issue of the renewal of the Trident submarines – did spark a lively dispute during the second TV debate between the three leaders, with Cameron and Brown criticising Clegg for his alleged support for nuclear disarmament (although he was simply proposing to postpone the renewal of Trident). But overall foreign policy was far from the heart of the election campaign.

As US President Barack Obama made clear several times in his speeches (as well as in meetings held with British political leaders of all the main parties), the special relationship with Britain only made sense to the extent that Britain did not isolate itself from its European neighbours. If Britain wants to count, it must contribute to the development of stronger community institutions, initiating debate on how to resolve the many crises around the world, reducing vetoing powers in European institutions. In short: it must play the Europe card. This view is consistent with an overall pattern of a changing transatlantic scenario, which contains also some

Table 10.1 Party positions on some European issues in 2010

Policy Area	Issue	Labour	Tories	Lib Dems	Coalition agreement: which party wins
Constitutions	**Future referenda on EU**	Yes on Euro	Yes, on future power transfers	Yes on EU membership and Euro (in favour)	Conservatives, but they renounced a UK Sovereignty Bill
Economy	**Adoption of the Euro**	Unclear position	Never	Yes	Conservatives
	Reform on communitarian budget	Vague promises of CAP reform, saving the rebate for the UK	Vague promises of CAP reform, saving the rebate for the UK	Vague reform promises, unclear positions on CAP and rebate for the UK	Not considered (n.a.)
	European supervision of financial systems	In favour with reservations	Against, if it entails transferring new powers	In favour with reservations	Not considered (n.a.)
Foreign Policy and Defence	**Political cooperation on defence**	In favour of greater cooperation	Against a European Defence coordination system	In favour of a European defence coordination system	Not considered (n.a.)
	Common foreign policy	Separation of the European diplomatic service from national policy issues	Separation of the European diplomatic service from national policy issues	Separation of the European diplomatic service from national policy issues	No major differences (n.a.)

		Support for the EU on current targets	Support for the EU on current targets	Support for the EU on more ambitious targets	
Environment	**Environmental policies**	Status quo		Status quo	Not considered (n.a.)
Social Policies	**Employment policies**		Opt out for most penalised economic sectors		Not considered (n.a.), Lib Dems in favour of softening the Tory objective to opt out of the Social Charter
Justice, human rights and immigration	**Establishing a European Public Prosecutor**	Against	Against	Not just one position	Conservatives
	Immigration and right to asylum	Partially in favour of greater integration	Against greater integration	Greater integration, particularly on asylum policies	Not considered (n.a.)
	Coordination of police forces and fighting crime	Status quo	No to new powers, opt out	Greater integration	Case by case, mix
	Immigration cap	Quota system on the Australian model	Yes	No	Conservatives

Source: Open Europe (2010), revised by author

paradoxical elements. Indeed, while Obama was greeted by Europe as a multilateralist, and hence a natural European ally, it soon became apparent that the US President was not comfortable with the standard European habits of having three or four leaders at the table speaking in behalf of the EU, as one could easily see in the Prague meeting in spring 2009.[7] The Obama administration itself is constrained in its international commitments, in part by the budgetary constraints exacerbated by the financial crisis (Jones 2011; Mandelbaum 2010), and therefore aspires for Europe to learn to speak with one voice in order to relieve the strain on the US. However, this is a distant ambition and for the moment Europe above all means NATO, then the most prominent nation states, with the EU as a whole occupying a marginal position, as far as the US is concerned.

The constraints facing British foreign policy require the coalition government to find a delicate balance not only between an increasingly Eurosceptic Conservative Party and a traditionally Europhile junior partner in the coalition, but especially between the aspirations of a country that still tries to 'punch above its weight' in the context of increasing financial constraints and a changing international scenario. And yet, when Foreign Minister William Hague set out the new foreign policy agenda on 1 July 2010, many thorny questions were avoided, and his speech was full of 'banal platitudes', including a vision of a 'distinctive British foreign policy' or a 'Britain active in Europe and around the world' (Williams 2011: 1). Equally vague and inconsistent was the simultaneous acknowledgement of the value of multilateralism together with the stress on an increasingly more 'bilateral world', without specifying what this could actually mean. The speech was perhaps most relevant for its omissions: no mention was made either of economic liberalism as a preferred approach to foreign economic policy, or of austerity (Williams 2011: 2), even though financial constraints were decisive in the first important international agreement reached by the coalition in its first six months in office: the Defence Co-operation Treaty, signed with France in November 2010, just days after the publication of the long-awaited British Strategic Defence and Security Review (SDSR).

Hague's stress on the importance of pursuing Britain's 'self-interest' goes to the heart of the question. For instance, one can see considerable continuity between the Brown and Cameron governments in their approach towards the Common Foreign and Security Policy (CFSP). Despite the arrival of a British politician – the Labour Baroness Catherine Ashton – at the helm of the new post of High Representative for Foreign Affairs and Security Policy created by the Lisbon Treaty, both main British parties remain highly sceptical about the EU's aspiration of a more cohesive European foreign policy. Of course there are many reasons for this – from the threat to national sovereignty to Atlanticism, to memories of Empire –

that contribute to explaining this scepticism. However, one should not forget that 'arguably the most important reason for Labour's shift [towards a more European friendly attitude] was the belief in Whitehall that developing a military capacity for the EU would actually help strengthen NATO' (Williams 2005: 61).

In opposition many Conservative MPs – including current Defence Minister Liam Fox – opposed Britain's participation in the Common Security and Defence Policy and, most recently, the Permanent Structured Cooperation (PSC), introduced by the Lisbon Treaty. The reason is simple: the latter is perceived as a means to revive the old 'federalist' dream of achieving a European army, something that threatens the core of the traditional principles of British sovereignty and is seen with particular hostility by the Conservative Party. Britain had cooperated with France over the formation of the European Defence Agency (EDA) in 2004 (O'Donnell 2011). However, the Brown government had resisted French attempts – during its EU presidency in the first semester of 2008 – to strengthen British involvement in CSDP in response to French reintegration into NATO's command structure (Bickerton 2010), and Fox has clearly moved along the same lines in asking for cuts in spending in the EDA (Hennessy 2010).The Franco-British agreement came just two weeks after the announcement of the defence cuts of about 8 per cent in real terms over the next four years: the biggest cuts since the end of the Cold War, but nonetheless less severe than those applied to other ministerial departments. Although the cuts were significant, they were a long way from undermining Britain's ability to meet its NATO commitments: UK defence spending, at about 2.3 per cent of national gross domestic product, remains the highest of any European Union nation. The decision to delay renewing Trident was taken in the context of cuts that will substantially reduce British military capabilities in the near future: British troops in Afghanistan will soon be reduced from 9,500 to 7,000, the navy and the air force will also see manpower reductions of about 5,000 each, while 25,000 will be cut from the Ministry of Defence's civilian payroll.

'No strategic shrinkage' declared Cameron when presenting further important cuts in the carrier, destroyer and frigate fleets. Yet doubts remain over Britain's ability to reconcile its new bilateral approach with the changing international context. The defence alliance with France is consistent with a pattern that, leaving aside the Iraq case, has seen cooperation between the two countries in most important international issues in the last quarter of a century. However, according to one qualified observer, by playing down CSDP, and 'by leaving EU efforts in a state of "malign neglect" and considering only some European countries as worthy partners for cooperation, the UK is harming its own interests' (O'Donnell 2011:

429). This demilitarisation of Europe has been vocally condemned by both the US administration and NATO's General Secretary Anders Fogh Rasmussen (O'Donnell 2011: 430). More generally, one can question the extent to which Britain can develop a sustained and coherent defence strategy in the near future under the current bilateral approach and with diminishing resources. As other experts have pointed out, there are several weaknesses and inconsistencies in the SDSR, which might seriously affect, in the near future, the ability of the UK to pursue a coherent national strategy (Cornish and Dorman 2011).

British foreign and defence policy in the first six months of life of the coalition government has been affected by important economic constraints and has brought about a new set of arrangements and agreements with Washington and Paris. This does not mean that a new 'triangular' transatlantic scenario will be established any time soon. Rather, it means that given the constraints that the US are also facing in their hegemonic role in international relations, and the more pro-American attitude demonstrated by the French return to the NATO integrated military command, Britain can pursue new opportunities of ad hoc alliances without necessarily following – for better or worse – the uncertain path of a pan-European defence alliance.

Conclusion

Cameron's coalition government came to office in a period dominated by the global economic crisis and, in Europe, the crisis of the Eurozone. The coalition government has inherited from New Labour a foreign policy that has somehow facilitated Cameron's task in keeping Clegg's more Europhile and multilateralist aspirations at bay. The Conservative leader has adopted a pragmatic approach, which has been successful in drawing a delicate balance between an increasingly Eurosceptic party and the international pressures – not least from Washington – to cultivate close relations with other European partners, especially in foreign and defence policy.

Traditionally, within the context of a regular Labour-Conservative alternation in government from which the Lib Dems had been excluded, the European issue came and went: periods of intense political confrontation over Europe alternated with periods of calm, when the issue disappeared from the front pages. Thus in the four decades since the UK joined the EEC the country's attitude towards Europe has been inconsistent. Blair eventually grew tired of the EU, Thatcher was initially enthusiastic but ended the decade as a Eurosceptic, Major had to switch from one position to another, and Labour Prime Ministers Wilson and Callaghan also had ambiguous attitudes towards Europe (Richards 2009).

Cameron has enjoyed more luck than his predecessors. The kind of push towards 'ever closer union' that could irritate the Eurosceptic fringes and encourage defections (of votes and MEPs) towards UKIP was largely absent in the early life of the coalition. Furthermore, the alliance with Clegg allowed the Conservative leader to embrace the pragmatism associated with the practice of coalition, while downplaying central Eurosceptic themes of the Tory campaign, such as the opt-outs on justice or the Social Charter. At the same time Cameron could claim, without fear of destabilising the coalition, that he had kept two crucial campaign promises: to stay out of the Euro and to hold a referendum on future European treaties. However, the volatility of the European issue suggests prudence in judging the ability of the new British Prime Minister to maintain effective leadership over European issues. Cameron would be advised to recall the remarks made by his coalition partner Clegg years ago: 'there is something in the political gene pool of British political leaders that makes them behave like this. By turns enthusiastic and cautious, defensive and arrogant, determined and aimless. In the end, they are all overwhelmed by events' (cited in Baker 2005: 34).

The Cameron government has had to make heavy cuts to public spending, which have also affected the resources available for foreign policy, as the Anglo-French defence agreement signed in November 2010 demonstrated. Great Britain and France are the two major European military powers, but today they are no longer able to maintain the defence expenditure characteristic of that status. The agreement is a pragmatic one, which has obliged Cameron to address Eurosceptic fears of a new European army, and Sarkozy himself has had to provide reassurances on French sovereignty. Cameron's Conservatives remain suspicious of the EU and wary of attempts to forge a more cohesive European foreign and defence policy: for all their newfound open-mindedness, they are still the party of the monarchy, the armed forces and the flag. They supported Blair's controversial decision over Iraq, while the Liberals, the heirs to pacifist internationalism, fiercely opposed it. However, the coalition government has every chance of balancing these opposing traditions, thanks to the common realisation that Britain can no longer aspire to a leading international role.

Notes

1 A clear example of this is the *Daily Telegraph* headline, 'God Is Opposed to Britain Joining EU's Single Currency' (cited in Carey and Burton 2004: 623).
2 Data from McKay (2006), and for 2008–2009 from www.mori.com.
3 A survey conducted in July 2009 on 144 Conservative MPs (out of a total of

209) found that on the relationship with the EU 47 per cent would like to reclaim some powers from Brussels; 38 per cent would like a renegotiation of the UK–EU relationship, and 5 per cent would like to leave the EU all together, with only 10 per cent stating to be satisfied with the current relationship (cited in Grant 2010: 2).

4 See www.votewatch.eu.

5 In comparison, the Green Party holds the cohesion record with 0.97, closely followed by the Socialists and Democrats (the new name of the PES) with 0.94 and by the EPP with 0.93. All data are taken from www.votewatch.eu and updated to the end of the summer parliamentary session in 2010; retrieved on 26 July 2010.

6 'Cameron's Ransom', *The Economist*, 31 October 2009.

7 'Europe and America', *The Economist*, 25 November 2010.

References

Anderson, B. (2010). 'David Cameron Is Relishing Foreign Affairs, But He Should Be Wary', *Daily Telegraph*, 22 July.

Baker, D. (2005). 'Islands of the Mind: New Labour's Defensive Engagement with the European Union', *Political Quarterly*, 76 (1): 22–36.

Baker, D., A. Gamble, N. Randall and D. Seawright (2008). 'Euroscepticism in the British Party System: "A Source of Fascination, Perplexity and Sometimes Frustration"', in P. Taggart and A. Szczerbiak (eds), *Opposing Europe? The Comparative Party Politics of Euroscepticism: Volume 1: Case Studies and Country Surveys*. Oxford: Oxford University Press, pp. 93–116.

Bickerton, C. (2010). 'Oh Bugger, They're in the Tent: British Responses to French Reintegration into NATO', *European Security*, 19 (1): 113–122.

Buller, J. (2009). 'The European Union', in M. Flinders, A. Gamble, C. Hay, M. Kenny (eds.), *The Oxford Handbook of British Politics*. Oxford: Oxford University Press, pp. 553–570.

Calleo, D. (1968). *Britain's Future*. London: Holder and Stoughton.

Carey, S. and J. Burton (2004). 'The Influence of the Press in Shaping Public Opinion Towards the European Union in Britain', *Political Studies*, 52 (3): 623–640.

Colley, L. (1992). *Britons. Forging the Nation, 1707–1837*. New Haven: Yale University Press.

Cornish, P. and A. Dorman (2011). 'Dr Fox and the Philosopher's Stone: The Alchemy of National Defence in the Age of Austerity', *International Affairs*, 87 (2): 335–353.

Davis, D. (2009). 'A Referendum Mr Cameron COULD Give the People', *Daily Mail*, 5 November.

Flinders, M. (2010). *Democratic Drift. Majoritarian Modification and Democratic Anomie in the United Kingdom*. Oxford: Oxford University Press.

Gamble, A. (2003). *Between Europe and America. The Future of British Politics*. Basingstoke: Palgrave.

Garton Ash, T. (2006). 'Why Is Britain in Europe?', *20th Century British History*, 17 (4): 451–463.

George, S. (1998). *An Awkward Partner: Britain in the European Community*. Oxford: Oxford University Press.

Gowland, D. and A. Turner (2000). *Reluctant Europeans: Britain and European Integration, 1945–96*. Harlow: Longman.

Grant, C. (2008). 'Why Is Britain Eurosceptic?'. London: Centre for European Reform.

Grant, C. (2010). 'Cameron's Europe. Can the Conservatives Achieve their EU Objectives?'. London: Centre for European Reform.

Hay, C. (2009). 'Globalization', in M. Flinders, A. Gamble, C. Hay, M. Kenny (eds), *The Oxford Handbook of British Politics*. Oxford: Oxford University Press, pp. 855–878.

Hennessy, P. (2010). 'Britain "To Veto European Defence Agency Budget Increase"', *Daily Telegraph*, 28 November.

Hood, F. (2008). 'Atlantic Dreams and European Realities: British Foreign Policy after Iraq', *Journal of European Integration*, 30 (1): 183–197.

Jones, E. (2011). 'European Security, Transatlantic Relations, and the Challenge to US Global Leadership', in R. Alcaro and E. Jones (eds), *European Security and the Future of Transatlantic Relations*. Rome: Iai Research Paper.

Lijphart, A. (1999). *Patterns of Democracy*. New Haven: Yale University Press.

Lynch, P. (2009). 'The Conservatives and the Europe: The Lull Before the Storm', in S. Lee and M. Beech, *The Conservatives Under David Cameron: Built to Last?* Basingstoke: Palgrave, pp. 187–207.

Lynch, P. and R. Whitaker (2008). 'A Loveless Marriage: The Conservatives and the European People's Party', *Parliamentary Affairs*, 61 (1): 31–51.

Mandelbaum, M. (2010). *The Frugal Superpower: America's Global Leadership in a Cash-Strapped Era*. New York: Public Affairs.

McKay, D. (2006). 'The Reluctant European: Europe as an Issue in British politics', in J. Bartle and A. King (eds), *Britain at the Polls 2005*. Washington, DC: CQ Press, pp. 78–96.

Norton, P. (1998). 'The Conservative Party. In Office But Not in Power', in A. King (ed.), *New Labour Triumphs: Britain at the Polls*. New Jersey: Chatham House, pp. 75–112.

O'Donnell, C. M. (2011). 'Britain's Coalition Government and EU Defence

Cooperation: Undermining British Interests', *International Affairs*, 87 (2): 419–433.

Richards, S. (2009). 'Blair Is the Only Man for this Job', *The Independent*, 30 October.

Riddell, P. (2005). *The Unfulfilled Prime Minister*. London: Politico's.

Rollo, J. (2002). 'In or Out: The Choice for Britain', *Journal of Public Policy*, 22 (2): 217–229.

Smith, J. (2005). 'A Missed Opportunity? New Labour's European Policy 1997–2005', *International Affairs*, 81 (4): 703–721.

Whitman, R. (2010). 'The Calm after the Storm? Foreign and Security Policy from Blair to Brown', *Parliamentary Affairs*, 63 (4): 834–848.

Williams, P. (2005). *British Foreign Policy under New Labour, 1997–2005*. Basingstoke: Palgrave Macmillan.

Williams, P. (2011). 'Hague's Blurred Vision of British Foreign Policy', *International Studies Today*, 1 (1): 1–2.

11

Conclusion: Cameron and Clegg's great experiment

Jonathan Hopkin

Introduction

The 2010 general election may or may not prove a turning point in recent British political history, but it certainly marked a decisive break with the past. After a string of predictable election outcomes since the early 1990s, the result of the 2010 poll remained unclear until the following morning, and for only the second time since the Second World War no party won an outright majority in the House of Commons. The usual choreography of a British election was turned upside down. The standard routine has the incoming Prime Minister heading for Buckingham Palace to meet the Queen just a few hours after the polling stations close, and the incumbent departing Number 10 Downing Street shortly after. In 2010, Gordon Brown remained – uncomfortably – ensconced in the Prime Minister's official residence for several days as party leaders negotiated.

The formation of a Conservative-Liberal Democrat coalition government marked another departure from post-war tradition. The hung parliament of 1974 had resulted in a second election, as Harold Wilson's Labour Party sought a parliamentary majority. In 2010 this option appeared untenable given the financial pressures facing the British state and the need to secure a stable government quickly. Perhaps surprisingly, the Conservatives opted for a formal coalition rather than seeking to form a minority government with outside support. Even more surprisingly, the coalition quickly moved to develop an unexpectedly radical joint programme to reshape the welfare state. Meanwhile, Labour was electing a successor to Gordon Brown, and the victory of Ed Miliband over his brother David in the leadership election seemed to suggest an abandonment of the centrist strategy that had characterised 'New Labour' ever since the early 1990s.

Where does this leave British politics? This concluding chapter will try to resist the temptation to make implicit predictions by gauging the historical importance of the 2010 election. However it will try to assess the possibilities of fundamental change in the British political system raised by this election, and the following pages will discuss developments in two broad areas: the set of political arrangements commonly described as the 'Westminster model' and the pattern of party competition that underpins them; and the British political economy, and specifically the role of the public sector in a period of profound economic stress.

Constitutional change: the end of the Westminster model?

The political system of the UK has occupied a stable place in the political science textbooks for quite some time as the most familiar exemplar of 'majoritarian democracy'. The Dutch political scientist Arend Lijphart drew on the UK to illustrate how some democracies tend to concentrate power while others tend to disperse it, providing us with the useful distinction between majoritarian and consensus democracy. The UK's Westminster model is a political system based around a 'first past the post' or plurality electoral system, in which just two political parties win most votes and parliamentary seats and alternate in power. Governments have solid parliamentary majorities and are able to follow coherent policy programmes, held accountable by a similarly cohesive parliamentary opposition vying to win control of government at the next election. No other substantial checks and balances are considered necessary or desirable: formal constitutional restraints are few, the upper chamber of parliament is weak, local or subnational administrations are subordinate to central government, and even the central bank is under direct ministerial control. The merit of this arrangement is the clarity of choice it offers voters and the cohesiveness of government activity; its downside is the ability of one political faction to wield a great deal of political power with little in the way of constitutional or practical requirements to consult more broadly.

In the quarter century since Lijphart's work was first published, British politics has moved steadily away from this ideal-typical representation. In 1997, the newly elected Labour government followed the example of all other advanced democracies by giving operational independence to the Bank of England, and soon afterwards passed legislation to establish independent legislative institutions in Scotland, Wales, Northern Ireland and Greater London, reversing the trend towards ever increasing centralisation of power around the central government (Flinders 2005). Although it took until 2010 for coalition government to finally become a reality, evidence of the decline of the two-party system, and the increasing fragmentation of the vote across a wider range of parties, had been accumulating for over three decades (see Patrick Dunleavy's chapter in this volume). Labour's dominance of the political scene for the decade following the 1997 election was exaggerated by the electoral system. Tony Blair's third electoral victory in 2005 was a tenuous one in terms of votes cast, with little more than a fifth of the total British electorate giving its active support to the governing party. The plurality electoral system for the House of Commons remains intact, but pressure for reform has been building, with forms of proportional representation adopted for the new devolved institutions, some local elections and European elections, and the 2011 referendum (albeit unsuccessful) on the reform of parliamentary elections.

The situation arising out of the 2010 election reveals with unusual clarity the workings of the British system of parliamentary government. Observers of the British political scene have been accustomed to UK politics resembling a form of attenuated presidentialism (Heffernan and Webb 2005), with elections revolving around a battle between the leaders of the two main parties. Margaret Thatcher in the 1980s and Tony Blair in the late 1990s and early 2000s were both frequently criticised for centralising power around a narrow clique of advisors and failing to consult parliament. The growth of the infrastructure of the Prime Minister's office, and the decline in the importance of the cabinet as a forum for collective decision-making, seemed to challenge the myth that the UK constitution rested on the concept of parliamentary sovereignty. The election of a hung parliament provides us with the ideal conditions to test out this interpretation of British politics.

The initial experience of coalition government gives contrasting signals. On the one hand, the coalition constitutes a break in the recent tradition of the Prime Minister exercising power as a kind of personal mandate. Without a majority, David Cameron has had to involve Nick Clegg quite closely in the policy process, and Clegg has shared the burden of explaining and justifying the most controversial government policies, at some cost to his own popularity. Although the two coalition parties agreed a common government programme presented in the Queen's speech after the election, and Liberal Democrats sit in the cabinet, policy still has to be negotiated with Liberal Democrat backbenchers. Moreover, the coalition government has already faced a number of parliamentary rebellions, with both Conservative and Liberal Democrat MPs voting against the government, most notably over university tuition fees, where the coalition's majority was reduced to twenty-one from a notional eighty-four. This more fluid relationship between the Prime Minister and the cabinet and parliament does seem to mark a shift away from the concentration of power characteristic of the Westminster model. On the other hand there are also some signs of continuity. The presence of the Liberal Democrats' key leaders in the cabinet, and Nick Clegg's apparent enthusiasm for the largely Conservative policy agenda of the coalition, imply that the parliamentary majority remains almost as subordinate to the authority of the Prime Minister as would be the case under a classic single-party government.

The lasting consequences of the coalition experiment will depend on two variables. First, the outcome of the coalition's proposals for constitutional reform. The Liberal Democrats, historically committed to proportional representation, were unable to convince the Conservatives to accept PR, but did persuade them to accept a referendum on the alternative vote, a referendum that was held in May 2011 and lost by a wide margin. AV is an electoral system currently used in Australia in which voters rank candidates in order rather than simply voting for one candidate as their preferred choice. The potential effects of AV on electoral dynamics in Britain were not entirely clear; since voters would still be electing MPs in single-member constituencies, the effects would not necessarily have been more proportional than the existing arrangement. Had the referendum succeeded, it would have undermined one of the lynchpins of the Westminster model (Sartori 1994), increasing the probability of coalition government becoming a regular feature of British politics. A similar point can be made about the proposal to elect the members of the House of Lords, which could fundamentally alter the nature of the Westminster parliament. The Conservatives are unlikely to support far-reaching constitutional change and campaigned vigorously against AV in the referendum, with the result that a likely defeat for the Liberal Democrats was transformed into an electoral humiliation.

A second key variable is the effect of the coalition experience on British voting behaviour. The hung parliament produced by the 2010 election is the culmination of a period of decline in support for the two main parties, which together averaged around 90 per cent of the vote in the 1950s, but only just around 65 per cent in the 2000s. Were the coalition to entrench the Liberal Democrats' pivotal position in the party system, allowing the centrist party to play 'king-maker' in future parliaments, then coalition government would not only become routine, but also likely result in institutional changes that would consolidate multi-party government (such as electoral reform). Opinion polls at the end of 2010 pointed in the opposite direction, however, with the Liberal Democrats dropping in support to around 10 per cent, while Labour and the Conservatives were effectively tied at around 40 per cent.[1] In other words, the short-term effect of the coalition was to reassert the two-party system, as the Conservatives took credit for their leadership of the government and Labour established itself as the sole party of opposition. Whichever of these trends dominates will determine the extent to which coalition government leads to a lasting change in the nature of the British political system.

Policy change: the end of the Keynesian welfare state?

Aside from the novelty of a coalition government for the first time in over sixty years, the 2010 election also determined the policy response to the worst economic crisis to have faced the UK for over seventy years. The incoming government inherited an economy that had suffered a massive financial crisis, requiring extensive government intervention to rescue major banks, followed by a brutal recession in which the UK's GDP fell for six successive quarters, returning to growth only in early 2010. The Brown government responded by adopting stimulus measures to supplement the automatic stabilisers in the welfare system, bringing forward government capital spending and cutting consumption taxes to encourage private sector spending. The sharp collapse in tax revenue and the increased public spending caused by the recession pushed Britain quickly into the red, with the government's borrowing requirement reaching 12.5 per cent of GDP in 2009 and forecasts suggesting a similar figure for 2010.

As a result, Britain's experiment in coalition government is taking place in an environment of deep economic scarcity and uncertainty. Moreover, although all the main parties had promised during the election campaign to act quickly in order to reduce the deficit, important differences remained. The Conservatives had adopted a hawkish stance on the deficit, arguing that it needed to be brought down rapidly in order to avert a crisis of Britain's financial credibility. The Liberal Democrats had adopted a softer line, emphasising the downside risks to the economy in too rapid an adjustment; Nick Clegg instead claimed that 'the conditions will be right for cuts from 2011–2012, but not before. So in our first year of office, we will recycle the money from any cuts we can identify'.[2] The coalition agreement clearly came down on the side of the Conservative position, with the extent and timing of the fiscal tightening planned by David Cameron and George Osborne emerging unscathed from the negotiations with the Liberal Democrats. The best Clegg's party could do was to obtain commitments on the elimination of income tax for the lowest earners and a redistribution of funding in favour of the poorest school pupils (the 'pupil premium').

The financial crisis had a dramatic effect on the political debate over the UK economy. In David Cameron's first period as leader of the opposition, the UK economy appeared to be performing well and the Labour government was expanding public spending on popular services, notably healthcare and education. As part of Cameron's strategy of pushing the Conservative Party towards the centre, he embraced growth in public spending, with the reservation that the 'proceeds of growth' should be 'shared' between increased spending and lower taxes. When the financial crisis hit, the Conservatives' initial reaction was panicked support of the emergency measures taken by Gordon Brown to shore up the financial system and stimulate a contracting economy. However, within a few short months Cameron signalled a change in strategy, adopting a vigorously confrontational style aimed at pinning the blame for Britain's economic problems squarely on the Labour government in general, and Gordon Brown in particular (Dorey 2009). As the banking panic mutated into a deep and durable recession, the party began to attack Brown's management of the economy over the previous decade, drawing a connection between Labour's rapid expansion of the public sector in the early 2000s and Britain's parlous budgetary situation after 2008. This strategy was epitomised by a Conservative campaign poster that depicted a new-born baby under the heading, 'Dad's Nose, Mum's Eyes, Gordon Brown's Debt'.

This change of approach reflected in part a short-term calculation that there was no electoral gain in recognising the broader nature of the UK's economic problems, and potentially much advantage in blaming the crisis on Labour's alleged profligacy. But the coalition's enthusiastic embrace of rapid deficit reduction in the June 2010 budget showed that the push for austerity was more than an electoral strategy, and rather part of a broader political project to halt and potentially reverse the public sector growth of the Labour years. It should have been no surprise that the Conservative Party, long wedded to the twin ideals of balanced budgets and low taxes, abandoned the 'sharing the proceeds' approach as soon as the opportunity arose. What was more surprising was the willingness of the Liberal Democrats to commit the party to supporting austerity, even though it had rejected this approach prior to the election and could have counted on the views of many authoritative public figures in continuing to do so.

In this respect, the coalition is engaged in a policy experiment as well as a constitutional and political one. There are few historical examples of successful fiscal consolidation on such a scale, and none in a similarly grim international context. If the gamble pays off, than the coalition will gain plaudits for rescuing Britain from a desperate economic crisis by taking tough decisions, and if it fails, than the coalition will be pilloried for ignoring the many voices calling for a gentler approach. But as well as the uncertainty over the outcome, there is also the question of how blame or credit are shared between the governing parties. Here, the Conservatives appear to enjoy the stronger position. If the policy is deemed a success, the party in charge of both Number 10 and Number 11 Downing Street is likely to gain disproportionately compared to its (very) junior coalition partner. The downside risk is perhaps greater for the Conservatives, particularly since the Liberal Democrats could conceivably leave the government if the need arose. However, early signs suggest that the Liberal Democrats are running the risk of acting as a lightning conductor for the government, with their about-turn over tuition fees attracting particular opprobrium.

The fiscal consolidation strategy is likely to have long-term consequences for the British welfare state. Some of the spending cuts imposed could easily be reversed by future governments through annual budgetary decisions, but a number of measures are more durable in that they establish new institutional mechanisms that would be more costly to change. For example, the reforms of the National Health Service, which will abolish the Primary Care Trusts and devolve greater decision-making to General Practitioners (family doctors) amount to a radical change in the functioning of the organisation, as do the proposed 'free schools' in the education sector. Some changes to benefits are also implicitly permanent, such as the adoption of a different inflation rate for calculating indexed increases in payments, which will tend to lag behind increases in prices in the broader economy. Moreover the social consequences of the deficit reduction policy could lead to further entrenching of some of the UK's acute social problems, as families living in poverty fall further behind average living standards and the unemployed fall out of the active population.

Although the coalition initially drew largely on the pressing fiscal crisis to justify spending cuts, the Conservative Party also proffered a more ideological foundation for its policies, revolving around the concept of the 'Big Society'. The Big Society idea has its origins in Cameron's search for clearer ideological definition to counteract the impression of superficial pragmatism given by policy inconsistencies on key areas such as taxation and welfare, green politics and social issues. Cameron's thinking drew on a critique of Labour's allegedly overbearing state interventionism while seeking to avert accusations of a return to Thatcherite rhetoric on 'rolling back the frontiers of the state' (Blond 2010). Cameronite Conservatives argued that the Big Society – volunteering, community work and civic participation in decision-making – is a better way of achieving community well-being than centralised targets and bureaucratic fiat. In Cameron's words, 'we need to turn government completely on its head. The rule of this government should be this: if it unleashes community engagement, we should do it; if it crushes it, we shouldn't' (cited in Kisby 2010: 484).

The Big Society is criticised for its vagueness and complacency. On the one hand, critics argue that it is not entirely clear what the Big Society means, when it comes down to concrete issues such as how to run the health service or allocate welfare benefits. However, the early signs in late 2010 were that the government had indeed taken steps to put Big Society ideas into practice, most notably in the education sector, where Swedish ideas about 'free schools' and measures to increase the autonomy of state schools from local councils were mooted. The difficulty the government faces in these areas is that the Big Society rests on the assumption that government 'crowds out' civil involvement, and that removing the heavy hand of the state would free citizens to become more active. However, if the 'crowding out' thesis proves wrong, than a policy-making vacuum could result.

A more aggressive critique of the Big Society from the left takes the whole project as a thinly veiled attempt to undercut the welfare state and weaken the redistributive structure that protects the most vulnerable. For example, relying on voluntary action and civic involvement could expand the advantages of higher income groups, who tend to have greater 'social capital' and the skills required to intervene in policy-making (Kisby 2010: 488). More generally, the 'crowding out' idea seems to imply that high levels of redistributive spending and state provision of services are at fault for undermining civic engagement, suggesting that the rolling back of the welfare state is in fact a core part of the Big Society project. The Conservatives have avoided making such claims, but the ambitious nature of the deficit reduction programme is likely to put the 'crowding out' thesis to the test, since a considerable part of the expansion of social interventionism under Labour is to be retrenched.

The Liberal Democrats, for their part, have also sought to reconcile the drastic implications of the government's fiscal strategy with their own ideology, with Nick Clegg making a brave attempt to redefine 'progressivism' in a keynote speech in honour of the late *Guardian* journalist Hugo Young.[3] In a similar rhetorical approach to Cameron's, Clegg juxtaposed the 'old' progressive politics of the defeated Labour government to his party's 'new' progressive politics: 'For new progressives, the test is not the size of the state, it is the relationship between the state and the citizen. Old progressives conflate the idea of progress with the control and reach of the central state'. By establishing that 'the question is not how much the state is spending, it is how it spends it', Clegg moved on to set a 'new progressive test' for government action: 'whether it liberates and empowers people'. Although Clegg was careful in this speech to leave space for government interventionism and redistributive spending, the emphasis on quality over quantity in the public sector and the concern for the risks of excessive state interventionism drew parallels with the Conservative idea of the Big Society. In this way, Clegg sought to reconcile the profound spending cuts of the coalition government with the concern for social harmony of the Liberal Democrat tradition.

The positions of both the Conservatives and the Liberal Democrats imply a clear rejection of New Labour's strategy of expanding public provision of services and addressing poverty through cash transfers and direct government action. The coalition, rather than adopting the middle ground, has therefore ended up participating in an increasing polarisation of the policy debate. In this regard, coalition does not seem to signal a departure from the competitive 'government against opposition' logic of the Westminster model. Instead, the 2010 election has acted as a further breakpoint in the long-running debate over the role of the state in Britain, which has seen policy oscillate from the privatising zeal of the Thatcher years to the expansion of the state under Blair and Brown.

Conclusion

This volume contributes to the developing debate on the nature of current changes to British politics, a debate that will continue as the consequences of the 2010 election become clearer. Taking a snapshot of this kind runs the risk of presenting apparently sound conclusions that quickly become anachronistic as politics moves in unpredictable ways. We have sought to capture the 'signal' rather than the 'noise' by looking at some of the fundamental structural shifts that appear to be taking place and moving beyond the issues dominating the twenty-four hour news cycle.

What is already clear is that the 2010 general election is a very important one in recent British political history. If coalition becomes entrenched in British political practice, it will require a good deal of rethinking about the UK political system, to move beyond the familiar categories of 'first past the post', 'cabinet government' and 'parliamentary sovereignty'. Equally, a reversion to the classic two-party system of the 1950s and 1960s – as indicated in opinion polls at the end of the year – is also possible, in which case 2010 would constitute a turning point of a different kind, at which the British electorate turned away from multi-party politics. However, this latter hypothesis runs up against the increasingly complex reality of political competition in Britain, in which voters are no longer lined up along class lines as in the immediate post-war period (Butler and Stokes 1974). Instead, the old class divisions are complicated by internal class differences, between the working and the non-working, the public sector and the private sector, the property owners and those cut out of the housing market. These cleavages around economic interests are supplemented by territorial, ethnic, religious and socio-cultural divergences, which are often more powerful than questions of material well-being. Multi-party democracy would appear the most plausible way of dealing with such complexity, but as we have seen, a number of factors in the British political tradition militate against it.

Although this book has focused mostly on events in the UK, it is important to recognise the comparative insights a broader perspective can bring. The 2010 election led to quite dramatic change in the nature of British government, but it was not simply the culmination of trends exclusive to the UK. The financial crisis sparked off in 2007 dragged Britain into a world economic drama of almost unprecedented gravity, the consequences of which will shape our politics for years to come. The success or otherwise of the coalition government's economic strategy will depend to a considerable degree on developments outside the UK, particularly in the United States and in the Eurozone. To this extent, the coalition's fate is not entirely in its own hands.

Notes

1 See UK Polling Report for extensive historical polling data tracking support for the main parties: http://ukpollingreport.co.uk/blog/ (last accessed 1 October 2011).
2 Nick Clegg's speech to the Institute of Public Policy Research, 16 March 2010, at www.libdems.org.uk/news_detail.aspx?title=Nick_Clegg%E2%80%99s _speech_on_winning_people_over_for_deficit_reduction&pPK=6f9f2878 -899b-4841–a558-0187fa80186d (last accessed 1 October 2011).
3 Nick Clegg, Hugo Young Lecture 2010. www.guardian.co.uk/politics /2010/nov/23/nick-clegg-hugo-young-text (last accessed 1 October 2011).

References

Blond, P. (2010). *Red Tory: How Left and Right Have Broken Britain and How We Can Fix It*. London: Faber.

Butler, D. and D. Stokes (1974). *Political Change in Britain*. London: Macmillan.

Dorey, P. (2009). '"Sharing the Proceeds of Growth": Conservative Economic Policy under David Cameron', *The Political Quarterly*, 80 (2): 259–269.

Flinders, M. (2005). 'Majoritarian Democracy in Britain', *West European Politics*, 28 (1): 62–94.

Heffernan, R. and P. Webb (2005). 'The British Prime Minister: More than Just First Amongst Equals', in T. Poguntke and P. Webb (eds), *The Presidentialization of Politics: A Comparative Study of Modern Democracies*. Oxford: Oxford University Press, pp. 26–63.

Kisby, B. (2010). 'The Big Society: Power to the People?' *The Political Quarterly*, 81 (4): 484–491.

Sartori, G. (1994). *Comparative Constitutional Engineering*. Basingstoke: Macmillan.

Index